D1613034

Books are to be returned on or b
the las

Aldham Robarts LRC

Liverpool John Moores University

Theorizing Modernity

*Inescapability and Attainability
in Social Theory*

Peter Wagner

SAGE Publications
London • Thousand Oaks • New Delhi

SAGE Publications Ltd
6 Bonhill Street
London EC2A 4PU

SAGE Publications Inc
2455 Teller Road
Thousand Oaks, California 91320

SAGE Publications India Pvt Ltd
32, M-Block Market
Greater Kailash - I
New Delhi 110 048

British Library Cataloguing in Publication data

A catalogue record for this book
is available from the British Library

ISBN 0-7619-5146-6
ISBN 0-7619-5147-4 (pbk)

Library of Congress catalog card number available

Typeset by Siva Math Setters, Chennai, India
Printed and bound in Great Britain by Atheneaum Press, Gateshead

Contents

Acknowledgements

This book is in many respects a sequel to *A Sociology of Modernity* (Wagner, 1994a). It tries to spell out some of those conceptual issues that had remained implicit or that were not sufficiently clarified at all. Work on this book proceeded slowly and has found some intermediate outcomes on which I draw (and to which I refer as follows): on Friese and Wagner, 1999a for the overall argument, on Wagner, 1995 for Chapter 1, on Wagner, 1998a for Chapter 2, on Wagner, 1998b for Chapter 3, and on Wagner, 1999a for Chapter 5. Parallel to the work on this book, I have continued investigations in the history and the philosophy of the social sciences, the results of which are scheduled to be published at about the same time as this book (Wagner, 2001).

Johann Arnason, Heidrun Friese, Hans Joas, Petr Lom, Björn Wittrock and Bernard Yack have read the entire manuscript and provided critical comments, for which I am very grateful. If I have in a number of cases not been able to take up their suggestions and address their criticisms, I hope to respond to them in a more adequate way in the future. I have also greatly benefited from discussing these ideas with the doctoral students at the Social Theory Centre at the University of Warwick and in seminars of the Centre. My intellectual indebtedness to Heidrun Friese is, to everybody who knows her work, too evident for words. Chapter 4, in particular, owes many of its reflections to discussions with her.

The terms inescapability and attainability are borrowed from Charles Taylor and Stanley Cavell respectively; the full references can be found in Chapter 3.

Prologue: Theorizing Modernity

'Human reason faces in one sphere of its cognition the particular fate that it is disturbed by questions that it cannot decline, as they are presented by its own nature, but that it cannot answer either, as they transcend every faculty of human reason.'[1] In Immanuel Kant's view, this is a situation that will need to be confronted. There are questions that are inescapable, even though firm answers to them are unattainable. It is the contention of this book that social theory and social science, in contrast, have aimed at arranging the sphere of cognition that is proper to them in such a way that there are, in principle, neither questions that cannot be declined nor answers that cannot be found. Social science has been inclined to reject the issues of inescapability and of attainability; they have been regarded as names for adversaries that need to be fought against.[2]

Kant was writing the *Critique of Pure Reason* in the late eighteenth century, at a time that has been interpreted in a variety of ways as a historical period of great significance. He was writing at the dusk of the Enlightenment, when the intellectual reactions to what was often considered as an exacerbated and unqualified praise of freedom and reason had already set in. But he was also writing at the onset of political modernity, which is commonly, and not unjustifiably, related to the advent of the American and the French revolutions. Furthermore, he was writing just before the emergence of a mode of reasoning that very soon after became recognizable as the social sciences by and large as we still know them today. At the time of his writing, however, their concerns and ways of arguing had not yet separated from philosophy in general and from political philosophy in particular.

In other words, the late eighteenth century was an historical period during which a major conceptual-intellectual transformation coincided with a major politico-institutional transformation (see most recently Heilbron et al., 1998). The concomitance of these two transformations made it possible – and often far too convenient – to associate the emergence of 'modern society' with the emergence of the social sciences as the form of reflexive self-understanding appropriate for modernity. In this sense, this double transformation would mark the establishment of modernity in both intellectual and institutional terms. I will try to argue, however, that while some significant relationship between the two occurrences exists, this relationship is far more problematic.

In terms of the intellectual transformation, the separation of concerns between *philosophy* and the emerging specialized *sciences* has often been hailed as a differentiation that made an enormous progress of knowledge possible. In this view, the sciences, including the social sciences, emancipated themselves from the tutelage of philosophy and threw off the chains that limited their development. It became their task and their accomplishment to systematically provide 'positive', empirical knowledge of the social world. In the view that I will advocate in the following, in contrast, this separation has at the same time incapacitated social science to address some issues that are of constitutive significance for its own intellectual programme and for its interpretation of modernity.

The separation from philosophy has allowed social scientists to embark on empirical research strategies and leave questions of epistemology to the sub-fields of the sociology of knowledge, the philosophy of the social sciences and the sociology of science. Debate in those sub-fields hardly ever entered back into the core of the social science activities. Since the obstacles the social world poses to human cognition, however, vary across situations and time, questions concerning the quality of its own knowledge and the means to acquire it have to remain in the centre of the social sciences (Chapter 1).

Contemporary academic institutions know a rather clear-cut division between the two empirical disciplines of *sociology* and *political science* (which stand in an often uneasy relationship to each other), on the one hand, and a normative discipline of *political philosophy*, mostly accompanied by an interest in the history of political thought, on the other. Historically, however, the social sciences have emerged from concerns that are now considered to fall into the realm of political philosophy. They have addressed those concerns, sometimes called the problem of social order but more appropriately considered as the question of the viability of the polity, by different means, but they do not reconnect those means to the ones adopted by political philosophy. Thus, they rob themselves of the faculty to reflexively understand political issues (Chapter 2).

The social sciences have developed an interest in questions of human selfhood only of late and systematically only from the early twentieth century. Furthermore, they have largely ignored ways of representing the human self that were proposed in other areas, in philosophy for instance, but maybe even more importantly in literature. Thus, they have tended to look at the question from the perspective of a fully developed, stable personal identity, rather than making the continuity and coherence of the self an issue open to investigation. This focus can hardly be understood otherwise than through the perceived needs to presuppose an ontological stability of the world to keep social science possible and to expect a political stability of the world on the basis of a presupposed coherence of human orientations and actions (Chapter 3).

One commonality stretches across the ways in which the social sciences have dealt with the questions of the certainty of knowledge, of the viability of the polity and of the continuity of selfhood: time has been rendered unproblematic. During the nineteenth century, the social sciences co-emerged with the *historical sciences* from under the umbrella of philosophy. The two new fields share what one may now call, by retrospective use of a common formula, the empirical turn. But, extraordinarily, they nevertheless develop as separate projects with quite different and often opposed agendas. The basis of the social sciences' claim to specificity was the assumption of the radical novelty of the contemporary social configuration. Assuming such a break of the present with the past, the social sciences inevitably employed a concept of the past and its relation to the present, but they rarely explicated their own view of the accessibility of the past (Chapter 4).

A similar problem exists with regard to future time. At least during the nineteen ِ century, emerging social scientists were aware of having inherited their problématiques not least from religion and theology, and they knew that a concept of eschatological time was part of this heritage. They claimed, however, that their thinking about the evolution of societies had progressively superseded the earlier intellectual form. In other words, the future had remained knowable despite the abandoning of the mode of thinking called *philosophy of history*. During the twentieth century, social science by and large – with notable exceptions, in particular during the 1960s – has become more cautious with regard to directly addressing the future. The interest in knowing what lies ahead in time remained awake, though, and theoretical constructions were developed that ultimately aimed at keeping the future transparent (Chapter 5).

Through a discussion of this sequence of issues, the aim is to show, first, that the project of social science and social theory, as it developed over the past 200 years, either ejected or relegated to sub-fields a number of questions that had been kept together in earlier reflection about the human social world. This claim is not novel as such, but it has been evaluated in highly different ways, both as a necessary advance and as a regrettable loss. While I do agree that considerable losses were incurred, this book does not aim to contribute to any nostalgic interpretation of intellectual history. Rather, second, it strives to demonstrate that the concerns that were ejected or relegated remained constitutive of social science and social theory, albeit in an implicit and unexplicated way.

Thirdly, and most importantly, it is to be shown that this particular way of historically separating a project of social science from other intellectual concerns and forms is related to a similarly specific way of conceptualizing modernity. Rather than connecting social science to modernity in terms of a correspondence of a form of knowledge to a socio-political reality, one should see existing social science as a specific way of interpreting a socio-historical experience. Or, to put it the other way round, social science, as manifold as it may often appear, has occupied but a rather limited space among the available possibilities to theorize modernity. It has tried to make answerable all questions that modernity poses by eliminating those from its concerns to which answers proved unattainable by means of its mode of operation. Rather than making its explanatory grip on the social world necessarily more powerful, it has thus largely disabled itself to follow the history of Western (and other) societies through transformations of modernity.

The History and Theory of Modernity

The relation between modernity and the social sciences is marked by an inherent tension. On the one hand, 'modernity' is the condition for the social sciences, as the reflexive knowledge of the human social world, to emerge and exist. On the other hand, it is the objective and task of the social sciences to conceptualize and analyse 'modernity' as an historical social formation. In the first meaning, 'modernity' refers to a philosophical and, in particular, an epistemological condition. In the second meaning, it refers to an historical, empirical instance. It is on these grounds that the context of their emergence, the alleged separation from philosophy, on the social sciences that would never again go away. And this ... omes especially visible when these sciences aim at dealing with ... *tout court*, as the entire societal constellation of which they them- ... re a part. In other words, the term 'modernity' inevitably carries a double ... otation; it is always both philosophical and empirical, or both substantive ...d temporal (Yack, 1997), or – to introduce my own preferred terminology – both conceptual and historical.

Anticipating more detailed discussion below, a first preliminary characterization of modernity – one that, unlike many others, acknowledges this tension – is required at this point. *Conceptually*, I will understand modernity generally as a situation in which a certain double imaginary signification prevails. The two components of this signification, ambivalent on their own and also tension-ridden between them, are the idea of the *autonomy* of the human being as the knowing and acting subject, on the one hand, and the idea of the *rationality* of the world, i.e. its principled intelligibility, on the other. To put it briefly, modernity refers to a situation in which human beings do not accept any external guarantors, i.e. guarantors that they do not themselves posit, of the certainty of their knowledge, of the viability of their political orders or of the continuity of their selves. Despite the enormous variety of specific conceptualizations of modernity, the great majority of them take it to be the key characteristic of modernity that human beings think of themselves as setting their own rules and laws for their relation to nature, for their living together and for understanding themselves. The assumption of autonomy and the quest for mastery constitute then the double imaginary signification of modernity (Castoriadis, 1990: 17–19; and elsewhere Arnason, 1989; Wagner, 1994a: Chapter 1).

The special commitment of the social sciences to modernity – which is at the same time the source of their limits – makes them often turn this double signification of modernity into an unquestionable starting-point of their mode of reasoning. Autonomy and rationality are made the founding assumptions of the social sciences. They are considered attained, or at least attainable in principle, not least in and through the pursuit of social science inquiry itself. They become presuppositions of inquiry that are themselves neither questioned nor at all questionable. Social science tends to conflate the imaginary signification of modernity with the reality of social life in Western societies. Or to put it in Max Weber's terms, rationalization is '*not* an increasing general knowledge of the living conditions to which one is exposed', but rather 'the knowledge or the belief that, if one *only* wanted, one *could* always get to know them' (Weber, 1975 [1919]: 17). The rise of modernity is characterized by the strengthening of the latter belief; it is not – or at least not necessarily – a social reality of the former kind, i.e. one whose inhabitants constantly increase their knowledge about their world. In the following, I reserve the term 'modernist' for approaches that mistake modernity for the latter. In this sense, much of social science is modernist – rather than 'modern'. The latter term is used here for an attitude that embraces the same imaginary signification of autonomy and mastery, but is both able and willing to reflect about the conditions of possibility as well as the consequences of the limitations of this modern ideal.

A first important consequence of this definitional step is to create a space of reasoning about modernity, an *interpretative space*, of which the modernist position occupies only a part. Modernism, namely, was certainly never unquestioningly accepted, not even in the social sciences. Critiques persisted over the entire history of modernist social science, but three periods can be singled out as being of particular significance. Romanticism, proposed already during the founding period of the social sciences at the turn of the eighteenth century, remains of lasting importance as an alternative to modernism in the social sciences (see for example, Rosenblum, 1987; Taylor, 1995a and 1995b). At the end of the nineteenth century, second, the famous disputes over epistemology and method signalled a revival of critical debate that led into what is now known as the classical period of the social sciences. Weber's own work, as has recently been rediscovered, remained torn between political philosophy and social science, to use the time-honoured terms, rather than being unequivocally locatable at the founding moment of modernist sociology.

Since the 1970s, thirdly, a new and wide-ranging debate about the orientations of social science has started. It has many components, including as diverse approaches as the 'linguistic turn' applied to concepts and discourses of the social sciences, a renewed interest in historical-comparative studies, the return of the anthropological perspective on Western societies, gender and post-colonial studies, the sociology of scientific knowledge. During the 1980s, attempts were made to sum up the critique under the name of postmodernism. While this label is – and has been – in many respects misleading, it has at least two advantages. First, it signals the emergence of a new form of critique. At a closer look, the form was not quite as new, since its ways of thinking were often related to, broadly, Nietzsche-inspired philosophy. But nevertheless it is distinguishable from the kind of critique of modernist social science that, by and large, reaches from romanticism towards Nietzsche and Weber. I will try to explicate the difference further below.

The other advantage of the term postmodernism – which, though, may have been bought at the price of giant misunderstandings on the part of both modernists and postmodernists alike – is that it re-introduced an explicit preoccupation with 'modernity' into social theory and political philosophy. Arguably, this mode of thinking gained momentum in the historical situation of the outgoing twentieth century for identifiable reasons, a question to which I will also return. The theorem that was often taken to suggest that modernity had exhausted its powers and had come to an end, ironically – but not entirely inadvertently – revived the reflection about the condition of modernity. If nothing else, the post-modernity debate reminded of the fact that the issue of modernity was much more far-reaching than modernism in philosophy and the social sciences were willing to accept. In the first instance, the prefix 'post' suggested a temporal dimension of modernity and thus returned attention to the double connotation of the term 'modernity', its being inevitably both conceptual and historical.

Historically, modernity often refers straightforwardly to the 'history of the West'. More specifically, it refers to the history of Europe, and from some time onwards also of North America. Modernity then, to cut across the range of views, begins at the earliest in the mid to late fifteenth century with the Renaissance, the invention of movable type and the voyages of discovery. At the latest, it starts in the early twentieth century with modernism in the arts and in architecture and with the new form of self-inspection provided by psychoanalysis. In between, economic modernity is said to begin with the market revolution and the Industrial Revolution, and political modernity has its take-off with the revolutions in America and France in the late eighteenth century. Scientific and philosophical revolutions towards modernity can be variously dated along this temporal line – from Cartesian rationalism and experimental method to the *fin-de-siècle* critique of science and metaphysics and to the Theory of Relativity. Regardless of precise dating, the advent of modernity is always assumed to mark a rupture that leads to some specificity of the West in global comparison. But any such historical description of a rupture also always stands in some tension to the conceptual understanding of modernity. Though some are better candidates than others, none of the cited events and processes can be seen to fully incarnate the positing of autonomy or the quest for mastery.

Similarly, the alleged end of modernity can take on two quite different, although not entirely incompatible, meanings. Historically, the theorem should refer to the end of the specificity of the West. There are then again two possibilities. Either the specificity got lost because Western forms of social life and modes of social organization have spread across the world. Or those forms were being abandoned or transformed to such a degree that their distinctness has disappeared. An assessment of these two possibilities could not proceed without further conceptual clarification. Is the 'end of modernity' a situation in which human beings no longer believe in the setting of their own rules but resign themselves to complying to systemic requirements or global power structures? Or is it the generalization of the double European liberation movement from the end of the eighteenth century, now known as 'democratization' on the one hand, and the liberation of the market forces on the other? Will human beings ultimately have become the true masters of the world, or have they become the powerless objects of the forces they themselves once unleashed? Any attempt at answering those questions will have to proceed through a socio-historical reflection on the double modern signification of autonomy and mastery, thus combining conceptual and historical inquiry.

Plurality and Possibility

This combination of inquiries in a critical spirit, however, occurred rather rarely. It was the error of large parts of the social sciences during the nineteenth and twentieth century to mistake a historically specific interpretation of a problématique for a general problématique of modernity. Thus, sociology tended to conflate the historical form of the European nation-state with the solution to the political problématique, or as it was often called: the problem of social order, which was expressed in the concept 'society'. And the error of much of modern and postmodern philosophy consists in either searching for general solutions to the problématiques of, say, the certainty of knowledge or the viability of the polity, or in taking such search for vain from the start. Trying to avoid those errors, my earlier book, *A Sociology of Modernity* (Wagner, 1994a) itself proceeded largely by historical exemplification rather than explicit theorization. This book will aim at explicating the social theory and philosophy that needs to accompany such re-description. It will however not move from the historical to the theoretical or philosophical form, but rather try to reconsider the relation between the two.

To illustrate this objective and at the same time illustrate further the possible understandings of modernity, the limits of *A Sociology of Modernity* may be briefly addressed. That book already contained a conceptual linkage between the theorizing of modernity and modernity's historicity. Not only did this relation remain largely implicit, however, it was also developed on doubly limited terms. Socio-historically, the book focused on Western Europe and contrasted the West European experience with the modernity of the USA, which at most times appeared comparatively more 'liberal', and the one of Soviet socialism, which rather consistently appeared more 'organized'. Conceptually, the analysis limited itself to employing basically two registers. The oscillation between historically more 'liberal' and more 'organized' modernities, first, refers to the tension between individualist and collectivist interpretations of autonomy. The second focus was on the relation between procedural and substantive interpretations of collective arrangements, and in particular on the tension between the two main substantive resources for organizing European modernity, the cultural-linguistically defined nation and the socially defined class.

This limitation entailed that the analysis could not fully unfold an understanding of what one may call the cultures of modernity, namely the variety of socio-historical interpretations of the double imaginary signification of modernity and the resources such interpretations draw on and mobilize. Within Western Europe already, for example, between France and Germany, or within the more broadly defined 'West', for example, between Europe and the USA, those resources are much richer and much more varied than the book shows (see now Wagner, 1999a; Zimmermann et al., 1999; and Chapter 5). Both richness and variety increase considerably as soon as one moves attention towards so-called non-Western societies. Under names such as 'varieties of modernity' or 'multiple modernities', a research perspective has recently developed that aims at analysing the plurality of interpretations of the modern signification (Arnason, 1998; Eisenstadt, 1998; the *Daedalus* issues of summer 1998 and winter 2000; Friese and Wagner, 2000). In terms of the analysis of entire societal configurations, this seems to be the adequate response, all qualifications in detail notwithstanding, to the spreading discourse on 'globalization'. The latter, as almost implied in the term, far too often assumes that the increasing density of relations of communication and transport necessarily leads to overall convergence of societies, to be captured by individualist-rationalist social theorizing and to be brought about by neo-liberal policy design.

The historical-empirical observation of modernity's variety has its conceptual complement in some constitutive openness of modernity – even of the project of modernity, if some readers prefer this accent. Under conditions of modernity, there is always a range of possibilities, even if some thinkable possibilities may remain remote from any actualization. But if the *history* of modernity knows both plurality and possibility, can there be a *theorizing* that captures all the present and past diversity as well as the possibilities that are open to the future without itself adopting some mode of plurality and possibility? This question has regularly been answered in the affirmative. Or, even more strongly, the necessity of a single and stable theoretical viewpoint has been asserted as a necessity, for otherwise neither firm analysis nor critique would be possible.

Thus, the philosophical discourse of modernity, to use Jürgen Habermas's formula (1985) has long searched for a stable and reliable solution to the basic problems mentioned above.[3] There seems to be, maybe most importantly, a modern way to ascertain the certainty of knowledge; equally, there is a modern polity; and there is a modern self. An answer to each of these questions exists, not least because it needs to exist since otherwise the viability of the modern project itself would be put into doubt. A number of contributions to discussions over the past two decades, the decades of alleged postmodernity, have in contrast posited that there can be, as a matter of principle, no answers to these questions. Epistemological relativism, the farewell to those 'grand narratives' that hold political orders together, and the de-centring of the subject are all seen as inevitable. Some commentators, most pronouncedly Richard Rorty (1989), saw indeed no problem at all in the emerging insight into the contingency of language, community and selfhood, but rather the dawning possibility of a postmodern liberalism.

It is my view, in contrast, that the historicity of modernity requires the elaboration and explication of a plurality of modes of theorizing that is adequate to the variety of modernity and to the problématiques that the modern condition poses for social life. In this book, thus, I try to further develop a viewpoint that differs from all those mentioned above. It holds that there are problématiques that have been and will remain constitutive for socio-political modernity. Modernity is characterized by problématiques that remain open, not by specific solutions to given problems.[4] Among those problématiques we find, in particular, the search for certain knowledge and truth, the building of a viable and good political order, the issue of the continuity of the acting person, and the way of relating in the lived present to time past and time future. Without some assumption of human autonomy, i.e. the ability of human beings to give themselves their own laws, these questions would not arise. That is why they are fundamentally modern. But this assumption cannot take itself for granted, and it does not lead towards solutions. That is why modernism unduly limits the variety of possibilities of conceiving these problématiques.

These problématiques co-emerge with modernity, and they can neither be rejected nor be handled once and for all by finding their 'modern' solution. Societies that accept the double imaginary signification of modernity are destined to search for answers to these questions and to institute those answers. Temporarily stable solutions can thus indeed be found – the 'thirty golden years' in Europe and the USA after the Second World War, for instance, were marked by a temporarily stable compromise between different possible sets of answers to the political problématique. In other words, the constitutive problématiques of modernity have always to be interpreted in their concrete temporality, at their specific historical location.

Inescapability and Attainability

In a way, the plurality of modes of theorizing that I call for indeed exists in current social science and social philosophy. But it is neither well elaborated nor explicated, since the positions are hardly ever put into relation to each other. It is indeed a quite familiar way to look at current social theorizing of modernity as a threefold intellectual field.

First, and most centrally in this field, modernity's achievement is precisely seen in having overcome the need for any substantive and particular foundations for the order of the social world and in having replaced them by universalist reasoning, in terms of practices often linked to ideas of procedure and communication. This may be called the classic modern view. Secondly, during the past two decades, it has often been argued that even such non-substantive foundations are untenable and, indeed, include hidden substantive ideas. The ensuing deconstruction of the classic-modern position then leads to what has often been called postmodernist thinking. Such alleged postmodernism maintains that foundations of any kind are neither needed nor justifiable; more appropriately, it should be considered as a radicalization of modernist thinking applying its own principles onto itself. Thirdly, one may also – and still – deny the validity of the classic-modern, anti-foundationalist proposition on different grounds and try to develop substantive ideas for grounding discourses and practices that, far from being merely 'pre-modern', might withstand the modern experience. Such a viewpoint would often be labelled a critique of modernity, which can appear in the guises of rather traditional, but also of more contemporary language.

In many of the recent disputes in social and political philosophy as well as in social theory and methodology it has been assumed that these positions are clearly distinct. They are mostly seen to provide mutually exclusive and incompatible answers. And the fervour of some such debates exactly stems from the perceived need to commit oneself (and others) to one of those positions and to regard other viewpoints as untenable, if not even (politically and/or morally) irresponsible.

Reviewing the central objections that can be raised from any one of these positions to any other one, however, one will rather find that each of them is untenable on its own, since the objections clearly have some validity, some degree of irrefutability. Let me very briefly illustrate this: modernist social philosophy holds that, with the advent of modernity, only traditional foundations are called into question and truly modern ones can be built in their place. But then the search for such solutions quickly proves futile (or aporetic), since there are no such truly modern foundations, no uncontestable basis on which to build a modern social order. The postmodernist conclusion then is that foundations are neither needed any longer nor even possible, once they have been questioned. But certainly, every society has practical understandings of, for instance, knowledge, politics and selfhood, contested as they may be, which are recurrently mobilized – as well as fought about – in social life. Finally, then, one may presume that the rejection of the modern 'adventure' (Lefort, 1986a: 23, 25) remains a viable option, even after the advent of modernity. If there are always some practically valid understandings, it has to be the task of philosophy and sociology to identify their foundations. But then again there is no return to 'origins' of any kind, once they have been called into question.

This brief play of refutations shows that indeed, in some kind of circular way, a valid objection can be raised from any one position against any other one. There is no end to disputes over justification, once different orders of justification are at play (see Boltanski and Thévenot, 1991). Furthermore, none of the modes of answering these questions could lay a specific claim to being modern. The impossibility to give any one superior answer together with the inevitable persistence of the questions is rather what modernity is about. It is only when taken together that the three positions open and map the interpretative space in which the theorizing of modernity can take place. Instead of focusing on the differences between these positions, my argument will insist on the commonality of the questions, of the problématiques, to which they intend to respond, and will aim to relate them to each other – without conflating them.

However, this interpretative space is not well understood in the forms of either the time-honoured opposition between 'traditional' (and 'conservative') and 'modern' understandings of the social world or the more recent one between 'modern' and 'postmodern' such views. The first step towards mapping this space thus has to be an attempt at re-describing the three positions. I shall try to do so by re-interpreting the threefold structure of the field as a double questioning of modernist conceptions.

Above, modernism in the social sciences was characterized as a thinking that takes the double modern signification of autonomy and mastery as an unquestionable starting-point of all reasoning. Thus, it thinks of human beings as giving themselves their own laws and as being capable of mastering the world. For both features to be fully attained, this human being needs to distance himself from the world, to step out of it and reach a superior position, to be able to consider the world as an object that can be both known and controlled. Such thinking pervades many areas of intellectual life. Often it is regarded as precisely the scientific attitude as such (see Chapter 1), although the distancing from the world can also be understood in terms of – to use a currently fashionable turn – a reflexivity that does not rely on a separation from the world. In political philosophy, such modernism can be found in the tradition of individualist liberalism, which rests its claim to superior insight on the construction of a decontextualized 'original position' (John Rawls, 1971) from where individual human beings enter into contract with one another (see Chapter 2). In terms of selfhood, the individual human being mastering the world by the power of his 'disengaged reason' (Charles Taylor, 1989) is often seen as the very incarnation of modern man. And generally, rationalist individualism, currently known in social thought as rational choice theory, a theorizing that is indeed an intellectually imperialist expansion of neo-classical economics (to be broached as an increasingly widespread mode of social theory in Chapters 4 and 5), expresses such modernist attitude.

What all these approaches have in common is a double intellectual move. They first withdraw from the treacherous wealth of sensations that come from the socio-historical world to establish what they hold to be those very few indubitable assumptions from which theorizing can safely proceed. And subsequently, they reconstruct an entire world from those very few assumptions. Their proponents tend to think that the first move *decontaminates understanding*, any arbitrary and contingent aspects being removed. And that the second move creates a *pure image* of the world, of scientific and/or philosophical validity, from which then further conclusions, including practical ones, can be drawn.[5]

Without opening already here a discussion of the merits of the first move in principle (see, in particular, Chapter 1), it has often been objected that such a move does not – and cannot – accomplish its objectives. Theorists have chosen a great variety of different starting-points; the double notion of autonomy and rationality is just the example that lends itself best to analyse the project of modernity. Whatever concepts are chosen, however, they are never pure, or merely procedural and formal, never devoid of substance. As a consequence, they cannot mark any unquestionable beginning from which thinking can safely start out, and doubts can be raised about any world that is erected on their foundations, that is, about the subsequent second move. However, it was exactly doubt about the multifarious perceptions of uncertain epistemic status that emanate from the world that made this thinking arise in the first place.

The critique of this attitude, in contrast, held that such modernist distancing was neither warranted nor achievable. It was not warranted since 'one doubts on specific grounds' (Wittgenstein, 1969: par. 458, a more appropriate translation may be: 'one doubts for specific reasons'); there are always – even for Descartes – claims 'beyond reasonable doubt' and knowledge would proceed from such claims. It was not achievable because unlimited doubt would even affect the proposition about such doubt itself. As Wittgenstein (par. 456) put it, 'If, therefore, I doubt or am uncertain about this being my hand (in whatever sense), why not in that case about the meaning of these words as well?' Wittgenstein himself observes the distinction between these two arguments, but also the difficulty to keep them always distinct. 'There are cases where doubt is unreasonable, but others where it seems logically impossible. And there seems to be no clear boundary between them' (par. 454).

Throughout this book, the focus will be on such twofold questioning of modernist conceptions, which are characteristic not merely of the debate on knowledge, but of the structure of current social philosophy in general. Each kind of questioning addresses a particularity of the movement in thought that is characteristic of modernism. The first questioning refers to the alleged necessity of 'modernity' to distance itself from its context as well to the adverse consequences of such an attempt. The second questioning focuses on the capability of modernity to do so and to elevate itself to a position from which it can act on its context from the 'outside'. Emphasizing inevitable requirements, or needs, the former thus focuses on questions that are inescapable. Emphasizing the power of modernity, in contrast, or more precisely the lack of it, the latter focuses on the attainability of answers, or more precisely, again on those answers that cannot be entirely satisfactorily attained. Both objections thus provide a critique of modernity. The one critique is irreducible to the other, because of the different directions of criticism – even though, as Wittgenstein underlines, they are also related to each other and sometimes difficult to tell apart.

Cautiously introducing historicizing terms, the modernist discourse can be associated – rather self-evidently – with the advent of modernity, if the latter is characterized by the early, 'original' attempts at a distancing of the human self, constitutively a knowledge-seeker and political being, from its context. Key thinkers to be named are Descartes and Hobbes, in the so-called early modern period, and some Enlightenment thinkers slightly later (see in more detail Chapters 1 and 2). Opposing this modernist view, the theorizing that insists on the need for a substantive, rather than purely definitional or procedural, attainment of selfhood, knowledge and politics and, thus, on the substantive inescapability of these questions is a *first intellectual response* to the principled limits of this attempt at distancing. Historically, romanticism is its first full expression, and this thinking marked much of the nineteenth-century *controversy about the viability of modernity*. The *second response*, in contrast, is better understood as an intellectual *reaction to the historical success of modernity*, of the original distancing. It is in this sense that Nietzsche becomes the key figure in this mode of thinking. Rather than offering an answer for the question of attainability, as the first response does, this second response underlines the principled and persistent openness of the question. As a consequence, it redefines the idea of inescapability, which is turned from the need to find an answer into a horizon of a problématique. The second response reconnects to the first one, but it is unable to maintain the strong substantive stand that characterized the former.[6]

Vanishing Points of Modernity

This book will deal with the questions of the certainty of knowledge, the viability of the polity, the continuity of selfhood, the accessibility of the past and the transparency of the future as inescapable questions to which lasting answers are not attainable. It would not be very fruitful to identify exhaustively the questions that cannot be declined but not answered either. Certainly, not all questions of social science are of this category, although one may well think that the lack of a once-and-for-all attained answer to those inescapable questions may have some impact on the ways other questions are answered. Instead of trying to deduce the inescapability of issues, the persistence of problématiques across the history of philosophy and social theory may suffice as an indicator. This criterion should not immediately be taken to merely refer to persistence across time; issues must also persist across modes of conceptualization.

My ways of posing the questions may be seen to entail a bias towards modernist theorizing. But I am only affirming the questions, not the modernist answers. And I indeed take it to be one of the merits of modernism to have posed those questions in a clear and radical way. That is why I draw on the modernist way of formulating the questions more than on the other modes. To make the questions clearly recognizable in the other modes needs historical illustration and conceptual translation, both of which will be provided in the subsequent chapters. On the other hand, my case for the irreducible plurality of modes of theorizing may be seen to entail a bias towards the second response, to emphasize the problem of attainability. And I do indeed hold that this second response, and only it, opens the space for a full reflection of the significance of the questions. But the centre of my argument is provided by the idea that the three modes need to be related to each other to create the space of possibilities within which answers can be found.

Thus, I suppose that across the modes of theorizing these questions are generally recognizable as important and principally unresolved issues. True, from each of those positions one would tend to look for answers in somewhat different ways. But each specific answer would lose some relevant aspect of the issue out of focus. Something always escapes from sight. That is why the spatial metaphor of vanishing points is useful. The issues whose inescapability and attainability is in question are located at the vanishing points of social theorizing. They structure the perspective on the world, but they cannot be grasped themselves. The vanishing lines reach from the three poles of the triangular space of social theorizing towards those issues. The issues can be taken in view by each of the three modes, but each view will characteristically differ from each other. It is their reference to a vanishing point that holds them together, and it is their difference that creates a space of possibilities.

This book proposes to reconsider some of these unattainable yet inescapable issues by looking at the ways in which they have been approached and have always again escaped. The mode of presentation adopted here is not predominantly philosophical. Rather, the search for solutions will be located in historical space and time. The perspective is one of a historical sociology of ideas and practices, even if it is one that stretches sometimes across large distances. Given the issues it deals with, it works at the same time at the boundaries of sociological reasoning. If it achieves something of what it is meant to achieve, it will connect ideas about how one can think about modernity to ways of researching social worlds in which the modern imaginary signification is prominent.

Notes

1 Kant, 1993 [1781]: 3 [A VII], translation altered.

2 'Social science' is a term the meaning and connotations of which have changed historically and have often been contested. My argument operates with, and relies on, a historiography of the social sciences – as both social research and social theory – that cannot fully be explicated here. If a fuller and often more explicit account may at times appear desirable, elements of it are provided in Wagner (2001). To avoid misunderstandings, I may also add that, despite all criticism, I do not necessarily want to posit my own thinking outside of the social sciences. Rather, my own project can be understood as aiming at broadening the meaning of the term.

3 When Habermas (1985: 57) perceptively describes Hegel as the first philosopher 'for whom modernity became a problem', the task of the philosophical discourse is already implied, namely: solving this problem. Habermas praises Hegel for having fully identified and accepted the inevitable diremption of modernity, but he criticizes him for having

abandoned the one promising way for solving the problem, namely via a theory of communication and intersubjectivity. The debate between Habermas and his critics could be more fruitful if it were focused on the possibility that one can accept such a theoretical standpoint but nevertheless argue that modernity remains 'a problem' for the key aspects of which there is a variety of mutually irreducible 'solutions'.

4 As will become clear in the course of the argument, this is neither to say that there are no solutions at all nor that some solutions are not better than others. However, solutions are historical and thus likely to be temporary. And the criteria for the evaluation of their quality may themselves undergo change, at least in the course of major socio-political and intellectual transformations within modernity, and are open to dispute.

5 Whatever dissonance there may be between sensations and this image will then be treated as the secondary problem of the relation between theory and empirical observation. Throughout this book, it is precisely this relation that I propose to reconsider for a social theory of modernity.

6 In an earlier attempt, we have formalized the terminology and have referred to a first, second and third mode of social thought (Friese and Wagner, 1999a). The intention was to avoid more specific terms – such as 'romanticism' and 'Nietzscheanism' – which have connotations that tend to conform to unwanted preconceptions about these modes of thinking and, in addition, tend to apply to some of the problématiques to be discussed better than to others. The price of such a formalization in terms of new misunderstandings, however, is very high. Thus, this presentation will try to do without, hoping that the two crucial objectives can nevertheless be achieved: to show that (a) there is an interpretative space of social theorizing filled by a plurality of mutually irreducible modes (for which combat terms are inappropriate) and that (b) these modes can be related to each other by demonstrating their sharing common problématiques.

1

The Certainty of Knowledge

Doubts About Certainty

'Man who lives in a world of hazards is compelled to seek for security.' Thus starts a book that was published in the USA on 11 October 1929. Only a few days later, Wall Street crashed. And very soon after this event, the world seemed out of joint and security in short supply. In the history of the twentieth century, the world economic crisis of 1929 and the years after marked the starting point for, or at least the acceleration of, a new search for securities. The temporary outcomes of this search – through civil war, war and totalitarianism – were the relatively consolidated Western democracies of the 'thirty glorious years' with their Keynesian steering of the economy, proliferation of welfare policies and empirical and applied social and economic sciences. Not aiming at institutional analysis in this book or this chapter, I want to ask the question whether and in which way the development of those sciences can be understood as a part of this seeking for security in a world of hazards.

The book was John Dewey's *The Quest for Certainty*, and the precise timing of its publication was only coincidentally related to the Wall Street crash.[1] However, there is a broader context of crisis to which it indeed responds. For decades, concern had already been growing about the relation between the truth claims of philosophers to the kind of knowledge the sciences had been producing with increasing success throughout the nineteenth century. Those sciences, including the social sciences, were seen as overspecialized and fragmented while at the same time highly successful in generating new insights and in transforming the world through science-based technology. Having initially developed under the shelter of philosophy, they seemed to make philosophy – just like religion – both superfluous and unsustainable, since no ontological or metaphysical claims about any continuity of the order of things, nor any ground for that order, could be upheld in the face of rapidly changing scientific concepts and empirical insights.

The 'crisis of the European sciences' was to be declared by Edmund Husserl (1970) in the 1930s, and at about the same time Max Horkheimer and Martin Heidegger made programmatic proposals on how to overcome it, both in inaugural speeches that should each in their own way become notorious. Horkheimer criticized the 'chaotic specialization' (1931: 11) of the social sciences in his lecture on the occasion of his becoming director of the Institute for Social Research in Frankfurt in 1931 and sketched the idea of a critical historical materialism that should bring social research and social philosophy together. Martin Heidegger gave his inaugural address as the rector of the University of Freiburg only two years later – but in a fundamentally altered political situation. He, too, criticized the 'encapsulation of the sciences in compartmentalized disciplines' and their 'dispersion in isolated fields and corners' (1983a [1933]: 13) and demanded their reconnection in and through the 'essentiality and simplicity of posing questions in the centre of the historical-spiritual world of the people' (1983a: 17). With all that separated the one speaker from the other, they were nevertheless united in the diagnosis of a crisis and in the demand for a renewal of the relation between philosophy and the sciences. Furthermore, this renewal entailed for both of them a revaluation of philosophy, even though again in quite different ways. Horkheimer resorted to the tradition of German idealism, not least to Hegel. Heidegger asked his questions more radically, returned to Greek philosophy and wanted science to be again the 'questioning, unprotected resisting in the middle of the uncertainty of Being as a whole' (1983a: 14). While Horkheimer set the corner-stone for the mode of thinking that should become known as Critical Theory, Heidegger's work was to become a key reference for post-structuralism, the other major mode of contemporary critical theorizing, or, as we may wish to say in the present context, of a critique of modernity.

At the turn of the twentieth century, Deweyan pragmatism is often seen as a critical inquiry into the modern condition that avoids the pitfalls of the approaches inspired by Horkheimer and by Heidegger. Moreover, it is sometimes held to be the only one to have survived the transformations of modern social life between 1968 and 1989. This alone would be reason enough to warrant a detailed appraisal in the context of a review of the social theory of modernity. While no such comprehensive appraisal can be undertaken in this study, my discussion of the epistemological problématique of modernity will revolve around Dewey's conception of knowledge.

Rather than arguing for a revaluation through a return to original concerns, Dewey's gesture waves farewell to philosophy as it was known. 'I don't suppose the title means much,' he wrote to Sidney Hook after having given the organizers of the Gifford Lectures a title early in 1929, 'but on the historical side it is a criticism of philosophy as attempting to attain theoretical certainty' (Dewey, 1984 [1929]: 267). In the concluding lecture he likened the recent development of the sciences to a 'Copernican revolution', borrowing the term from Kant, the implications of which for philosophy he aimed to have spelt out.

> We have seen how the opposition between knowing and doing, theory and practice, has been abandoned in the actual enterprise of scientific inquiry, how knowing goes forward by means of doing. We have seen how the cognitive quest for absolute certainty by purely mental means has been surrendered in behalf of search for a security, having a high degree of probability, by means of preliminary active regulation of conditions. [...] The old centre was mind knowing by means of an equipment of powers complete within itself, and merely exercised upon an antecedent external material equally complete in itself. The new centre is indefinite interactions taking place within a course of nature

which is not fixed and complete, but which is capable of direction to new and different results through the mediation of intentional operations. (1984: 231–2)

Dewey thus puts knowing and the knower firmly into the world. Where philosophy was concerned with epistemologically grounded certainty, his active, operative understanding of knowledge is set in the context of a search for security that is always related to problems and situations. Dewey is closer to Heidegger than the different gestures of writing suggest – as Richard Rorty (1980) among others recognized. And if Rorty were right in seeing Dewey, Heidegger and Wittgenstein as the most important thinkers of the twentieth century, then the question of epistemic certainty should long have been put to rest and epistemology overcome (Taylor, 1995a). However this was far from being the case. Half a century after *The Quest for Certainty*, another 'report on knowledge' underlined the fact that the sciences of the twentieth century had continued to make unwarranted claims to superior knowledge. The author, Jean-François Lyotard (1984 [1979]: 25–7), resorted to Wittgenstein's notions of language games and their irreducible plurality to explain why such a claim could not be upheld. He thus became one of those who triggered off a new debate on epistemology, often now referred to in the context of discussions about postmodernity. Similarly, Stephen Toulmin, in his introduction to the 1984 edition, underlined the continued importance of *The Quest for Certainty* for its critical look on 'twentieth-century natural science, as well as (sic) on philosophy' (Toulmin, 1984: xiv). It seems then as if Dewey's call to abandon the quest for certainty has not been heeded. Or vice versa, if we consider the outraged reactions to the so-called postmodernist challenge to epistemology, it seems as if philosophers and scientists continue to see themselves engaged with the quest for certainty rather than with a Deweyan search for security.

In this context, this chapter returns to an analysis of what in my terminology would be called the modernist quest for certainty. However, it aims at broadening the issue by giving special consideration to the social sciences and their epistemological issues and by asking whether the further history of the twentieth century obliges us to review Dewey's diagnosis.[2] But the first look is at Dewey's proposal itself.

The Modernist Quest for Certainty

In the centre of Dewey's criticism was what he called the 'spectator theory of knowing' (1984: 195), namely the view that the world is exposed to the human gaze and that it is exactly this distance between the knowing subject and the object to be known that allows for certain knowledge. This idea is sometimes – and arguably wrongly – traced to Plato's distinction between a realm of essence and a realm of appearance. However, it acquires its particular modern guise when it is developed in response to radical doubt about the certainty of the world. As such, the main reference is to Descartes's *Discourse on Method*, inaugurating modernist rationalism on the basis of a radical positing of subjectivity, and later to Kant's *Critique of Pure Reason*, aiming to conclude the dispute between Cartesian rationalism and Humean empiricism.

The spectator theory of knowing thus starts out from a radical scepticism, from the attitude that nothing can be taken for granted. And it is in response to the doubts about the world around us as we experience it that the quest for certainty needs to proceed through a distancing from the world to gain an 'outside' look at it. The distancing from the sensations of the world was considered a precondition for the identification of those very few indubitable assumptions on which claims for valid knowledge can be erected. By the same move, the question of epistemology itself emerges as the problem of the relation between the 'reality' of the world and the 'representations' that human beings provide of the world in their philosophy and science. The preference in the philosophy of science was for a long time, as Dewey points out, for an epistemological formalism that presupposes this distance between the knower and that which is to be known. Thus emerges the *modernist* conception of knowledge. It went along with the quasi-sociological idea of separating out a social realm in which the pursuit of knowledge was possible in independence from other concerns of social life.

Dewey provides a forceful critique of this conception, and he shows how its adoption has created endless and futile debates in the philosophy of the sciences. It is exactly the force of the argument, however, which leaves one wondering how such an erroneous view could be held in the first place. There certainly are explanations that proceed via a denunciation of the interests of those who hold that view – be it the striving of humans for godlike power or be it the successful social distinction of professional philosophers from manual labourers (Toulmin, 1984: xiv). These explanations are disingenuous, however, in that they do not take into account the reasons given by the people in question themselves. Once the activities of philosophers and scientific researchers are considered as practical engagements with the world and not as a priori distinct from other activities, then it becomes possible to identify the particular problématiques they intended to address in specific situations. Dewey's philosophical critique, in other words, would need to be complemented by an interpretative history of philosophy, in particular of those key moments in philosophy – and their authors – that have become regarded as major turning-points of modernist thought.

Some recent writings in the history of philosophy and the sciences have indeed pursued, more or less consciously, such an agenda. As we have seen, Descartes has long been accused of promoting the unachievable and ultimately damaging project of grounding certainty beyond the specificity of experience. And to the present day, Hobbes's *Leviathan* is one of the key references when the similarly misleading attempt at grounding political order on an abstract conception of the individual human being and its rationality is discussed. While such critiques are well justifiable, they remain within the mode of denunciation and fail to grasp the core of those intellectual projects (for a critique of denunciation as a mode of theorizing, see Boltanski and Thévenot, 1991). More recently, Descartes's discourse on method has been read in context, that is as addressing the question of 'security' in human social life at a time when the consequences of the Reformation and the religious wars signalled one major step in the destruction of the foundations of certainty (Toulmin, 1990). Similarly, the long-neglected controversy between Hobbes and Boyle about the grounding of knowledge in experience marks another case in which the fervour of the attempts to re-establish certainties can hardly be explained otherwise than through the impact of violent religious strife on the consciousness of the authors (Shapin and Schaffer, 1985; Latour, 1993; Stengers, 1993).

In such a more contextual perspective, the specificity of both Descartes's and Hobbes's attempts is a high awareness of an inescapable dilemma. On the one hand, there is a deep intellectual consciousness of contingency, of the lack of stability and certainty. Radical doubt is indeed the starting point of the reasoning. In this sense, these episodes are rightly regarded as high points in the history of modernist thought, indeed inaugurating modernist discourse in philosophy and in political theory. On the other hand, Hobbes and Descartes were also driven by the conviction that humankind could not live well without some categories of social and natural life which impose themselves on everybody, and such categories would only impose themselves if and because they were undeniably valid. The situation of uncertainty that was experientially self-evident in a situation of devastating religious and political strife had to be overcome by appeal to an instance that in their view could only be outside such experience. The coexistence of these two, apparently incompatible, convictions gives their work a character which one might label dogmatically modernist: radical in their rejection of unfounded assumptions, but inflexible in their insistence on some definable minimum conditions of cognitive and political order that could, and would have to, be universally established. Or, to use Dewey's terms, that is how their fully understandable attempts to seek security ended in the claim for a superior rationality and truth that, in turn, Dewey was to interpret as part of the misconceived quest for certainty.

What, however, if we interpret the writings of Descartes and Hobbes strictly as activities in Dewey's sense that perform an operation on the world with a view to giving that world a new direction? Then, the authors would be identifying a problématique in a given situation, would aim at problem-solving and would be driven by a situation-specific sense of urgency – rather than aiming to provide a timeless truth of philosophy or political theory (which, of course, was how they themselves described their activities). And their project would in no way be distinct from what Dewey urges us to do. I suggest that the history of philosophy and the sciences should also be read from such an angle.[3] Such an approach would be able to address two issues that cannot be addressed by either a generalized pragmatism of Dewey's kind or by any of the philosophies that persist in the 'quest for certainty'.

First, it would resolve a tension in the pragmatist critique of philosophy that comes close to a performative self-contradiction. Pragmatism emphasizes that knowing is an activity and an operation in the world rather than anything happening in an entirely separate realm. However, it appears to deny such a worldly status precisely to those writings in which the case for an entirely separate realm of knowledge is made, i.e. the modernist approach to knowledge. The insistence on knowing as intelligent problem-solving in a given situation has to allow for different kinds of situations – not least situations with greater or lesser degrees of (experienced) security – and for different proposals to solve the problems at hand – not least solutions that work by generalization and solutions that work by specification. Modernism would then no longer fall into a separate category of knowledge-seeking, but would merely be that approach that insists on the need for generalization in – and because of – situations characterized by high insecurity.

As a consequence of such differentiation, second, this approach would allow for varieties in the search for security rather than remain content with working with a fundamental distinction between the legitimate desire for 'security' and the illegitimate striving for 'certainty'. (For this reason I will abandon Dewey's terminological distinction in the following and will interpret philosophy and science in the light of a more broadly understood search for certainty.) More specifically, it would invite to re-read the debate about 'the crisis of the European sciences' as a dispute about various ways of engaging the world. The dispute was certainly marked by the diagnosis that an instrumental concept of knowledge lending itself to the transformation of the world by means of technology was about to become predominant. In the first instance, however, it relied on the possibility of making distinctions between various conceptions of knowledge. As such, such a re-reading permits a consideration of the place of the social sciences in the quest for certainty – a question that is but very insufficiently addressed in *The Quest for Certainty* (see Chapter 8 of Dewey, 1984; of particular interest are pp. 169 and 174).

As to the question of the variety of quests for certainty in general, a few indications must suffice here. Most contributors to the debate in the early twentieth century worked with a strong distinction between philosophy and the sciences. In many of the European contributions, the loss of the hegemony of philosophy over the sciences was central to the problem. The initial observation of the fragmentation and compartmentalization of the sciences as a consequence of the loss of the philosophical umbrella led later to diagnoses such as the hegemony of instrumental reason – and thus the 'eclipse' of reason in a more comprehensive, objective sense – in Horkheimer and the emergence of modern technology as a new metaphysics in Heidegger. The alternatives these authors offered in their early writings pointed into different, but similarly viable and important directions for a rethinking. This was towards a historicization of knowledge for Horkheimer, although one that remained constrained by its Hegelianism. And this was the posing of the question of Being for Heidegger, although one which, despite its emphasis on temporality, did initially not allow any socio-historical contextualization and later only a very problematic one.

The alternative approach was to reject any return to philosophy, however conceptualized, and to embrace the new sciences. In different ways, this was what the (neo-) positivism of the Vienna Circle and American pragmatism both proposed. In Dewey's terms, positivism would transfer the – misguided, in his view – quest for certainty from philosophy to the sciences. It basically works with a model of a mind-independent reality and draws a clear boundary between knowing and acting. As a philosophy of science, positivism tries to establish the claim for the certainty of superior scientific knowledge in a new form, based not least on logic and mathematics, which for Dewey are merely one pole of possible knowledge. It is in this sense – and only in this sense – that *The Quest for Certainty* can be read as a critique of modern science, as Toulmin suggests. Dewey himself, however, embraces the sciences, not least because he sees them undergoing a decisive change in orientation as a consequence of Heisenberg's discovery of the principle of indeterminacy. In Dewey's view, the quest for certainty is therewith refuted and replaced by the search for security. Science will no longer want to discover laws of motion of antecedent objects, to which human beings have to conform, but will move to 'constructing enjoyable objects directed by knowledge of consequences' (Dewey, 1984: 217).

Important conclusions follow from this step. In the first instance, one might say that the road towards an analysis of the condition of knowledge in modernity remains open in Dewey, although he does not advance on this road himself at all. The reign of instrumental reason or of unfettered technology, in Horkheimer and Heidegger the outcome of their philosophy of knowledge and technology, is from Dewey's stand-point a mere historical-empirical possibility, the realization of which would need to be analysed (and Lyotard remains peculiarly undecided between those two positions). However, Dewey provides very little in terms of tools for an analysis of knowledge developments in society, not to speak of the absence of any actual such analysis. An occasionally very optimistic tone, which appears to take the forward change in knowledge for granted, is the only indication for his attitude and was often – not quite justly – criticized, especially by European readers, as displaying a 'hands-on' attitude to social change.

Beyond Dewey, a comparative-historical analysis of the sciences, and *mutatis mutandis* the social sciences, is required that sees those practices as the search for alternative ways to certainty after the insight into the absence of other – religious and metaphysical – foundations had become more widely accepted. Major parts of the scientific activities since the so-called scientific revolution (but also earlier) can be interpreted as precisely problem-solving activities in Dewey's sense. Exactly because they entailed action, not just observation, the sciences could create certainty rather than merely postulating it. But these activities have also always been accompanied by attempts to legitimate the special validity claims for scientific knowledge by recourse to philosophies of science and epistemologies that would fall under Dewey's verdict. An understanding of the relation between those two readings of science, and by implication of technology, is what is at stake in the early twentieth-century debate about the crisis of the sciences.

This discussion, however, shall not be pursued any further here. The remainder of this chapter proposes to read specifically the history of knowledge claims in the social sciences in the light of this problématique. This reading will be guided by two ideas. It is supposed that the history of the social sciences can largely be interpreted as a version of the quest for certainty, but that this quest takes particular forms in the social sciences. And, more specifically, it will be argued that the historicity of forms of knowledge, and by implication of forms of epistemic certainty, becomes particularly visible in an analysis of the social sciences.

The Quest for Certainty in the Social Sciences

Sociologists' convictions about the knowledge they produce are highly variable. The degree of certainty with which sociologists convey their findings differs individually, of course. But there are also broad changes in the sociological moods over time. The epistemic certainty of the 1960s stands out as an extreme case that provides a useful point of reference. About 1960, many sociological texts exuded an air of confidence over the validity of concepts and methods and over the degree to which social scientists would actually analyse and explain social phenomena adequately. Robert Fraisse (1981), a former French research administrator, reviewing his experience called this attitude 'epistemic optimism'. By 1980, such optimism had clearly waned and had given way to profound scepticism, persisting up to this day, as to the possibility of understanding societies sociologically. Such observations lead into reflections on the conditions for epistemic certainty or uncertainty in the social sciences.

In the historiography of the social sciences it is not unconventional to identify a long-term intellectual transformation that began during the 'classical' period at the beginning of the twentieth century and ended in the 1960s with the establishment of the 'modern' social sciences. The implication is often that the major epistemological, theoretical and methodological problems have been resolved over that period so that smooth progress of knowledge may occur from then on. While such a description indeed captures an important change, it argues from the point of view of fully established epistemic certainty at the end of this period. Indeed, a modernist approach to social science is fully established by the 1960s and becomes then dominant. However, I find it preferable to understand its emergence – in a long and contested process – as part of a major redefinition of the historical situation rather than as an unquestionable breakthrough (see Wagner, 1990; Wittrock and Wagner, 1992, 1996 for more detailed analyses). The requirements for epistemic certainty, which were not fulfilled at the beginning of this process, were being fulfilled through societal transformations that were related to this redefinition of the situation (on requirements for epistemic certainty, see Wagner, 1995). To sketch this historical trajectory an intellectual history or a history of the sciences alone will not suffice; an inquiry in political sociology is needed.

During the nineteenth century, the work of social scientists was often directly linked to state concerns, with a view to orienting social knowledge to policy-making. Such state-oriented social science defined the major political issue of the time, which in many countries was called 'the social question' or 'the labour question', in terms of finding a smooth way to exit from the earlier restrictive liberalism (or even, as in Germany, old regime). The growth of state involvement, while necessary, was mostly not seen as a radical break with earlier practice. Social élites just had to be more responsive to the needs of the population than they had been. Empirical social analysis was meant to both demonstrate the need for reforms, also against élite resistance, as well as develop and propose the type of measures that were required. Towards that end, no particular epistemological or ontological issues needed initially to be confronted; broadly, a sober empirical realism appeared to be sufficient for such a problem-oriented social science. Accordingly, a soft version of positivism prevailed among policy-oriented social scientists after the middle of the nineteenth century, committed to the extension of positive knowledge, and sometimes even evoking Auguste Comte's name, but without the religious fervour of the original project of a positive science of society.

Towards the end of the century, however, the historical situation was increasingly seen as one of rising uncertainty. It can thus be analysed in terms analogous to earlier situations in which a 'quest for certainty' was strongly voiced, such as the era of religious wars (p. 18) or the aftermath of the American and French revolutions (to be discussed in Chapter 2). In this case, it was the transformation of the restricted liberal modernity of the nineteenth century into a fully inclusive social configuration. By the end of that century, such transformation was widely regarded as impossible without major upheavals, and as highly undesirable in many views, but often enough also as inevitable (Wagner, 1994a, Chapter 4). The rise of the workers' movement and the resistance of the established élites to its demands appeared to offer a future of permanently incompatible interests and of continuous class strife that threatened the social order. The cultural-intellectual debates known as the *fin de siècle* laid bare the questioning of all foundations of the intellectual order. The advent of the First World War and, in a different way, of the Russian Revolution seemed to confirm many gloomy perspectives.

In this situation, many social scientists, such as importantly the 'classical' sociologists, were well aware of the event of a major social transformation and of the inadequacy of much of the accepted social knowledge of the time to understand this transformation. The shift in political orientations, i.e. increasing doubts about the viability of liberalism, was paralleled by a shift in epistemological orientations, i.e. renewed skepticism about the other central tenet of the Enlightenment tradition, the intelligibility of human action and the social world. The period around the turn of the century is now known as an intellectually extremely fruitful, even a classical era in many fields of social science, most notably sociology, psychology and economics. At that time, however, much of the work was pursued out of a sense of crisis, a feeling of inadequacy of many of the epistemological, ontological and methodological assumptions of earlier social science.

In terms of epistemology, social science saw itself forced to largely abandon the idea of representing social reality and accepted the view that conceptual constructions were dependent both on the means and forms of observation and perception and on the interest of the observer in the social world. American pragmatism is the most explicit case of such a reorientation, but similar, often much more tension-ridden, discussions were led in European debates, a prominent example being Max Weber's methodological writings. As a consequence, the formation of concepts became also much more problematic. Key concepts that had been taken to be self-evident were exposed to scrutiny. In particular, this applies to the set of collective terms, such as society, state, people and religion, and the set of terms referring to the human beings and their sense of continuous existence, terms such as individual, action, self, psyche. Certainty about these concepts was especially important, because in some form or other they were indispensable for theorizing the political order, in terms, namely, of some stable relation between the collective phenomena and the individual human beings. Epistemological and ontological questionings had repercussions on methodology. Statistical approaches, for instance, always rely on some assumptions about the aggregates, mostly states, and their components, mostly individuals or households. If certainty about these concepts was shaken, the ground for any research methodology also appeared unsafe.

As a consequence, the turn-of-the century approaches were less convinced about a determinist course of human history than earlier social science, and also less persuaded of the direct insight into any laws of the social world from empirical observation. Such uncertainty should, first of all, be expected to restrict the usability of social knowledge for purposes of action. The earlier call had been for better, 'positive' knowledge that would lead to better action; according to such a conception, action based on uncertain knowledge should entail uncertain outcomes. And indeed, the turn-of-the-century debates were marked by a chasm between social philosophizing that tried to live up to these insights, on the one hand, and empirical research that continued and even expanded rather unconcerned by such issues, on the other.

Through the early decades of the twentieth century, however, novel conceptions of the relation between knowledge and action were proposed that turned out to lend themselves to a greater involvement in policy than before. The world-political crisis of the First World War and the persistent instability of the inter-war period had the effect of giving such considerations a sense of urgency and of focusing the debates. It is in this sense that the coincidence of the publication of *The Quest for Certainty* with the crash at Wall Street gains significance for politico-intellectual history.[4] The epistemological critique of a misguided quest for certainty was voiced against the background of the experience of insurmountable uncertainty in socio-political life. Confidence in the orderly course of the social world seemed no longer that which was demanded, as the legacy of the Enlightenment wanted it for nineteenth-century social science. Rather, the acceptance of uncertainty was seen as a precondition for a search for knowledge that would guide change rather than conform to laws (see in more detail Wagner, 1999). This was also Dewey's view and expectation for future knowledge-seeking in the natural as well as the social sciences.

The Quest for Certainty Answered: the Discursive Constitution of the Social Fact

The further history of social science can nevertheless not easily be written in such terms. The critique of determinism was indeed linked to an emphasis on the feasibility of goal-directed political action, namely by the fundamental and critical epistemological presupposition that the social world is in important respects not found and discovered but made and invented. This novel combination, however, provided merely for one strand of debate in the inter-war social sciences. The other major strand severed its ties with turn-of-the-century social theory entirely and put social science on completely new foundations. And this latter strand was to have greater importance for social-scientific modernism. The key element here is the 'scientific world-view' of the Vienna Circle and the unified science movement, which created a similarly unprecedented linkage of positivist philosophy, socialist thought and modern sociological research, or what has also been called a blend of Comte, Marx and behaviourism. In an intellectual and political context of doubt and uncertainty, its proponents hoped to reaffirm the societal project of modernity by reproposing sociology as a science of equal epistemological standing with the allegedly more advanced natural sciences. Even though the direct impact of the

Vienna Circle remained limited, its broader perspective informed the overall reorientation in the social sciences.

For an example, we may turn to the history of statistics and of empirical social research. In statistics, the period between the end of the nineteenth century and the 1930s witnessed intense debates about a seemingly very specific methodological question. The problem was how to generalize observations collected from the study of a part to statements about the whole. Its solution was a number of statistical techniques summarized under the label of representativity. These techniques were developed simultaneously in debates within the statistical profession and about the design of social insurance arrangements. An institutional, a cognitive, and a political transformation were closely interlinked, 'the nationalization of social statistics, [...] the diffusion of the "representative method" and of random selection, and [...] the beginnings of the development of the Welfare State' (Desrosières, 1991a: 228). The transformation of the conceptually liberal state into a welfare state involved the 'substitution of the homogeneous language of statistics and social research for the contradictory language of rights' (Donzelot, 1991: 171; see also Österberg, 1988).

During the inter-war period, mathematical techniques spread to other areas of empirical research, not least to the emergent fields of opinion research, of business cycle research and of research into the social structure of society. Special research institutes were created, during those years and particularly after the Second World War, that were to provide the data to which those techniques were to be applied. From the late 1920s onwards, thus, the contours of an empirical positivist social science, being oriented towards application and developing in special institutions, which then should dominate the image of those sciences in the second post war era, are recognizable. This social science liberated itself from the doubts of the 'classical period' by methodologically circumventing the problem of relating the individual to society under conditions of mass society through (a particular version of) empirical social research. The doubts about epistemological and conceptual issues could not be entirely removed, but they could be dealt with, it was assumed, by starting from the most secure elements one could find, i.e. the empirical observation and collection of data on the preferences and behaviours of individual human beings. Conclusions referring to the larger scale of society and politics were arrived at by aggregation of those data; and the questions towards the answering of which data were generated or analysed were derived from policy needs for 'social control'. Thus, a 'soft' behaviourism aligned with a similarly 'soft' pragmatism.[5]

Such behavioural social research recognizes the individual human beings and their doings as a methodological starting-point, and it mostly rejects any prior assumptions about behaviours as 'unfounded' or, in Vienna Circle terminology, 'metaphysical'. Thus, it may be seen as drawing one – certainly not unproblematic – conclusion from a basic tenet of political modernity, the primacy of individual autonomy. However, it is a very different kind of individualism than the one assumed in either liberal political theory or neo-classical economics, where individual rationalities are postulated. In behavioural social research, social regularities can only be discovered through the study of the utterances or behaviours of individuals, not in any way derived. But after such regularities are identified, they may be reshaped by altering the possibilities of action.

On such a basis, the social sciences posed after the Second World War as methodologically, ontologically and epistemologically mature (see for more detail Wagner, 1994a: Chapter 7). Of particular relevance in the present context is the attempt to reach epistemic closure, which was pursued by much of the philosophy of the social sciences of the 1950s and 1960s, which measured the achievements of the social sciences against the alleged standards of the natural sciences (see for example, Nagel, 1961: Chapters 13–15). We could see here a 'modernist' grounding of epistemology, if we wanted to. The move is modernist because it rejects religion and metaphysics, but it provides for a grounding nevertheless, since it makes a claim for superior knowledge on the basis of allegedly unavoidable methodological and ontological decisions. Such a self-understanding of modernist social science could be exposed to a Deweyan critique. However, there is another possible interpretation. This social science can be seen as knowledge guiding human action towards the creation of future opportunities. This then would be a science as Dewey envisaged it. This interpretation is arrived at if we see this social science not as requesting certainty from a philosophical epistemology but as constructing certainty itself by its conjoint observation-intervention.

The cognitive process at work in data production, statistical procedures and processes of classification, as they are characteristic of contemporary social science, is not merely descriptive; it involves a labour of making equal, an 'investment in form' (Thévenot, 1985: 26). This labour is being performed to establish, often only temporarily and involving many efforts, a stable relation between persons and/ or things, thus reducing the uncertainty about the identification of a situation. The living conditions of those being identified as 'poor' according to a statistical analysis may vary strongly, and the people themselves may be unaware of any commonality among them. Being 'unemployed' becomes a strong and unequivocal statement on one's position only after an agreement over the use of the term has been reached; and again, the situations of those classified as such may differ widely inside this new group. Very often in the social world and in the social sciences, indeed, terms that were already in use may be redefined, or familiar situations may be put under a new term; a fact which explains the particular social labour that has to accompany conceptual innovation (Stengers, 1993: 113).

Such work of 'making equal' is a prerequisite for collective action. Those engaging in collective action will envisage a certain commonality with others, at least with regard to what is relevant for their common activities. There is a close linkage between 'addition (rendering equivalent) and coalition (action)', as Alain Desrosières (1991b: 200; also 1993) emphasizes, who titles his analysis of the relation between social sciences, statistics and the state programmatically 'How to make things which hold together'. Orders have to be created by assembling diverse elements to groups of equals.

Much effort in the modernist social sciences was devoted exactly to the construction of categories, and to the means of measuring them, that made it possible to deal with human beings as well-ordered groups with predetermined interests and ambitions instead of a great variety of idiosyncratic strivings.[6] By these means, the social scientists extended the reach of their concepts and were able to include ever more beings; that is how they often saw themselves, Paul Lazarsfeld for instance (Pollak, 1979), as constructively responding to the needs of mass society. These efforts showed a cognitive affinity to the state-centred construction of institutions of oversight and monitoring of human beings, of the all-inclusive, well-stratified social configuration now known as the interventionist welfare state, or of 'organized modernity' (Wagner, 1994a).

If this brief analysis of modernist social science as a transformative practice holds, how is it related to the apparently contradictory observation on the attempts of endowing this social science with strong epistemological validity claims? The paradox is resolved by pointing out that claims to certainty may have to be made to render knowing as an activity successful. The trajectory of the social sciences that I tried to describe is constitutively historical in the sense that a double – socio-political and intellectual – process of construction was at work in which the success of the one validates the success of the other. The social-scientific quest for certainty was made under conditions of great uncertainty. This quest for certainty was answered by a socio-political transformation that – by and large – produced those social relations and structures that had epistemically been hypothesized at the beginning. Conceptual rigour in the social sciences was often a very practically oriented means to deal with situations of great uncertainty. The quest for certainty posed as a want for epistemological purification. However, the desire for certain knowledge is nothing but the desire to lay the foundations for practices such that a legitimate call can be made on everybody to pursue their intellectual (and political) reasonings from the same, limited and well-defined, premises so that certainty over the actions of others will be achieved.

In periods of strife during the twentieth century, approaches to social science aimed at offering a minimum of descriptors of the social world on which everybody could agree. Among those approaches we find: the work of social statisticians, as mentioned above, already from the end of the nineteenth century; the 'scientifica-tion of work' early in the twentieth century, and Keynesian economics slightly later, as means to transform industrial relations into a co-operative positive sum game (Maier, 1970; Thévenot, 1985); opinion research as a foundation for an enlightened interaction between élites and masses between the wars; and the 'scientification of politics' after the Second World War. These endeavours all marked major steps in the development of the modernist social sciences and in the construction of a language for social action that was common for actors otherwise situated in conflictive relations. The claim that the language was, and should be, common could be made if its concepts and propositions could be referred to as higher-order knowledge. The epistemic claims of the modernist social sciences provided the material to do so. Nevertheless it would be wrong to conclude that epistemic reasoning merely served to legitimate political projects. Both projects shared the search for common foundations for practice; and they did so particularly intensively in periods of far-reaching dissent and strife. In all of the cases men-tioned above, innovations in the social sciences have not merely been new, 'more adequate' descriptions of the social world, but they have been active interventions into that world, attempts to create a coherence of social action.

The epistemic optimism of the 1960s then stemmed from the perception that such foundations had been successfully laid, that the language that had been developed actually described social phenomena, that 'things' as they were produced in the social sciences actually 'held together'. By that time it appeared as if the efforts social scientists had put into the discursive constitution of social facts, since the 1930s and partly earlier (in some European countries only from a later point onwards), had paid off.

Epistemic Certainty Reconsidered

If I appear to have argued that much of twentieth-century social science has been an intellectual artifice that tries to hold social things together, there is no element of denunciation in this argument as such. The social sciences are part of the discursive self-understanding of social life; and their attempts at creating a coherent intelligible order cannot be separated from other such attempts. It is vain to try to distinguish the kind of certainty that was searched for and socially produced in the modernist social sciences from any 'true' epistemic certainty over the reality of the world. The actions of others are an important part of the reality of the world. If somebody, thus, succeeds in prescribing permissible ways of reasoning and acting, then valid knowledge of the world is obtained exactly in as far as these rules are observed.

The term 'holding together' describes the emergence of activities around a phenomenon so that it is actually constituted. The concept 'unemployment', for example, used to hold together in our societies, at least until the recent past, because it was sustained by a legal definition; an institution that declared individuals to be in this state or not and that distributed objects as proofs of such status (identification cards as well as money); and theories of explanation and justification for the phenomenon, partly emanating from the economic sciences. Actualized practices, often sustained by objects and discourses, are the precondition for such concepts to 'hold'. If this is the case, then people may also agree that they hold sufficiently together. It is not even necessary for this to be the case that practices, objects and justifications fully cohere. Not all individuals who consider themselves unemployed need to be recognized by the official institution as well as endowed with the respective material objects, and share one of the common theories on the phenomenon. However, the term 'unemployment' becomes very unspecific, once the situation is no longer tied to an institution that endows the status with rewards (placement priority and/or benefits) and once the theories of justification can no longer sustain the normality of waged labour. It is not only that the concept becomes 'theoretically' difficult to uphold; it vanishes and disappears also as an empirical phenomenon when people no longer report their status, because it does not 'make sense' to them.[7]

For about three decades now, an increasing questioning of the cognitive conventions, of the 'conventions of evidence' in the social sciences is observable (Friese and Wagner, 1997; Fyfe and Law, 1988; Wagner, 1994a: Chapter 9). All of the features of modernist social science that I have discussed in the two preceding sections are being questioned. These conventions have themselves been very gradually established, as I argued above, in a long, contested process from the late nineteenth century onwards and have been in place as widely accepted conventions only for a short period, the 1950s and 1960s, obviously with variations between countries. By 1960 hardly any text on sociological epistemology could be found that did not – implicitly or explicitly – insist on the principled superiority of sociological knowledge.[8] By the 1990s, it was very common to criticize the lack of distinction between sociological and other knowledge of the social world, on the one hand, and – not without tensions in the argument – the distorting work of modernist sociology on the social world, on the other. At the same time, the very existence of 'social structures', and even more so its determining impact on human action, was doubted. In intellectual practice, structural sociology, very broadly understood, loses out to 'thick' descriptions of unique histories and cultures, on the one hand, and to a-structural individualist theorizing, on the other.

The debate on postmodernism in sociology has been the most explicit expression of the new epistemological uncertainty. The postmodern challenge is often seen to question the possibility of attaining valid knowledge at all, as a general philosophical proposition, so to say. It inevitably leads into relativism, as many observers argue, i.e. into a situation in which a plurality of knowledge claims exists, but no means to decide between them.[9] The idea that there always is a strong moment of undecidability between validity claims, most commonly associated with the label 'linguistic turn', integrates the study of language itself into social philosophy and insists on the relative openness of the languages of description of the social world. It obviates thus the presupposition – as a presupposition – that the language of social theory provides an adequate mirror of the social world. In a more empirical mode, research in the 'new' sociology of scientific knowledge since the 1970s has aimed at analysing scientific practices symmetrically, i.e. without any presuppositions regarding the validity of knowledge claims. Taken together, these two strands of thinking and research have significantly questioned the access routes of social theorizing to valid statements about the social world. In turn, the proponents of these strands have been accused of opening the door to a dangerous principled relativism and of entirely abandoning the search for valid knowledge (see Fuller, 1998; Outhwaite, 1999 for recent critical assessments of the issue for social theory).

On the one hand, this debate reflects increasing incoherence of social practices, in the sense in which coherence was defined by the modernists: many practices tend to hold much less together (Wagner, 1996). On the other hand, this debate is exactly a response both to the kind of epistemological claims made in modernist social science, now deemed unjustifiable, and to the mode of concept-formation, now seen as involving reification. The discourse on postmodernity criticizes modernist social science as being founded on notions, a priori, of the intelligibility of the social world, of the coherence of social practices and of the rationality of action. The criticism has culminated in radical reconstructions of the problématique, sometimes leading to positions from which any social science, regardless of its form, becomes difficult to conceive. As mentioned earlier, Richard Rorty's celebration of contingency (1989) is a major example for such reasoning; and it is relevant in our context not only because the author situates himself with the pragmatist tradition.

The critique of all attempts at grounding basic concepts of philosophy and the social sciences leads Rorty to a general conclusion on the need to start out from the assumption of contingency. By discussing language, selfhood and community under the aspect of their contingency he effectively undermines the ground on which social science takes place – only however to raise to prominence two other concepts, cruelty and solidarity, or more precisely, solidarity in the face of cruelty. There are two ways to read this proposal. Either it is interpreted as a philosophical statement of the classical kind – despite all its author's disavowals. Then, it reiterates themes to be found in Dewey, Heidegger or Wittgenstein, but its dogmatism of contingency fails to provide any insights for a sociology of solidarity (Friese and Wagner, 1999b). Or it is read as a social philosophy of our time. Then, it underlines the recent fairly radical restructuring of the social world that entailed the decomposition of many of the key categories of the social sciences, including those that have most often been considered as indispensable, the individual human being ('self') and the society ('community'). By implication, the language of the social sciences is demonstrated to be of a contingent and not of an epistemologically superior nature.

If read in the latter way, Rorty would argue for a reflection on our languages and on the concepts and forms of community and selfhood as permanent tasks of the social sciences – especially, but not only, in situations of serious doubt like the present one. The latter qualification is important. Dewey (1984: 195) reserved a strong verdict for a philosophy that sticks to its quest for certainty:

> Any philosophy that in its quest for certainty ignores the reality of the uncertain in the ongoing processes of nature denies the conditions out of which it arises. The attempt to include all that is doubtful within the fixed grasp of that which is theoretically certain is committed to insincerity and evasion, and in consequence will have the stigmata of internal contradiction.

In the light of our earlier considerations this statement may be read as an indictment of the modernist social sciences. They rested on assumptions about the certainty of the social world, and that is indeed where they failed – proved both contradictory and evasive, sometimes also insincere – when nature proved to be more uncertain than expected.

Nevertheless the reference to 'the reality of the uncertain' contains a significant openness. It invites the question about the degree of certainty that is attainable in different states of the real. Rather than embracing contingency, the social sciences may better aim at understanding socio-historically variable degrees of attainable certainty. Commonly, sociology has worked with either of 'two restrictive definitions [...], which presuppose the safeguarding of order and refuse to deal with the doubt: a) a unanimity or similarity of behaviour subject to common material constraints or well mastered by shared ideas (beliefs, representations); b) a diversity of actions integrated through systematic articulation (division of functions, of roles)' (Thévenot, 1993: 276; on the following see also Wagner, 1994b).

'Limited spaces of action in which the permanence of a universe of objects and routines guarantees stability and similarity of conduct' may and do exist empirically (Thévenot, 1990: 57). However, a basic theoretical terminology cannot presuppose such restrictive understandings, but must be able to account for two different types of situations likewise. In social life, there are such 'moments in which the activities of persons hold together, [people] adapt to each other and achieve agreement over an order of things, moments that tend to allow for notions of objective constraint, social norm, equilibrium, successful communication, fulfilment of the speech act and the like.' But there are also those 'moments in which unrest dominates the scene and reveals disputes over what is at stake, moments of uncertainty, of more or less critical doubt.' (Thévenot, 1990: 57–8) The important insight is that the latter, not the former, make for the analytically more general case. The latter should not be treated as a deviant case of the former; rather the former emerges analytically (not necessarily empirically) from the latter through creative human action.

Such reversed perspective renounces 'any conception that regards the unity and cohesion of a group as the product of a substantive similarity between its members and of an objectively shared interest'. Attention will instead be directed towards 'the immense historical labour that is necessary to unite disparate beings around the same system of representation, to constitute the reality of such a heterogeneous ensemble, to inscribe it into devices (*dispositifs*) through an intensive effort of objectification and to endow it with a common interest' (Boltanski, 1990: 70). At the heart of the epistemic certainty of the 1960s is no epistemological, conceptual or methodological achievement in the social sciences, but rather the successful accomplishment of such historical labour.

Historicizing Epistemology

In the light of the preceding historical observations, the question can now be posed anew of what it means to overcome or abandon epistemology and whether this is a feasible project. On the one hand, a (broadly understood) pragmatist conception of knowledge seems the only one that is defendable. And since this conception rejects the assumption of a clear-cut separation of a mind-independent reality from the human knowledge about such reality, it undermines the traditional epistemological question. If this is what it means to overcome epistemology, then the case can be considered closed. For a social scientist, however, the problem remains that human beings in the social world persistently make arguments for forms of knowledge that are held to be superior to others. The persuasive force of those arguments may have an impact on whether knowledge will be widely accepted and whether people will act on the basis of such knowledge and transform the social world. Even if epistemology in a traditional sense is overcome, actual claims for knowledge and their impact will have to keep being investigated.

Rather than pretending not to know anything about history, as Rorty implicitly does, such epistemic claims need to be investigated in the historical context in which they are made. As I tried to argue above, much of the history of the social sciences and of social philosophy can be read as knowledge claims being made in problematic situations and with the practical aim to solve those problems. This observation can be formulated in such a way that the difference to the position adopted by pragmatists is emphasized: epistemic claims are made as a part of solving problems. Such statement opens a research agenda for social theory and philosophy that pragmatism cannot address. Pragmatism tends to consider the epistemic problématique as overcome once knowledge-seeking is understood as problem-solving. Thus, it underestimates the significance of the argumentative means to settle disputes in situations in which the interpretations of the 'problem' as well as the proposals to deal with it are diverse and contradictory. One cannot rest content with a general refutation of epistemically formulated validity claims. Such claims should be read less as statements about the world, statements which could indeed be denounced by a critique of epistemology, than rather as ways of questioning the world, whose 'truth' resides always in their nature as action on problems. Thus our question may now be reread as to why specific ways of questioning the social world appeared particularly plausible at certain times. In this light, we can return to the history of the social sciences and their epistemic claims, in particular during the twentieth century.

Up to the end of the nineteenth century, most of social science had proceeded on the assumption that radical doubt about that which held the social world together was unwarranted or 'unreasonable', to use Wittgenstein's term. By and large it applied a more or less systematic empirical-observational approach with a view to solving social problems and took the rootedness of social life in customs and habits, in a loose sense, for granted. In the terminology I proposed earlier, it hardly was modernist at all. Social science had emerged, however, against the background of quite different traditions of political philosophy and of political economy. The former had taken its inspiration from Hobbes, Locke and Kant who, at various points in European history, had seen the need for a radical distancing from the situations they lived in to provide an angle from which to solve its problems. (The relation of political philosophy to social science will be systematically discussed in the following chapter.) The latter emerged from moral philosophy, but adopted an increasingly formal approach to exchange relations between individual human beings, in parallel with the unfolding of a capitalist economy. These traditions, which as a shorthand we can call the liberal-individualist and rational-individualist approaches respectively, promoted modernist social theorizing. Both contained promises for certainty, namely a contractual agreement on societal order in the former case and automatic self-harmonization of social life in the latter.

In the early twentieth century, it appeared very strongly that these promises could not be kept. These versions of modernist theorizing lost their persuasiveness when the constructions erected according to their principles seemed to fall apart. In the turmoil of industrialization, urbanization and workers' protest, however, the established versions of social thought could not gain plausibility, since the very idea of substantive rootedness of social life seemed to refer to a 'traditional' past. This is the problématique with which the 'classical' sociologists struggled, and from this context modernist science gradually emerged as an alternative source for certainty. The precariousness of the situation encouraged the adoption of a strong version of what Dewey called the quest for certainty.

The critique of science and philosophy developed by Nietzsche, Heidegger, Dewey and Wittgenstein between the late nineteenth and mid twentieth century shifted the emphasis from the 'unreasonableness' to the 'impossibility' of radical doubt. Thus, it inaugurated the second response to modernist social theorizing. From our brief analysis two conclusions about this step can now be drawn.

First, this critique of science has a particular historical context of emergence. It followed upon the rapid development of the scientific disciplines during the nineteenth century and the increasing application of their findings in what is often called the second industrial revolution at the end of that century. Its problématique is circumscribed by the exigency to develop a critical perspective on the impact of modernism on the one hand, but the lack of plausibility of any recourse to 'tradition' or 'embeddedness' of social life, which would appear as an impossible return in time, on the other.

What is characteristic in this respect about the inter-war period, i.e. Dewey's time of writing *The Quest for Certainty*, is that the situation is not the same for the social sciences. There is as yet no fully spelt-out modernist perspective in the social sciences (excluding neo-classical economics, which, however, was still rather marginal), i.e. one that displays a coherent set of epistemological, ontological and methodological assumptions. The difference between a creative social science based on a pragmatist epistemology (or rather, pragmatist epistemic considerations, to avoid a contradiction in terms) and a technocratic social science based on an epistemology of certainty cannot be named. In contrast to Dewey's view about philosophy and the sciences, both such forms of social science would see themselves as problem-solving activities. The latter would only make the additional claim that an idea about superiority of knowledge is required to convince social actors about the adequacy of the solution that is proposed.

After the Second World War and the growth of the social sciences during the 1950s and 1960s, a debate about the forms of social knowledge and their various relations to action develops. In this debate, the so-called post-structuralist analyses of 'the discourses of the human sciences' propose a novel mode of theorizing that, it appears, is not yet sufficiently recognized as such – both in terms of its contributions and in terms of its limits. Derrida, Foucault and Lyotard, to name the most important contributors, continue the critique of epistemology and ontology and apply it consciously to the social sciences. Foucault in particular, and to some extent Lyotard, also develop a critical perspective on the relation between those forms of knowledge and power in contemporary societies. However, the situation of social theory and philosophy after this critique is only alluded to and never explicated. The observations above suggest the need for a historicization of epistemology rather than its overcoming. Epistemic claims need to be taken in their historical context to understand the problem they aim to address.

The second conclusion after this critique may appear surprising, but to some extent it follows from the first one. Despite its most recent appearance and its critical force, this theorizing cannot be taken to invalidate or supersede the other two modes. Dewey's programme for intelligent problem-solving seems to imply that 'intelligence' will arrive at the one or best solution for a given problem without epistemic grounding. His argument then appears, at first sight, to be compatible indeed with a universal pragmatics and to lead further than both Wittgenstein's and Heidegger's reasoning, as those authors are allegedly marked by a 'deficit of reflection' and an 'a priori of contingency' (see, for example,

Apel, 1991: 49 and 68). If there were the space here to complement the short history of twentieth-century social science with a history of other proposals for solving the 'same' socio-political problems, the historically doubtful character of such an argument on implicit universalism would become evident. But also in theoretical terms, an understanding of human intelligence as creative (Joas, 1996) would have to allow for the possibility of a plurality of interpretations of any situation as 'problematic' as well as of a plurality of solutions to what is determined as the 'problem'. To introduce a moment of openness and thus undecidability is precisely what distinguishes this more recent theorizing from modernism, which has an abstract and procedural solution, as well as from the first, rather nineteenth-century response to modernism, which has a solution whose roots are antecedent to the 'problem'. If these are the indispensable advantages of the recent critique of modernism, its deficits would also disappear once this theorizing took its own and often repeated call for historicity seriously (see for a similar argument Skirbekk, 1993).

Such historicization would focus attention on situations that are embedded in spatially and temporally widely extended contexts. Available languages of evaluation are neither a priori universal nor mutually untranslatable, but will have developed across reconstructable periods and spaces. They are the resources to deal with arising situations of conflict and diversity in which agreement needs to be reached or in which, at least, some interpretations and solutions of the problem at hand require that agreement be reached. In such a situation, which we may call political, a recourse to something that is outside the situation itself is necessary. Participants in the dispute will have recourse to orders of justification and, even without invoking the term epistemology or talking about certainty, they will argue why their solution is more adequate than others to the situation (Boltanski and Thévenot, 1991). At this point, conventional terminology suggests that we shift terrain and move from epistemology to political philosophy. There is a shift indeed, but to fully recognize its significance some continuity of problématique must be preserved. It is part of my argument that the social sciences narrowed their epistemic basis for what at first sight appear as 'extra-epistemological' reasons, namely for reasons of the viability of the polity. This aspect will be explored further in the next chapter.

Notes

1 The publication was rushed after the presentation of the Gifford Lectures, on which the book is based, in Edinburgh in the spring of that year, and the reason for the rush was Dewey's forthcoming seventieth birthday on 20 October.

2 Toulmin (1984: xiii–xiv) suggests boldly that Wittgensein's – rather than directly Dewey's – related ideas had a considerable influence on the development of the human sciences and on 'social theory'.

3 The first volume of Hannah Arendt's *The Life of the Mind* (1978) is such an attempt to re-read the history of philosophy in the view of thinking as an experience, the full reach of which seems to me not to have been sufficiently recognized.

4 And both events also fell into the year when the report on *Recent Social Trends*, commissioned by President Hoover, was delivered by William F. Ogburn. The report is a

major example of a social-statistical attempt to grasp the main lines of societal developments with a view to enabling government action.

5 This formula was suggested to me by Dorothy Ross in a comment on Wagner, 1999b.

6 Only to a much more limited extent can we recognize the intellectual intention to render human beings able to act collectively by themselves.

7 Vice versa, one might also argue that the neo-liberal critique of unemployment benefits – that cases are reported which are not 'real', to obtain the benefits – can be voiced more strongly now that the concept is already weakened.

8 In an assessment of the achievements of sociology during the postwar period, Christopher Bryant (1990: 76) identified three major advances since the 1950s, namely the 'widespread recognition of the problem of foundationalism, near-universal acknowledgement of the linguistic turn, and a growing interest in social science as moral inquiry.' Now, while I am in full agreement both with the analysis and with the evaluation, I doubt that every sociologist regards these developments as progress. To some, the foundations of the discipline as a realistic, value-neutral study of social facts, healthily in place at about 1960, will appear as shaken and on the verge of demise today.

9 In the social sciences, this claim receives a specific, dual form. Postmodernism may voice doubts about the intelligibility of the social world either because of certain specific features of the philosophy of the social sciences – the double hermeneutics, for instance – or because of recent changes in the social world that made it less intelligible than it once was. Thus, a rather theoretical-philosophical postmodernism can be distinguished from a rather empirical component of contemporary epistemological debates (see also Wagner, 1992).

2

The Viability of the Polity

What is the social outcome of the actions and interactions of individual human beings? This is presumably one of the key questions of any social science. Toward the end of the eighteenth century, the emergence of what came to call itself social science meant a deep transformation in the range of possible answers that could be given to this question. One key element of the emerging conception was the view that the social outcome of such human strivings, if left uncontrolled, would not be disorder and warfare. A well-intelligible and potentially stable order of social relations would emerge, based, in a very broad sense, on exchange (Hont, 1987). This view was built not least on the idea that to leave human strivings on their own, without any detailed moral commands and external agency to enforce those commands, may not necessarily open social interactions to all contingencies. A certain predictability and stability could be inferred to passions and interests.

Regardless of its validity, one very peculiar feature of this thinking is worth noting. Emphasizing the predictability and stability of human inclinations and their results is an eminently political move. It is a concern for the practical order of the world, which was to be sustained by the identification of some theoretical order inherent in the nature of human beings and their ways of socializing. It has become customary to describe the intellectual developments between 1750 and 1850 as a transition from political philosophy to social science (for example, in Heilbron et al., 1998; Pagden, 1987a). However, political concerns do not disappear from the rising social sciences, rather they are decisively transformed. In this chapter, my objective is to trace this transformation of thinking about politics in the social sciences over the long-term, up until the present.

Rephrasing Foucault (1966: 355–6), I will first argue that, while the transformations of the human sciences marked indeed a major 'event in the order of knowledge', this event was decisively shaped by the experience of the so-called democratic revolutions in North America and in France. The restructuration of political orders and their modes of justification created aporias that should accompany political thinking until the present. Political philosophy in the aftermath of these revolutions has often been seen as being on the decline. I will try to show that all the transformed ways of understanding political matters that emerged during the nineteenth century can be read as modes of dealing with the post-revolutionary aporias. They were centred, affirmatively or critically, on the liberal idea of the polity, but – as social sciences – they insisted that liberal-individualist political philosophy on its own was insufficient to understand a social order.

Two notes of caution may here be appropriate. First, any kind of highly synthetical presentation as I intend to give here can only be very cursory, and will sometimes even risk being caricatural. In my view, though, the unfolding of such a large map can nevertheless be of help in understanding events in intellectual history, not least in terms of identifying rifts across large discursive formations when each small change seems to be smooth. Second, as to the substance of the map, a possible reproach could be to have presented merely a sophisticated version of a Whiggish history of individualism-cum-liberalism, in particular in the light of recent attempts to revive pre-liberal, republican thinking through a revised historiography (see, for example, Pettit, 1997; Skinner, 1997). In this chapter individualism-cum-liberalism will indeed appear as an organizing centre for social and political thought during the past two centuries. By presupposing, even if only hypothetically, a reason-endowed individual as the starting-point of analysis, individualist liberalism provides for a modernist form of political philosophy. This clear-cut presupposition gave this discourse its strength and coherence. Although the very presupposition simultaneously invited for criticism, this discourse thus gained a centrality in the discursive field, which meant that hardly anybody could avoid referring to it, be it affirmatively or critically. Nevertheless my observation of such centrality should not be misunderstood as implying that a commitment to 'modernity' irrefutably demands a commitment to liberal-individualist discourse. The analysis in terms of a history of concepts overlaps with a history of political modernity that starts out from the American and French revolutions but hardly embarks on any linear path of institutionalization of liberal forms. What I aim to show is therefore, in the first instance, a kind of historical, but not a theoretical, inevitability of individualism-cum-liberalism. This historical analysis is then meant to re-open the debate about possibilities of political philosophy, a debate that I take up at the end of the chapter.

Starting out from the revolutionary events, two main lines of post-revolutionary thinking can be distinguished in the course of the nineteenth century. One line emphasizes that politically relevant features of social life pre-existed the formation of the polity and remained significant; this is the political form of the first response to modernism. The other line points out that the rules of the polity created social structures which, in turn, determined political life; this leads into modernist social science, i.e. another form of modernist theorizing, one that relates to, but transforms the modernist form of political philosophy. In other words, this reading will demonstrate that the social sciences, as they developed over the past two centuries, remained deeply impregnated with the problématiques of political philosophy, even though they transformed them decisively. It will also contribute to understanding the discursive alliance of individualist liberalism and modernist social science, as two versions of modernist discourse, that dominated the political self-understanding of Western societies during the 'thirty glorious years' after the Second World War. The hegemony of this alliance seems to be waning at the end of the twentieth century when the debate about the need for a 'rethinking of the political' signals a re-opening of issues. Since the modernist concepts of both the polity and the political subject are questioned, these most recent developments will be presented as the emergence of the second response to modernism in political thinking.

Liberty and Certainty: the Aporia of a Science of Politics Under Conditions of Modernity

The pervasiveness of political issues in the early social sciences, i.e. in authors like Smith, Condorcet or Hegel, is plainly evident. In political terms their modes of reasoning were, however, marked by a curious paradox. These authors were working in the shadow of liberalism (in a very broad sense), namely accepting the right of human beings to self-determine their individual and social lives, even though not always without important qualifications. At the same time, though, they were holding that the free action of human beings would not actually generate, as one might innocently assume, a very wide range of possible individual and social forms and orientations of behaviour. Given complete autonomy, human beings would reveal themselves not to be free in a radical sense, but driven by a limited number of well-intelligible inclinations. One might even infer that it was exactly this predictability and order that gave grounds and reasons – to these authors themselves and to more hesitant others – not to reject the normative project of liberty. And this linkage of freedom and predictability became particularly important in the historical moment when the externally imposed barriers to free deliberation were threatened to be removed, the moment of the American and French revolutions.

These revolutions gave institutional expression to the political aspect of a broader culture of individual autonomy that is a key element of modernity. In this sense, much of this era can be seen as a liberation of human beings from imposed ties, but this liberation was far from unproblematic. As Claude Lefort (1986b: 214–15) once described this feature of modernity:

> When he is defined as independent, the individual does not exchange [...] one certainty against another one. [...] The new mode of existence of the individual within the horizons of democracy does not merely emerge as the promise to control one's own destiny, but also and not less as the dispossession of the assurance as to one's identity – of the assurance which once appeared to be provided by one's place, by one's social condition, or by the possibility of attaching oneself to a legitimate authority.

Liberation is here interpreted as an increase of contingency and uncertainty in the lives of human beings.

If this view were unequivocally valid, one should expect a philosophy of contingency – in Richard Rorty's style, for instance – linked to a liberal-individualist political theory to dominate the intellectual scene forever after the successful revolutions. However, historically this was not at all the case. I have briefly mentioned above the customary view that political thought declined throughout the nineteenth century, precisely after that historical point when the free and open deliberation about the things people have in common could be seen to be moving from the mere realm of discourse into actual social practice. To quote just one recent author's view, 'the historical moment, about which we speak, emerges in such a way that the real rising of the political instance entails its theoretical abatement' (Manent, 1994: 123).

At the same time, one might also have expected any kind of reasoning to fall out of fashion that assumed that the actions of human beings were somehow shaped and controlled by forces beyond their immediate reach. Social factors such as one's 'place', 'social condition', or attachment to an authority, to return to Lefort, should have played more of a role for human social life, and for thinking about human social life, before these revolutions than after. The beginning of modernity should have been a deeply anti-sociological occurrence. Again, however, almost the opposite turned out to be true. 'Society' as the object of the social sciences has been a 'postrevolutionary discovery'; or, to put it even more succinctly, 'the sociological point of view constitutes itself in the moment when the notion of liberty becomes the principal articulation of the human world' (Manent, 1994: 75 and 113; see Therborn, 1976, for an earlier analysis of the emergence of sociology 'between two revolutions').

Such apparent paradox reveals the aporia of political thought after liberation. Very generally speaking, the social sciences are exactly a part of the response human beings gave to their new condition of – self-incurred, one might say – contingency and principled uncertainty. Being unable to rely any longer on externally defined certainties, political thinkers started searching, sometimes almost desperately, for regularities and continuities which exist without being commanded. The social sciences have been a means to decrease contingency (as I tried to argue in much more detail in Chapter 1). It is not least in this context that inescapable questions were reformulated such that answers became attainable.

Earlier political thought had already recognized the inevitable circularity of a reasoning in which unity should rise from diversity as well as, at the same time, impose itself on diversity. At that time, however, there was room to try to approach the issue by mere conceptual construction and theoretical determination. As long as there were barriers to the practice of liberty, every conceivable view on its outcomes and consequences for the polity could be held. The mode of reasoning was bound to change when those barriers were removed and experiences were made and when practical issues, such as the founding of political institutions, had to be tackled. The American and French revolutions strongly suggested to study what held human beings together, how they would actually organize their lives – individually, in 'associations' or 'social movements', and in the polity and the 'nation' – and what kinds of regularities and orders could be expected, if people were permitted to do so on their own, without imposed restrictions. This is the search for social ties that is one major root of the social sciences, and it is in this sense a politically motivated search.

If, in contrast, we see with Hannah Arendt (1958b), politics as human activity, that by its nature, is open, plural and diverse, then such a cognitive linkage of free action and predictable outcome is inconceivable. Orderly outcomes can only result from planned or routine activities, work and labour in Arendt's terminology, over which certainty can be established before they are started. In contrast, political action in a context of liberty must go along with contingency of outcomes.

From an Arendtian viewpoint, thus, those early social scientists established an impossible connection. If they were heading for a 'social science' trying to identify laws and regularities of human action and societal development, then they necessarily abandoned the heritage of political philosophy, the emphasis on creative agency, irreducible diversity and the permanent possibility of unpredictable beginnings. The discourse on politics was then bound to decline. However, even if some of the emerging ways of thinking may have assumed so, things political would not vanish. They can be detected, though often in submerged and distorted forms, in the social sciences, which no longer call themselves 'political'.

Modernity and the Decline of Political Thought

The Emptying of the Political Space

Political philosophy, in its pre-revolutionary versions from Machiavelli and Hobbes onwards, had gradually developed an understanding of that which people have to regulate in common on the basis of the assumption that they do this on their own, without any external demands. The line of thinking that leads from Hobbes to Locke and Rousseau is often seen as the source of Western liberalism. It is most often presented as the theory of the social contract in which the individuals relinquish some of their rights in exchange for security and the regulation of the common realm provided by the state. In recent years, however, it has become common to distinguish the Hobbesian from the Machiavellian tradition. In this view, liberals define liberty as non-interference. The Hobbes-Lockean state, founded by free contract, dominates over the individuals, but it interferes with their liberties only to the degree in which the maintenance of order makes this necessary. The liberal tradition needs to draw a strong boundary between the public and the private, and since non-interference of the public into the private is the supreme principle, it can only have a 'thin' concept of membership in a polity. Significantly, the concepts of the state and of membership can be developed in the abstract, since they are based on a reasoning each rational individual is seen to arrive at, regardless of the situation. On these grounds, such liberalism can here be characterized as a modernist political theory.

In contrast, republicans define liberty as non-domination. Drawing via Machiavelli on Roman political thought, non-domination is conceptualized in stronger terms than non-interference; it requires security against interference. Such security stems at least in part from the ways in which citizens relate to each other, so that there is a less sharp divide between the private and the public and a 'thicker' concept of membership than in liberalism (see Pettit, 1997; Skinner, 1997, for recent accounts). As a consequence, the shape and substance of each republican polity is specific, since it depends on its members and their deliberations. Most contributors to this recent debate emphasize the distinction between liberalism and republicanism to underline that individualist liberalism, i.e. modernist political theory, was not the only alternative available to provide the discursive underpinning of political modernity at its onset. This is an important observation, to which I will return at the end of this chapter. However, they also agree that republicanism was by and large abandoned towards the end of the eighteenth century, and liberalism, though it neither appeared particularly powerful nor coherent before, very soon emerged as the pivotal political theory in post-revolutionary polities.

At a closer look, it is not too difficult to understand such an intellectual shift through a look at the deep shock the revolutions meant to political thinking. The revolutions were certainly inspired by republican thinking. Looking at them in the somewhat stylized way that an emphasis on the French experience has long suggested, we recognize, however, that they aimed at combining two objectives that proved to be practically impossible to hold together. On the one hand, they aimed at transforming state sovereignty in the hands of the monarch into popular sovereignty, i.e. they worked with extended notions of citizenship and liberty. On the other hand, they held such a transformation of the polity to be conceivable only in the form of the existing territorial state and within its dimensions.

Such double transformation entailed, first, that the existing relations between the people, tainted with the suspicion of domination and privilege characteristic of feudal society, had to be weakened or abolished. Thus, however, a major available resource for a substantive, 'thick' grounding of a modern republic was rejected. Second, the idea of extending political rights widely cast doubts about the viability of a demanding concept of liberty such as the one upheld in the republican tradition. Caution seemed to demand, not least for some more conservative observers, to limit the substance of the concept at the moment at which its reach was extended.[1] As a consequence, the public realm, the state, was robbed of most of its substance and the formal process through which common deliberations were reached was emphasized instead. About such processes, though, there is much less to reason in politico-philosophical terms. The liberal conception that things regulate themselves as soon as atomistic individuals are endowed with the right and the capacity to follow their own interests and passions makes political thought almost superfluous. It suggests that nothing beyond some basic assumptions and rules as to how to set up such processes is needed (though, of course, such rules are much less innocuous than it may have appeared to some of the revolutionaries).

This change is most visible in the context of the foundation of the USA, at least in a reading of it, inspired by Gordon Wood, that tries to go beyond the debate over the republican or individualist beginnings of the American polity. In their reaction against obtrusive and illegitimate government, the Americans consciously tried to build institutions so that 'power may not actualize itself anywhere'. The 'disembodiment of government … goes along with a disentangling of power, of the law, and of the knowledge of the ultimate ends of a society' (Lefort, 1991: 27). Many of the most important themes of earlier political philosophy were simply ejected from reasoning about political institutions as illegitimate. As Claude Lefort (1991: 27) puts the 'change that is at the origins of modern democracy': 'For the first time, the place of power is easily recognized as being empty.' The Americans of the revolutionary generation had, as Gordon Wood (1998 [1969]: 614 and 612) summarizes, 'broken through the conceptions of political theory that had imprisoned men's minds for centuries' through the renunciation of any substantive foundation of the polity and 'a total grounding of government in self-interest and consent'.

Even in the American context, this deliberate political construction could not exorcize all concerns about the substantive foundations of the public realm. Beyond the calls for republican virtue during the early period, the search for a preordained unity emerged in the nineteenth century, pursued often by Americans with some German intellectual background (Gunnell, 1991). However, such political science could not establish itself as a dominant paradigm and was mostly abandoned after the end of the nineteenth century. In Europe with its long-established statist institutions, the idea of unity was not abandoned, but it was rather radically transformed. As in the USA, the observation seemed undeniable that, once the reasonable will of the human beings had been cast into institutions, the political order must be seen as intrinsically satisfactory (Manent, 1994: 228–9). In this organized context, however, the fear that such new order based on human liberty might turn out unsustainable was much greater than in North America 'The effect of liberty to individuals is, that they may do what they please: We ought to see what it will please them to do, before we risque congratulations', as Edmund Burke (1993: 8–9) put it in his reflections on the French Revolution.

In this situation, individualist liberalism provides the less demanding concept of ('negative') liberty as non-interference that may live up to Burke's requirements under the proviso that the state is capable of maintaining order for and above the individuals. However, there is another way out of the aporia of liberty, namely the attempt to arrive at knowing 'what it will please them to do' by other means. In Europe, indeed, the idea of an emptiness of the political space did not fully emerge. In the Enlightenment combination of freedom and reason, the state was rather reinterpreted as the incarnation of reason once the expression of human freedom fed into its construction. This is one of the central themes of Hegel's writings, but it can be found in many other contemporary works as well (for example, Wuthnow, 1989: 315). This linkage of knowledge and politics, the idea of 'legislative reason' (Bauman, 1987), was characteristic of much of the early social science thinking during the revolutionary period in Europe. Reason, rather than merely serving as an ideal point of philosophical orientation – which it also continued to be – was to be made practical in the elaboration and application of the rules of politics. The movement to transform political reason into a science of politics found its most ardent spokespersons in France where politics had most radically been put onto new foundations. Beyond the voluntary commitment to construct a new social order, there was also a feeling of dire necessity to do so on well-informed grounds, not least motivated by the shock of revolutionary terror. The writings of Saint-Simon and Comte mark one major line of such thinking.[2]

The hope and aspiration was that the moral and political sciences should and could now achieve 'the same certainty' as the physical sciences (Baker, 1975: 197; see also Brian, 1994). Certainty was a requirement of some urgency, since the new political order needed assurances of its viability. But it was also regarded as an historically new possibility, since political action was liberated of the arbitrariness of decisions by rulers of doubtful legitimacy and given into the hands of the multitude of reason-endowed human beings. The 'blend of liberalism and rationalism', which Keith Baker (1975: 385) observed in Condorcet's convictions, can thus be explained as stemming from the same source, the Enlightenment linkage of freedom and reason – admittedly, though, in possibly its most optimistic version.

This linkage, if it could be sustained, made a science possible, where according to the classical view it would have been unthinkable, in the realm of the political. Condorcet subscribed to the new concept of free expression of political wills, but for him there was no contradiction between that view and the possibility of scientific analysis. In Baker's words (1975: IX and 193), 'societal choice' could well be transformed 'into the rational decision-making of the idealized republic of science.'

The Remaining Foundations of a Political Science:
the Rights-endowed Individual
The rights-endowed individual became thus, in such views, the only conceivable ontological as well as the methodological foundation of a science of political matters after the revolutions. Once the rights of man had been generally accepted as self-evident and unalienable, it seemed obvious, to Turgot and Condorcet for instance, that they were also 'the logical foundation of the science of society' (Baker, 1975: 218). In rights-based liberalism, the individual is the only category that need not, often in fact, cannot, be debated. The individual is simply there, whereas everything else – for instance, what criteria of justification are to be applied when determining the collective good – needs to be argued about. Substantive aspects of human interaction are subject to communication and consensus. And, to make the issue even more complicated, with whom one should enter into communication, that is, the boundaries of the community, is itself not given, but subject to agreement.

Once this assumption was accepted, basically two avenues of constructing a science of the political opened. Both of these are modernist forms of social theorizing as we have defined it for the purpose of our analysis; they connect modernist political philosophy, i.e. individualist liberalism, to a science of the political. One possibility was to try to identify by theoretical reasoning the basic features of this unit of analysis, the individual human being, and its actions. Since this unit was conceived as an ontological starting-point, devoid of all specific, historical and concrete ties to the world, its characterization was to proceed from some inherent features. From earlier debates, those features had often been conceived as twofold, as passions and as interests. In the late Enlightenment context, the rational side of this dichotomy was regarded as the one amenable to systematic reasoning. It thus allowed the building of a scientific approach to the study of at least one aspect of human interaction with the world, namely the production and distribution of material wealth. This approach inaugurated the tradition of political economy, later to be transformed into neo-classical economics and, still later, into rational choice theory. As briefly mentioned in the prologue, the moral and political philosophy of the so-called early modern period split into a political theory based on the idea of the social contract and a rationalized moral theory based on the idea of exchange. In both cases, the individual is the starting-point and unit of the analysis.

While political economy was based on a highly abstract, but for the same reasons extremely powerful, assumption of human rationality, the other conclusion from the individualist foundational principle was possibly even more reductionist but much more cautious. Avoiding any substantive assumptions on the driving forces in human beings at all, the statistical approach, often under the label of political arithmetic, resorted to the collection of numerically treatable information about human behaviour. The space of substantive presuppositions was radically emptied in this thinking, but the methodological confidence in mathematics seemed to have increased in inverse proportion (Brian, 1994; Desrosières, 1993).

Thus, two strands of political thought that had been proposed and elaborated for some time rose to new and greater prominence: political economy and political arithmetic. The denominations by which these approaches were known in the late eighteenth century referred explicitly to political matters. Both were to lose these attributes in the nineteenth century when they had consolidated their ways of proceeding and when the application of these cognitive forms had established predominance over political deliberation in decision on common matters, at least in the view of many economists and statisticians. Mostly, this terminological change has been interpreted as an autonomization of cognitive approaches and as a differentiation of the sciences into disciplines. However, it is not exactly appropriate to say that economics and statistics separated from politics. Once the approaches of the former two are accepted as valid, there is nothing political left to study.

Critiques of such a Foundation

The acceptance of the economic and the statistic ways of conceiving of the social world did not go without criticism; and they were never accepted as the only possible ways anywhere. However, the critiques and alternatives that were proposed most often accepted the fundamental change in political reasoning after the construction of a polity based on liberal-individualist rules.[3] After such a polity had begun to come into existence, new problems were identified. These were now essentially liberal problems; they resulted, one might say, from the observation that not everything that was needed for organizing a liberal polity could indeed be derived from an 'original position'. Two main types of problems may be distinguished by reference to the hypothetical original position in which individuals meet under a veil of ignorance.

On the one hand, the range of conclusions that could be drawn from the assumption of free and equal individuals was too limited. These individuals' relations were structured by the existence of politically important 'pre-political' social facts, of orientations and links between human beings that were seen to exist already before individuals entered into political communication and deliberation. On the other hand, the working of the liberal rules would themselves produce new kinds of social relations, 'post-political' relations, which would have a structuring impact on the polity in turn. The first of these arguments is to be discussed in this section; the second in the succeeding one.

Several different attempts were made to theorize the pre-political relations. They all start out from the critical observation that the human being who enters into political relations is not such a kind of individual as liberal political theory described it, and that the hypothesis of any original position would lead to serious flaws in the conclusions. This thinking emphasizes the rootedness of the singular human beings in contexts from which their ways of giving meaning to the world stem. Thus, it provides a first response to the modernist formula for dealing with the political problématique. The broadest intellectual movement of this kind has been the cultural-linguistic theory of the boundaries of the polity, which inaugurated culturalist thinking in the social sciences and at the same time became one source of later nationalism.[4]

In the latter, nationhood was regarded as a constitutive boundary in terms of social identity. In many European countries, not least Germany and Italy, political intellectuals fused the idea of a liberal polity with the search for a somehow natural collectivity that should form this polity. The notion was developed that there are such collectivities of historical belonging in Europe, and that they are defined by their common, historically transmitted, culture and language. In Germany, Johann Gottfried Herder proposed the concept of *Volk* (people) as an ontological unit. And Friedrich Schleiermacher, in a move that now appears as almost postmodernist, linked the very possibility of knowledge to common linguistic practices and concluded that one should strive to keep the speakers of a common language together.

Nationalism (or, in broader terms, theories ontologically based on cultural-linguistic entities) was increasingly widespread in Europe throughout the nineteenth and into the first half of the twentieth century. Such theories co-existed with, say, classical sociology – as well as Marxism (see pp. 48 and 53) – at the turn to the twentieth century; they were even widely taught from university chairs. And European polities were also at least partly constituted on the basis of national integration and this was reflected, even if in highly diverse and often mediated ways, in the sociological concern about social integration. Nevertheless, theories of nationalism hardly developed into a body of socio-political thought that aspired to internal coherence and empirical validity in the way it was increasingly demanded in academic institutions.[5]

Without committing themselves to such a substantively well-defined notion of pre-political relations, other scholars developed related thoughts on social ties between human beings. Most of Hegel's political writings can be read as an attempt to reconcile, after the French Revolution, the ideas of individual liberties and of moral unity. While he was referring to the state as a unifying institution above and beyond the human beings, he also pointed to different human modes of recognizing the other, of which the legal relation of liberal theory was only one among others (Honneth, 1995; Smith, 1989). Alexis de Tocqueville even went actively searching for social foundations of democracy and meant to identify the intense associative life in the USA as a source, and possibly precondition, for a viable liberal polity (Kelly, 1992). These latter thinkers, among others, maintained a predominantly politico-philosophical approach to the study of the social world. Even de Tocqueville, one of the more empirically minded of them, would not subscribe to the view that there could be a science of action that could provide individuals and groups with certitudes (Lamberti, 1983: 302).

Factually, such thinking, which retained a certain primacy of philosophy over sociology, found itself in long-term gradual decline through to the late twentieth century. But, significantly, it appears to be now being revived after the sociological line is often seen to have exhausted its cognitive-political potential (I will return to this issue on p. 54).

The Impregnation of the Social Sciences with the Heritage of Political Philosophy

Whereas the above-mentioned critiques of an individualist foundation of political thought did not feed into the tradition of the social sciences as it is commonly written, the other main line of 'post-revolutionary' social thought did. It started out from the insights, first, that the basic liberal assumptions, once they were cast into effective rules, would have durable and important effects on what social scientists would soon call the 'structure' of social relations. In this sense we can refer to those relations as being conceived as 'post-political'. And second, the question of such relations was forced onto the agenda of social and political thought by the fact that the liberal assumptions on their own did not suffice to create and justify a political order.

By insufficiency of the liberal assumptions I refer to the fact that the set of rules on which viable political institutions could be built needed propositions beyond those that could be derived from the basic assumptions of individualist liberalism. The concept of self-determination needed, for instance, procedural rules of participation in communication and in deliberation. Since such rules could not unequivocally be derived from the principles themselves, the issue of representation emerged. In response to the French Revolution, Edmund Burke (1993 [1790]) argued that, while there was a practical issue of representation (best handled in line with grown traditions), there was no specific legitimacy attached to representation. Statements like this earned him the – not entirely deserved – reputation as a conservative. Thomas Paine (1993 [1791–2]), in contrast, linked most forcefully the idea of the sovereignty of the people to the representation of the people in the governing bodies. The controversy between Burke and Paine 'marks the turning point of two ages of representation' (Sternberger, 1971: 594; see also Kraynak, 1990: 211–14 on Burke). As soon as any position closer to Paine than to Burke was accepted, debates on modes of representation, such as those that had already occurred in both the American and the French constituent assemblies, became inevitable. And it was in conjunction with this inevitability of disputes over representation that the creation of 'post-political' social effects of the liberal rules moved to the centre of attention (for a recent discussion of the post-revolutionary disputes over representation see Cedroni, 1999).

Beyond fixing rules, the observation of structures of representation also served the interest of enhancing some stability and certainty in political procedures that could appear to be opened to all contingencies by the abolition of any legitimacy of preordained orders. Typically, we find here again the two main strategies for rediscovering certainties, systematic observation and reflective conceptualization.

The one seems to be more typical for American thinking, where the structure of the vote was of key interest, whereas European social thinkers focused on what came to be called social structures behind the vote, most importantly the social question. These two intellectual responses to the political problématique inaugurate two further modes of social theorizing, the behaviouralist and the structural-functional one. Since these approaches, unlike the culturalist one, do not have recourse to sources outside and prior to political modernity, they are versions of modernist theorizing. Unlike economics and statistics, however, they do not make individualistic assumptions but aim at grounding socio-political life in purely social forms.

Behaviourism: the American Way

'Politics as voting is', as Judith Shklar (1987: 346) noted, 'a subject for constant investigation, because it is uncertain and yet it needs to be grasped.' When she claims that the emphasis on voting studies is a key feature of American political science from Hamilton onwards, she stretches her point somewhat.[6] Still, it seems true to say that all intellectual efforts to introduce more substantive reasoning into American political thought, which were in considerable number undertaken during the nineteenth century, failed to persuade academics and politicians likewise. And from the early twentieth century onwards, when the American Political Science Association was founded and the discipline acquired an institutional profile, Shklar's argument on American political science becomes clearly valid. Voting studies that tried to reveal stable patterns of electoral behaviour without any theoretical or conceptual a priori assumptions, became the core of the field. In a political space that was radically emptied, empiricist behaviourism is almost self-justifying as an approach and places all other considerations under the onus of the argument. 'The prime concern now was to discover, not how people should behave in order to achieve the best possible political arrangements, but how they will behave under specific and analysable circumstances' (Pagden, 1987: 16).

Social-interest Theories of Representation: the European Way

European socio-political thinkers after the revolutions would often broadly agree with such a view, but they were less convinced that the empirical study and later aggregation of individual behaviour was the only remaining means to that end. A 'social science', some of them held, would be able to identify an order of the social world that organized individuals into larger groups and could serve as an objective, scientific basis for rules of representation.

Elements of such a social theory of representation were proposed already before the Revolution as a means to reform the monarchy. Mirabeau, and following him Turgot and Condorcet, had accepted the idea that interests are something constant and reliable that could be used to build a social order. Abbé Sieyès used the same argument in a revolutionary reasoning. Society is to be represented rationally, and that can best be done on the basis of social interests. His theory of representation was built on a progressive, productivist view of society, in which identification of the rational interests of social groups and their recognition in the organization of the political order would enhance social progress. At the same time, it introduced the tension between the political logic of the unitary will – ahistorical and unsociological, if one wants to say so – and the social logic of interest positions according to the division of labour (Baker, 1990).

This tension made itself increasingly felt during the nineteenth century. Starting out from the concern for solidarity already in the French Revolution, the expectation among many republicans in France was that the establishment of the desired political order, the republic with universal suffrage, would take care of all other problems, since everybody concerned would have a say in collective matters. At the latest, however, the failure of the Second Republic to satisfy the material needs of its electorate – a failure that entailed the early end of the republic itself – made evident that the so-called social question would remain a key issue even for a democratic polity. 'The social question, thus, first appears as the recognition of a deficiency of social reality with regard to the political imaginary of the Republic' (Donzelot, 1984: 33; see also Procacci, 1993).

This problématique of the early republic appeared to demonstrate that the modern polity, all individualism and egalitarianism notwithstanding, showed internal social structures that somehow would have to be taken into account in its political practices. In this sense exactly, the social question can be seen as giving rise to sociology, as the liberal awareness of the persistence of problems of social order. In France, such transformation of classical liberalism was clearly linked to the formation of a social group with specific demands, the workers. In the liberal atmosphere after the July 1830 revolution the workers turned optimistically to the new regime with their demands, but were rejected. They 'responded by developing a new political and organizational language that met the regime on its chosen terrain: the discourse of liberty. In doing so, the workers embraced, but also modified and elaborated, the liberal language of the French Revolution. Class consciousness, in other words, was a transformed version of liberal revolutionary discourse' (Sewell, 1986: 60). In the course of the nineteenth century, then, a philosophical idea of representation, based on Enlightenment reasoning, was transformed into a sociological one, based on a theory of industrial society (d'Arcy and Saez, 1985: 9; see also Seidman, 1983).

After the claim for a social science had been made by authors like Saint-Simon or Comte, the themes of the emerging social sciences formed around the observation of this internal structuration of societies. In Germany, Lorenz von Stein reported about the 'social movements' in France that announced a major change in the social order. At mid-century, Robert von Mohl diagnosed a transitory situation after the Ancien Régime had disassembled and no liberal order had been able to assert itself in the German states, while beginning industrialization and urbanization placed new demands on the political orders (Maier, 1980; Wagner, 2000). Karl Marx gave a central place in his social theory (and philosophy of history) to the newly forming social phenomenon, the 'working class'. And Émile Durkheim provided a representation of society in which the elements of the social order were defined according to their position in the division of social labour and their relations regarded as interlocking in the form of 'organic solidarity'. Steps like these marked the construction of a sociological viewpoint which was clearly identifiable around the turn to the twentieth century. 'Society' emerged as a structured and dynamic entity relatively independent of the state, of the polity, to which it stood in a complementary but tension-ridden relation.

The starting-point and driving-force of the argument is the observation that oneness is a key ingredient for all political philosophy, be it academic or practical, be it religious, legal or sociological. 'God, law and society are seen in the image of the King.' The single figure of the ruler and its claim to well-grounded legitimacy provides 'the principle of the legibility of society' (Murphy, 1997: 31). In other words, the central problématique for political modernity was to arrive, from the basis of the diversity of human strivings, since such diversity was now recognized and acknowledged, at unity for matters to be handled in common. This is already a transformed religious problématique, and it can never entirely cast off this heritage. Political modernity faces the question of the 'permanence of the theologico-political', as Claude Lefort (1986c) puts it (see Assmann, 2000 for a reversal of the issue). Or, in Émile Durkheim's (1976: 443) words: 'In all probability, the concepts of totality, society, and deity are at bottom merely different aspects of the same notion.'

In a recent analysis of the relation between law and social science, which echoes many of my concerns, Tim Murphy underlines the multiple consequences of the emergence of 'society' as 'an independent idea, a theme in its own right' (Murphy, 1997: 35). It lent itself to formalization, instrumentalization and objectification of knowledge production, on the one hand, and to professionalization of legal practices, on the other, in ways that were unknown before. Weber's discussion of rationality can then be read as a sign of both the ideological triumph and the epistemic exhaustion of law. And the social sciences are seen as establishing conceptualizations and methodologies that together 'come to serve as surrogates of "experience"':

> The emergence of modern social science heralded a surreptitious change in the nature of 'speculation' and 'theorizing', insofar as these activities now came to presuppose the possibility of constructing a 'factual' substratum to demonstrate the 'truth' of the social. Two related processes, that is, were at work: first, the emergence of new conceptual frameworks; secondly, the emergence of positivities which both filled out and underscored these conceptual frameworks, because it was known that the construction of such positivities was possible, at least in principle. (Murphy, 1997: 120–1)

In this way, the internal structuring of the modern political order became the key concern of an emerging sociology. The new discourse came to replace the discourse of political philosophy, for two very different reasons. To some, the basic ideas of liberal philosophy appeared to be generally accepted and no longer an issue of debate. Attention needed to be paid to issues of 'post-political' structures instead. To others, the same basic liberal ideas needed to be rejected, but the possibility of a convincing rejection seemed to be very dim on the plane of philosophical reasoning alone. As the very themes of the emerging social sciences showed that liberal theory did by far not solve all political questions, there was more hope of factually undermining liberal assumptions on this more concrete terrain. That the loss of interest in political philosophy was so ambiguously motivated makes for the politically equivocal profile of the 'sociological tradition', having been labelled both conservative and progressivist or socialist.

Such works mark the shift from a political philosophy to an empirical social science, a shift in which the basic questions are maintained, but are answered by different means. I try to say here two things at the same time, which are only apparently contradictory. First, classical sociology, if we take these works as a major point of reference, continued on the main themes of political philosophy. Far from heading towards a comprehensive study of all aspects of a societal configuration, most of the works of these authors remain focused on the political problématique. Second, they decisively transformed this problématique by introducing substantive social ontologies into a mode of political theorizing that had socially mostly been rather thin. This transformation entailed a reformulation of a key aspect of what politics used to refer to.

Political Philosophy and Sociological Reasoning

Agency and Determinism

Long before the intellectual developments discussed here, the notion of politics had acquired an ambiguous double meaning. On the one hand, it continued to refer to communication and deliberation about the common good, to the collective regulation of the realm of life human beings had in common. On the other hand, it was increasingly used to refer to the state, to an institutionalized sphere of power, and to the interests of that state, the *raison d'Etat* (Sellin, 1978: 808–9). This ambiguity contained a seed from which two entirely different and incompatible understandings of politics should grow during the so-called transition from political philosophy to social science.

The classical interpretation of the term, often called Aristotelian, emphasized essentially unconstrained human interaction, human beings engaging others through action and speech. In Hannah Arendt's reading, this was a view on the world that insisted on the potentially unlimited plurality of human lives and the possibility to make beginnings in the world. Power is here the capacity to convince in communication. During the intellectual transformation at issue here, observers became less and less persuaded that action and speech were the only, or even the most important, modes of human interaction. They increasingly pointed to common needs that united humankind and to modes of work that linked human beings to each other. Places of production and chains of material exchange acquired new attention; these phenomena should enter into the language of the new social sciences under names like markets and the division of social labour.

This shift of importance between modes of human interaction had an impact on notions of agentiality in the human sciences. There is a way rationally to reconstruct this shift. Needs and work had been confined to the household in the prior mode of thinking; political action could then be seen as rather free and unconstrained. In the emerging social formation, however, needs and work became the key node of social organization, which thus became dependent on ongoing flows of goods. That is why it became necessary, in many views, to talk of social structures, as the girders of the social building, and of 'society' as the ensemble of all those structures (Wagner, 2000).

This shift was not merely the replacement of one representation of the social world by another one. The place of the human beings in the picture was not left unaffected. The newly emerged or detected structures were seen to limit human plurality and agentiality. They limited plurality because human beings were now located at specific places in a given order of the social world. Thus, they could be grouped with others at near places into collectives of approximately similar outlooks on, and interests in, the world. The structures also limited agentiality because the girders, which might be enhancing stairs or ladders for some kind of activity, would turn into walls or fences impeding others. Agency was certainly not completely excluded; not all social scientists of the nineteenth century were strong determinists (though some were). But it would run against objective tendencies of history in Marx, against functional exigencies in Durkheim, or against the self-produced 'buildings of steel' in Weber.[7] Agential capacities could be strongly enhanced if they related to these structures, but they would be strongly constrained if they did not do so.

Against the background of my prior reasoning, this inclination towards determinism can now be understood as a way of dealing with the political problématique after exterior assumptions to control political action have been ruled out. It proceeds, in a first step, via a reintroduction of a substantive ontology that is now claimed to be internal to the social world. In a second step, it is argued that these phenomena have causal effects on human action, i.e. that identifiable determinants of human action emanate from them. Above I have argued that economics and statistics in their strong versions should not be seen as springing off from political philosophy by way of intellectual differentiation, but that they make a claim to replace it, each in its own way. The preceding argument now leads to the conclusion that the sociologies of the nineteenth century, again at least in their strong interpretations, can be read in a similar way.

In terms of political thought, the so-called transition from political philosophy to social science can be read as a shift in emphasis regarding one major underlying problématique of any political theory under conditions of modernity, namely the effort to reconcile the commitment to liberty with the quest for certainty. To establish a valid 'scientific' discourse on political modernity meant to reason on the basis of the recognition of liberty and contingency of human social life, but to strive for order and certainty under those very conditions. The discursive outcome that prevailed in post-Second World War Western societies was a combination of the political philosophy of individualist liberalism, with its emphasis on the validity of procedures in the limited sphere of politics, and the modernist social sciences, which were to analyse the determining socio-economic framework within which politics could take place. Or in the terms of the terminology introduced here, a modernist political philosophy finds its complement in a modernist social theory.[8]

The possibility of politics is severely limited in this conception. It can be understood in one of two ways, or a mixture of the two. In the first view, the administrative aspect has come to dominate the political one. Politics is much more about the efficient management of large-scale social phenomena than about crucial and contested decisions about the common life. This view can be traced to the revolutionary period and the conviction that, once impediments due to privilege are removed, good knowledge can and will guide society. In extreme versions, it can similarly be found in scientific Marxism and in the idea of the scientification of politics prevalent in the post-Second World War era of the alleged end of ideology.

In the other view, which is not entirely incompatible with the former one, politics is not replaced by administration but by the self-harmonizing capacities of the social structures. The social structures linking human beings to each other through various modes of exchange are then seen to be endowed with self-regulating mechanisms, such as most prominently the market. In a mixture of normative and analytical arguments, which is difficult to disentangle, it is held that 'society' and 'economy' are relatively autonomous and should be left rather to their own to create harmony in the social world. If such a view is accepted, the former realm of political will, now embodied by the state apparatus, will be confined to managing the relations between self-developing entities.

However, rather than adequately analysing a change in social practices, such observations marked a change in the cognitive order. The 'invention of the social', often accompanied or followed by the 'administration of the social', was not least a way of reordering cognitive tools for understanding social processes.[9] From my earlier reasoning it became evident that a number of different motivations entered into this shift. It could be seen, optimistically, as the beginning of a rational order of the world, in which liberty and reason became one. It could be seen as a necessary conclusion from the liberal opening of political liberties, which had created a radical contingency that needed to be decreased. Or it could be a 'reactionary' conclusion from the observation of post-revolutionary strife arguing that radical liberation is unfeasible and that laws of the 'natural order' need to be observed. Regardless of motivation the shift meant a reductionist rethinking of issues of choice and agency which has marked the social sciences almost up to the present day.

The Political

The preceding remarks may have sufficed to show that it can indeed be claimed that a major intellectual transformation occurred in 'the political sciences' at the turn of the nineteenth century. However, this transformation is so profound that it would almost be more appropriate to say that political thought did not survive the political revolutions. We are left without any founding assumptions in political thought, in striking contrast to the rather solidly established foundations of economic, statistic and sociological thought. During the twentieth century, the modernist social sciences developed on those foundations, while the very heterogeneous academic discipline of political science combined electoral, administrative and institutional studies with a sub-field of political theory that remained limited to the history of ideas and the consolidation of individualist liberalism. Now one may want to argue, in line with my introductory remarks on the rise of individualist liberalism, that the absence of any foundations for political theorizing is exactly what political modernity is about. Still, this absence is not unproblematic and, at the very least, its significance itself needs to be thought. At the end of the twentieth century, it was indeed possible to trace an initially thin, but gradually strengthening line of thinking that aimed at a revaluation of 'the political' in the light of what was seen as its reduction under the combined hegemony of individualist liberalism and modernist social science.

Speaking about 'the political', a language Carl Schmitt seems to have inaugurated, means emphasizing the autonomous character of political action. It marks a distinction from the concept of 'politics', which is often seen to imply a sphere or realm of activity with determinate relations to other realms, in particular the economic one. The revaluation of the political takes its starting point from a reconsideration of the revolutions of modernity as acts of self-foundation of a collectivity, and as such the exemplars of the assertion of political freedom. Under conditions of modernity, human beings are obliged to exercise collective autonomy in the founding of their polities. The absence of any pre-given foundations for political rules, in addition, demands of them political will and the exercise of choice. While these assumptions are shared by all attempts to rethink the political, emphasis is laid on various aspects of this situation in a large variety of ways. I propose to distinguish two principal forms of such re-interpretations of the revolutions in the course of the twentieth century, which I label pre- and post-totalitarian respectively.[10]

Pre-totalitarian political thinking agitates against the loss of political will and agency predominantly in the light of an increasingly economic self-understanding of society. In Lenin's adoption of Marxian thought, the primacy of politics has to be restored by revolutionary action against the economic domination imposed by the bourgeoisie. In theoretical terms, Western social-democracy can be regarded as having revised its Marxian heritage by asserting the possibility of a regulation and containment of economic matters through the workings of a separate political-administrative sphere. By implication, it thus also accepted the containment of politics in this latter sphere.[11] Lenin aimed beyond such a compromise through elaborating a stronger notion of the political based on the exertion of revolutionary power and violence. In the history of Marxian thought, an economic determination of politics, which lent itself to attentism and revisionism, has been accepted alongside a republican one, which is recently being rediscovered, and the revolutionary one of Marxism–Leninism. Despite Lenin's uncoupling of the revolutionary moment from the development of the productive forces, there remains nevertheless a residual substantive grounding of his political theory in an economic sociology of class society.

Carl Schmitt similarly deplored the decline of politics in Europe, but rather than overcoming bourgeois rule, he aimed at restoring political will to a bourgeoisie that had lost its power of decision when the terms of class struggle were imposed on it. He shared the decisionism with Lenin, but was not inclined to see it substantively grounded on class analysis. His entirely formal grounding of politics on the distinction between friend and enemy made him the more radical, more modern thinker compared to Lenin. Some of his writings, in particular the treatise on Hobbes (Schmitt, 1996), reveal nevertheless his own attachment to a cultural-religious foundation of political order. Both thinkers develop a strong critique of procedural liberalism, which they see as unable of providing its own basis, against its own claims. They move towards a political theorizing that questions the possibility of rational political deliberation to step out of the fire-line, as assumed by modernism, by emphasizing the principled openness and contested character of political action under conditions of modernity, defying all theoretical determination. However, they both assume rather without questioning the unity of the political will of a collectivity, which is indeed a precondition for their decisionism. While they thus have moved towards a form of reasoning that I called the second response to modernism, they are also inclined to re-introduce substantive elements, i.e. remain in the form of the first response, to determine (or, normatively, to recommend) the direction of this will, with reference to class in the one case, to religion in the other. Their theories could thus be used to prepare and justify the major forms of totalitarianism of the twentieth century: Stalinism and Nazism.

Post-totalitarian thinking of the political shares with the pre-totalitarian one the insight into the absence of any foundation for the polity under conditions of modernity.[12] However, it operates with an interpretation of the historical experience of totalitarianism as one of modernity's political possibilities – rather than as a rejection of modernity through a return to full substantive grounding of politics. Post-totalitarian thinkers share the critique of procedural liberalism and of modernist social science with Lenin and Schmitt, but they explicitly reject totalitarian conclusions from these critiques. The major theoretical step towards such rejection is the identification of the residual substantivism and determinism in pre-totalitarian thinkers of the political. While some conception of oneness is needed for a viable polity, Claude Lefort (1986c: 273), as mentioned earlier, emphasizes that the 'place of power is empty' in democratic modernity. Each attempt at occupying it substantively entails a denial of the 'adventure' of modernity. And Hannah Arendt (1958a: Chapter 1) underlines plurality as the core characteristics of the human condition under modernity.

At this point, I need to recall the discussion above of the revolutionary events, in particular in America, as giving occasion for the hegemony of individualist liberalism and behavioural political science to emerge. It is worth noting that both Hannah Arendt and Jacques Derrida, in slightly different ways, have interpreted the American Revolution as a political beginning which needed neither the certainty of a science nor any absolute, irresistible foundation. Instead it is read as based on the common practice of a performative act (Arendt, 1965; Derrida, 1986; see also Honig, 1991). The reasonings of both Arendt and Derrida show how it is possible to reject any kind of foundationalism, i.e. to be 'modern', without having to accept scientism and individualism, which go along with the more conventional versions of the modernist project.

A view of political modernity as a plural adventure without foundations of certainty – 'without bannister', as Hannah Arendt used to say – requires an understanding of human beings in their singularity and their always singular relations to others, as Jean-Luc Nancy (1991) emphasizes. The pre-totalitarian thinking of the political kept evoking a community that emerges from a decision and has the power to decide. Derrida, in contrast, points to undecidability in the face of infinite responsibility as a constitutive feature of the political problématique. And Nancy develops an understanding of community as 'inoperable', i.e. not based on any prior commonality or determinate relation between its members. As Massimo Cacciari (1997: 37–9) points out, such a view of the polity neither cuts the relation to needs or the past entirely nor does it fully rely on present procedures. Like a boat sailing between the islands of an archipelago, which is his image of a polity, political deliberation is always on the way to somewhere else, but never cuts entirely loose from its own 'interior'.

In denying the existence of any guarantee for its viability, post-totalitarian thinking of the political poses the question of the attainability of a stable polity under conditions of modernity as a key theoretical question. It accepts the question of the viability of the polity as inescapable, but it doubts the claim of modernist political theorizing to have found a procedural, non-substantive answer to this question. And it resists the desire in more substantive political theorizing, including the residual elements in pre-totalitarian thinking of the political, for a grounding in general terms, beyond the specificity of a situation.

Inescapability and Attainability in Current Political Debate

If forced to give an unequivocal answer, it appears that the dominant mode of self-understanding of the 'Western' democratic polity remains the modernist discourse of individualist liberalism, the most recent systematic treatise on which is John Rawls's *A Theory of Justice* (1971). This discourse claims that viable rules of the modern polity have been attained on the basis of formal-procedural reasoning and that other concerns that have haunted the history of political philosophy can be escaped from. Over the last two decades of the twentieth century, this thinking revived in both of its components, as neo-liberalism in its economic-political form and as neo-modernization theory in its socio-historical form.

At the same time, however, a movement in political philosophy and in the history of political ideas has emerged that aims at questioning such self-understanding. Major parts of my preceding analysis are a part of that movement, which demands that the transformation of European – or more generally Western – societies over the past two centuries should not unequivocally be understood as increases in political rationalization. Instead the focus should be on shifts in political rationalities from which no linear line of historical progress can be derived.[13] In contrast to the master discourse of a political modernity the basic principles of which have been firmly put in place by liberal political philosophy, first, and by the democratic revolutions, second, the critics tell stories of abandoned or repressed alternatives. Those alternatives, in the view of these authors, all have in common to be preferable compared with individualist liberalism in the one or other respect.

Versions of communitarianism, as they were proposed in the early years of the recent debate between 'liberals' and 'communitarians', rely on commonality of values in a political community and thus present a substantive form of political theorizing, partly referring to the broader tradition of romanticism. They have been succeeded by what seems to be the currently most intriguing such historical alternative to individualist liberalism, namely republicanism or, as Quentin Skinner (1997) now puts it, neo-roman political theory (see first Pocock, 1976). This theorizing is said to have flourished during the seventeenth and eighteenth centuries, to have had considerable impact on the Glorious and the American revolutions, but to have been suppressed by the hegemony of liberalism after the French Revolution. Quite in line with my own analysis, the advantage of republicanism is seen in accepting and acknowledging the persistence and permanence of the political problématique of arriving at substantive rules for the life in common under conditions of liberty and diversity. Individualist liberalism, in contrast, is seen as a device to limit the impact of this problématique by setting a firm boundary between the private and the political and exempting the former, which includes the economic, from the reach of political deliberation.

The import of these historians' work for current political theorizing lies in the rupture with a historiography that implicitly presupposes linearity and in their insisting on the lasting significance of the political problématique. To some extent, however, they suggest an image of history that just mirrors the one of their opponents. Where the latter assume nothing mattered any longer that happened before the advent of political modernity, the republican historians suggest that the societal changes over the past two centuries were of little or no importance for our ways of thinking the political. They cannot imagine that the political problématique may persist as a problématique but nevertheless change with the particular social and historical situations in which it appears (Pettit, 1997 is a partial exception). This assumption is reflected in a research agenda in which the nineteenth and twentieth centuries are of little relevance because of the hegemony of liberalism.

From my analysis, however, it emerges that the social sciences were a complementary response to the advent of political modernity, in addition to liberalism. And it is only in their combination that they succeed earlier thinking. Indeed elements of republicanism can be found in the early social sciences of the nineteenth century (as Skinner, 1997: x, admits for Marx). Instead of merely deploring the loss of the political problématique, one needs to understand how it was transformed during the nineteenth century and what arguments were provided in favour of its transformation. In a second step, then, one can try to identify the forms in which it re-emerged during the twentieth century. The preceding analysis is meant as a contribution to such a project.

We have seen that throughout its recent history individualist liberalism, the modernist discourse of political theorizing, has been opposed, with various strengths, by discourses that insist on some need for substantive rooting of the polity. Such grounding could be located either in prior commonalities among the members of the polity, not least commonalities of language and culture, or in the systematic consideration of substantive concerns of needs and social interest in its institutional rules. A closer look at contemporary polities will also reveal that the relatively stable political orders of the 'thirty glorious years' (Jean Fourastié) in the West after the Second World War were indeed not based on the pure proceduralism of individualist liberalism. Rather they showed signs of a compromise between liberal justifications and both those of a linguistic-cultural and a social nature, and tied those justifications together by recourse to an empirical science of politics and society, the employment of which was never free of technocratic undertones.

In terms of political philosophy and social theory, then, the current indications of a crisis and transformation of those polities should be seen as a questioning of this compromise and of the orders of justifications that enter into it. There we find again a substantively orientated critique in the guise of nationalism and, in weaker terms, (some versions of) communitarianism, which criticize the thinness of liberal notions of political membership and communication and aim at providing stronger substantive underpinnings. Beyond this quest to shift the balance between modernist justification and justifications in terms of the first response to modernism, however, the reopening of the compromise takes the form of a broader questioning that employs figures of the second response. I have traced elements of such thinking to the beginning of the twentieth century. Some republican theorists may argue that it has been a part of their tradition all along, with Machiavelli giving it its first explicitly modern form (see Vatter, 2000). The condition for accepting such a view, however, would be to give priority to a republicanism of political action and new beginning over a republicanism of participatory community.

In terms of contemporary politics, the current institutional and intellectual restructurings entail the reopening of the political problématique, which was temporarily closed (or 'frozen') as an effect of the stability of the post-war – and Cold War – institutional compromise over justifications. It can safely be asserted, on the one hand, that a novel answer to this political problématique needs to be found, an answer that restabilizes a version of the old compromise over justifications or, rather more likely, one that introduces additional elements or an unprecedented balance of justifications. The problématique is inescapable. But, on grounds of the inevitable plurality of modes of political theorizing, it seems equally safe to state that no 'pure' answer will be found. Any answer that resorts to one mode of justification exclusively is unlikely to provide a sustainable solution. This means that an answer to the current political problématique is not only unattained, but whatever temporarily stabilizable answer may be reached, this answer will at any moment remain within the thinking of the attainable that is not yet reached, i.e. it will never be fully attained. It may have been a throwaway remark when Derrida (1994: 89) recorded that it was suggested to him that the Russian term *perestrojka* should be translated as 'deconstruction'. But the connection that is created here between a political restructuring and an intellectual proposal captures indeed the linkage between a problématique and a situation that defines the urgency of a socio-philosophical quest.

Notes

1 This description has benefited not only from the account given by Pettit (1997, Chapter 1) but also from a discussion with Wyger Velema about the failure of the Dutch to transform their 'ancient', federated republic into a 'modern', national one at the moment of the revolution.

2 On Saint-Simon's view, for instance, that 'the critical and revolutionary philosophy of the eighteenth century must be superseded in the nineteenth century by a philosophy of organization', see Wokler (1987: here 334).

3 Since nineteenth-century polities all worked with restrictions that are incompatible with a full fledged individualist liberalism, one should say more precisely that such a polity was put on the horizon of political debate through the revolutions, rather than made actual in institutional form.

4 This thinking is much richer than both culturalism and nationalism, as some recent re-appropriations, for instance by Charles Taylor (1989, 1995b and 1995c) show. This, however, is not the place to discuss in detail the conceptual merits of this approach.

5 But see, for example, Schnapper (1998) and Balibar and Wallerstein (1991) for recent attempts to reconsider the questions of nation and ethnicity in the history of social and political thought and of political institutions.

6 Shklar goes on to argue more generally that the study of past occurrences, of 'history', had become the only available means to counter the principled 'unpredictability' of human action; see Chapter 4 on this issue. In Shklar (1991), a more plural picture of the field of political science is painted.

7 Weber's '*stählernes Gehäuse*' is not in the first instance, as the translation into 'iron cage' suggests, a prison. It is a dwelling-place that provides protection as much as it limits freedom.

8 This entire chapter works with a distinction between philosophy and science that is close to the one that drives Claude Lefort's effort at rethinking the political (see, for example, 1986a, but also already 1972). Rather than trying to elaborate on a distinction between these two cognitive-intellectual modes – an effort that is always prone to misunderstandings due to the multiple connotations of these terms, and particularly so in this case in which that distinction intersects with my own distinction of modes of social theorizing – I shall let the historical presentation of the political problématique accomplish this task (for my own brief explicit discussion of Lefort's work see Wagner, 1999b).

9 Instead of entering here into a discussion about whether the changes in the 'real' structure of social relations between 1750 and 1850 warranted this major intellectual turn in talking about the social world, I refer back to the analysis of epistemic certainty in the social sciences in Chapter 1 above. The more specific answer, in brief, would have to elaborate on the fact that the language change 'responded' to some extent to observations, but that it introduced a new order of language that could not be said to be derived from observations.

10 A more standard distinction is between right-wing and left-wing thinkers, with Schmitt being in the former, Lenin in the latter category. With increasing historical distance from the relevance of that distinction, however, the picture has been blurred, with the emancipatory potential of Lenin's project being doubted (for example, Dutschke, 1974) and with Schmitt being appropriated by former Marxists (for example, Mouffe, 1991, 1999). While completing this chapter, I have benefited from reading Eckard Bolsinger's Ph.D. thesis at the European University Institute (Bolsinger, 1999).

11 The theoretically most sophisticated version of this argument is probably provided by Jürgen Habermas in *The Theory of Communicative Action* (1987).

12 The term 'post-totalitarian political theory' should in general refer to all political theorizing that is decisively shaped by the advent and experience of totalitarianism (see Wagner, 1998). While the authors I mention in the following all are critics of a procedural and individualist liberalism, there are other post-totalitarian thinkers whom the experience induced to move closer to liberalism. I include here importantly Central and East European intellectuals who found residence or exile in England, such as Isaiah Berlin and Karl Popper. Jürgen Habermas's communicative liberalism can also be mentioned in this context, although (as just mentioned) it has a stronger statist, 'interventionist' component. It may be Habermas's particular significance to be the first German thinker of democracy, as Alain Touraine once suggested (in a seminar at the University of Warwick in 1997).

13 The work of Michel Foucault and his political-theory disciples in France, of Quentin Skinner and the Cambridge historians in England, and to a more limited extent the

'conceptual historians' around Reinhart Koselleck in Germany need to be mentioned in this context. The formula in the phrase above draws on Münkler (1998). With reference to my remark about evolutionary thinking in the prologue, it may need to be underlined that such a statement does not amount to a denial of progress or even of the possibility of progress. It just implies that progress may rather easily and consensually be measurable only within a discursive formation. Across discursive formations, the very concept of progress will require more fundamental debate.

3

The Continuity of Selfhood

Political philosophies, as discussed in the preceding chapter, need ways to conceptualize both the collectivities of human beings that form polities and the members of those collectivities. Under conditions of political modernity, the singular human being has become the predominant form of understanding the unit of membership in political collectivities. Many formalized discourses of the human sciences – such as law, liberal political philosophy and neo-classical economics – work with a notion of the singular human being as a unit that is characterized by its indivisibility, for those reasons also called the individual. Historically, to be precise, a condition that I called restricted liberal modernity has long prevailed, a condition under which the unit was not the singular human being, but the family represented by the father or the household represented by its head or the company represented by its owner. As de Tocqueville already recognized, however, the discourse of political modernity had a strong leaning towards conceptualizing the singular human being as the unit citizen.

To arrive from the individual members at ways of constructing stable collectivities, an additional assumption about the guiding orientation or behaviour of the members needed to be introduced in the human sciences. In the discourses mentioned above, this assumption is basically one of rationality, with specific variations. In liberal political theory, the capacity for rationality leads the individuals to enter into a social contract for their mutual benefit and to restrict the play of their passions to the private realm. In economics, rationality translates into interest-guided behaviour and the sum of those behaviours into the optimization of wealth. In legal thinking, the adult individuals can be taken to be responsible for their actions because of their endowment with the faculty of reason. Furthermore, the continuity of such individuals over time needs to be presupposed to allocate responsibility for past actions. Even those sociological and anthropological discourses that were proposed in critical reaction to the presupposition of rationality remained dependent on a prior notion of rationality (Joas, 1996). In the preceding chapter, I put forward the argument that such limitation of the intellectual space for understanding the singular human being in the human sciences stems at least in part from the fact that those discourses were predominantly developed with a view to addressing the political problématique.

However, a common view of the history of social life in Europe holds that a 'culture of modernity' spread gradually over the past five centuries. This 'is a culture which is individualist [...]: it prizes autonomy; it gives an important place to self-exploration; and its visions of the good life involve personal commitment' (Taylor, 1989: 305). Such an emphasis on individuality and individualization is quite alien to the more formalized discourses of the individual. In European intellectual and cultural history, there is very little connection between these two discourses. Philosophy and social theory proceed predominantly by presupposition and show little interest in actual human beings, who tend to be taken into account only as disturbances the more they enter the public scene. In literature and the arts, in contrast, the experience of modernity is in the centre and, as an experience, it concerns in the first place the singular human being (Berman, 1982). Michel Foucault's lecture 'What is Enlightenment?' very succinctly distinguishes between those two readings of modernity. Modernity as an attitude and experience demands the exploration of one's self, the task of separating out, 'from the contingency that has made us what we are, the possibility of no longer being, doing, or thinking what we are, do or think' (Foucault, 1984: 46). It is counter-posed to modernity as an epoch and a set of institutions, which demands obedience to agreed-upon rules.

Today, one way of discussing this historical separation of discourses is to see it as a long period during which issues of selfhood were neglected in the social sciences. A genuine interest in such issues, so the story goes, arose only in the early twentieth century. The ground was prepared outside of what is conventionally recognized as social science, namely by Friedrich Nietzsche, and later by Sigmund Freud. Nietzsche radically rejected the problems of moral and political philosophy and thus liberated the self from the impositions of the rules of the collective life. Freud located the drives toward a fuller realization of one's self in the human psyche and connected the history of civilization with the repression of such drives. Against such a 'Nietzschean-Freudian' background (this is Richard Rorty's way of speaking), Georg Simmel and George Herbert Mead could observe the ways selves are formed in social interaction and conceptualize variations of self-formation in different social contexts. From then on, a sociology and social psychology of selfhood has developed which is characterized by important advances and insights. It no longer relies on presuppositions about some essence of human nature, and it is at the same time able to connect its findings to both child psychology and phenomenology. It emphasizes the socially constructed nature of selfhood, but remains capable, at least in principle, to analyse the specific social contexts of self-formation thus working towards a comparative-historical sociology of selfhood. And without having to presuppose the self-sustained individual of modernity it can demonstrate how autonomous selves develop through social interactions over certain phases of the life-course (Joas, 1998; Straub, 1998).

This account is in many respects convincing, and it is without doubt true that the understanding of human selfhood in the social sciences has become considerably more complex due to the reflections of Simmel and Mead earlier in the twentieth century. There remains, however, quite some lack of clarity about what one is actually studying, and what one is interested in, when dealing with selfhood. In recent years, the suspicion that selfhood may be among those 'essentially contested concepts' (Gallie, 1955–6), of which there is a considerable number in philosophy and the social sciences, has been raised again when the notions of the 'de-centring of the self' and of the 'post-modern self' have been introduced. The former apparently is a theoretical notion demanding a rethinking of what selfhood is. The latter refers predominantly to the alleged empirical observation that selves are much more transient and fugitive than even sophisticated sociology and social psychology used to allow for. As a consequence of the emergence of these themes, a new separation of discourses can be observed. There seem to be dividing-lines of thinking that are almost impossible to cross. In this context, this chapter will head for an exploration of the conceptual field of selfhood not least with a view to identifying some points of passage between those discourses.

Both the ideas of a 'de-centring' and of a 'post-modern self' question some major implications of the more standard sociological view of selfhood, namely the existence of the human self as a unit and its persistence as the 'same' self over time. It will need further considerations below to see whether and to what extent such propositions are indeed held. That the assumption is not entirely unjustified, however, can be gathered from the fact that the term 'self' is often – and, it appears, increasingly – used synonymously with the term 'identity'. This latter, though, in most understandings precisely posits existence as an entity and sameness with itself over time. 'Identity' in current social science means 'continuity of selfhood'. We shall start our considerations at this point.

Selfhood and Identity

'Roughly speaking, to say of two things that they are identical is nonsense, and to say of one thing that it is identical with itself is to say nothing at all' (Wittgenstein, 1984a: par. 5.5303; see also 1984b: par. 215–16). The insight at which the young Wittgenstein arrived seems to be largely forgotten today, at least in the social sciences. Identity is a term that has gained considerable popularity. Wittgenstein's rough remark remains significant, however, as the prevailing confusion in current discussions about identity shows. Should one succumb to the temptation to separate the nonsensical from the void, one easily arrives at the point where any vague hope for a remainder of valid and significant insights threatens to disappear. That, at the latest, would be the time for a halt and for rethinking the rationales of the search. Before aiming at understanding 'identity' and 'selfhood', it seems wiser to gain an understanding of the ways those terms are used.

Evidently, there is no obligation to share Wittgenstein's scepticism.[1] Regardless of whether one agrees or disagrees with him, however, his statement should convey the need for every reference to 'identity' that there be a 'thing' that is identical with itself or not. (To be precise, there should be two things – the object of consideration and the one with which the former is identical. I will return to this question below.) That is why it comes as a surprise that 'identity' occurs without an object in many titles of recent books or articles. The current discussion about identity seems to have liberated itself of this requirement. It has become possible to speak about identity without indicating who or what is identical to itself or something else. Careless use of language does not seem to be the only or even main reason; uses of language often indicate problems of thought. Let me cast this problem, which will accompany all of the following discussion, initially as follows: the discussion about identity aims at firmly conceptualizing something that it avoids naming with any precision in more empirical terms.

A closer look allows the preliminary sorting of some issues. In the social sciences the term 'identity' is used predominantly in two forms. As a shorthand for 'self-identity' or 'personal identity' it refers to a human being's consciousness of the continuity of her existence over time and of a certain coherence of her person, to 'a subjective sense of continuous existence and a coherent memory' (Erikson, 1968: 7). The terms 'social' or 'collective identity' expand the idea and refer to a sense of selfhood of a collectivity, or the sense of a human being to belong to a collectivity of like people. 'Identity' then means 'identification' of oneself with others (see the detailed discussions in Assmann and Friese, 1998 as well as Friese, 2001a). A consciousness of sameness within a group implies the idea to be different from those who do not belong to this group. This phenomenon is currently discussed under terms such as alterity or strangeness and the setting of boundaries between that which is one's own and that which is of others.

The otherwise useful distinction between self-identity and social or collective identity tends to obscure the relation between the two. Self-identity will usually be 'social' in the sense that a relation to particular other human beings is seen as giving a significant orientation to one's own life. Collective identity, on the other hand, will, it seems, only emerge if and when a multiplicity of singular human beings draw a sense of significance for their self-identities from the same collectivity. More basic clarifications are needed to disentangle the strands of the debate around selfhood and identity. A further step can be taken by trying to discern the cleavage lines between those various strands.

We can start with some illustrations. Erik Erikson's works are a central point of reference in that part of the debate that may be considered as the mainstream of psychology and social psychology (see Lapsley and Power, 1988; Slygoski and Ginsburg, 1989). Psychological and psychoanalytical analyses from a feminist perspective, in contrast, can often do without a single reference to Erikson, even when they start out from a history of ideas and mention Nietzsche, Freud and Simmel (such as in Weir, 1996). A comparison of modern and post-modern identities is now regularly made in culture, media and communication studies. Without doubting in any way the plausibility of the findings and the adequacy of the presentations, one has to note that the theoretical references are often very diffuse and haphazard (for example, Kellner, 1995; Morley and Robbins, 1995). A great variety of orders of reference thus emerges behind the apparent consensus expressed through the term 'identity'. In this light, some doubts can even be cast on the assertion that there is a growth of common interest in 'identity' at all.

In what follows I will try to demonstrate that the debate on selfhood takes place in a semantic space in which the idea of personal identity is variously connected to notions of meaning, of modernity and of difference. The emphasis on continuity and coherence of the self, as mentioned above, will be considered as the modernist position in this debate. It is conditioned by the need to maintain a notion of human autonomy and agentiality as a basic tenet of what *modernity* is about, namely the possibility to shape the world by conscious human action. Such modernism is not strictly tied to the atomist and rationalist individualism of some versions of economic and political thought, most notably neo-classical economics and rational choice theory. It is open towards important qualifications in terms of the corporeality, situatedness and possible non-telelogical character of human action (see Joas, 1996 for such a conceptualization). However, it cannot abandon the link between identity and agentiality and, therefore, needs to insist on some important degree of continuity and coherence of the self.

Objections against such a conceptualization can go in two different directions. On the one hand, it can be argued that every form of selfhood is dependent on the cultural resources that are at hand to the particular human being when giving shape to her or his important orientations in life. Human beings give *meaning* to their lives by interpreting their situations with the help of moral-cultural languages that precede their own existence and surround them. Cultural determinism is the strong version of such theorizing, mostly out of use nowadays, but many current social theories adopt a weaker version of this reasoning which indeed sustains the notion of the continuity of the self but sees this self as embedded in cultural contexts rather than autonomous.

On the other hand, doubts about the presupposition of continuity and coherence of selfhood employ notions of difference and alterity that are not reducible to the idea that selves are formed by relating to others, by intersubjectivity. Such notions rather underline the non-identitarian character of being by casting the issue of 'the other in me' (see Critchley, 1998 for a most recent account on Lévinas and Blanchot) as a philosophical questioning rather than a straightforward sociological one. While most prominent in the writings of Jacques Derrida, such a view is not at all confined to post-structuralist thought. In another strand of discourse it can be found, for instance, in Hannah Arendt's (1978: especially 183–7) insistence on the 'two-in-one', on the relation to oneself as another, as the very precondition for thought.

In the remainder of this chapter I shall first try to demonstrate that, despite some points of intersection, these three discourses pose the problem of selfhood in highly distinct and mutually irreducible ways. An analysis in some detail will show that the first two discourses bear signs of tension as a consequence of a recent confrontation of their conceptual terminology with findings of empirical research on current social situations and configurations. The direction of conceptual critique then points towards the third discourse. This discourse, however, has been but little received in the social sciences, not least because it raises basic questions as to the possibility and form of theorizing in the social sciences. It also will not be able to replace the other two, because it cannot address the issues they address. However, a comprehensive understanding of the problématique of selfhood requires its inclusion into the debate.

Discourses About Identity

Identity and Meaning

In the discourse on meaning, the term 'identity' is evoked to name a form of connection between human beings that is in principle capable of holding together a social order. Even if this is not always apparent, such discourse forms part of the tradition of cultural analysis that reaches back at least to Gottfried Herder. Elements of such thinking have persistently been present in cultural anthropology and in those strands of sociology that emphasize questions of the normative integration of society, such as in Durkheim and in Parsons.

'Culture' refers to shared beliefs, values, norms and forms of behaviour. Cultural theorizing thus tends to presuppose that human beings know the cultural features of their own societies, at least to such an extent so as to enact them, even though they may not always be able to explicate them or to assess in how far and with whom those cultural features are shared. In most cases, as cultural theorists tend to argue, human beings have some conception of the community to which they belong. This sense of belonging is their collective identity. In a cultural perspective, the collective identity is the most significant connection between those human beings (for a discussion of recent culturalism, see Friese and Wagner, 1999b).

Such an understanding of identity appears to have removed the notion of interest from the central position the latter had until about two decades ago in those strands of the social sciences that focused on societal integration.[2] Social life was then described in the language of structures and systems, and human beings were seen as determined by their roles and interests, which in turn could be derived from the position of those human beings within structures. In more recent discussions, in contrast, social life is ordered through meaning and values. Human beings live together in cultures, and they no longer recognize the similarity or strangeness of the other through their class position but rather through their identity (see similarly Griswold, 1994: xiii; Lamont, 1992: 179–80; Lash, 1994: 214–15; Smelser, 1997: Chapter 3). Under conditions of the late twentieth century, however, such return to cultural interpretation could not be effected without modifications.

In the history of cultural thinking, linguistic commonality was the assumption that should lead to the idea of national identity as cultural-linguistic identity. Human beings who share language and values have a primordial commonality that lends itself to the formation of political communities. Such ideas were developed in Germany at the end of the eighteenth century, not least in reaction to the Enlightenment and the French Revolution, both of which were reproached with resting on empty abstractions. The French Revolution itself founded the political identity of the nation on an idea of membership through political orientation and choice and thus in opposition to language as a criterion of membership that precedes the conscious life of a particular human being (see Chapter 2).

Such an assumption of cultural and linguistic homogeneity, while always having been contestable, became empirically untenable for contemporary societies. More recent discussions about cultural identity have therefore introduced concepts of 'cultural complexity' (Hannerz, 1992) and the possibility of co-existence of several cultures – including sub- and counter-cultures – on the same territory. Vice versa it is now also recognized that cultures may expand across large spaces without excluding or dominating other cultures (as it was assumed for national cultures). Jewish culture or the 'culture of science' are evident examples. But even cultures that used to be the traditional object of anthropology, such as the culture of the Samoan islanders, have been analysed as 'multi-local' cultures by

rlining both the spatial extension through migration and the simultaneous
stence of ties of belonging (Sahlins, 2000).

__me of those partial identities within a territorially defined society that are
currently the focus of attention are implicitly or explicitly analysed in relation
to the hegemonic identity group in that society. The term 'ethnic identity', for
instance, is predominantly used for minority groups, such as Afro-Americans in
the USA. Similarly, the discussion about gender identity, which was started from a
feminist viewpoint (even if it now goes beyond it), is concerned with female identity in a male-dominated society. Identity becomes relevant under conditions of
boundary-setting and exclusion, and is accordingly thematized by the marginalized
or excluded groups. In turn, one may conclude that identity is not a significant issue
for hegemonic groups, who may show an inclination towards universalizing reasoning on the terms of which particularity cannot persist.

If all these modifications of the classical concept of culture and cultural identity are taken as an ensemble, they tend to undermine the original quest of the discourse of meaning that resided in the search for identity-constituting commonalities
between human beings in their modes of interpreting the world. Such commonalities were seen to precede the concrete human beings and to be genuinely collective. They are constitutive for social life as such. Singular human beings are of
interest in this perspective only in terms of what they have in common with others.
The sum of the recent modifications of this discourse, however, amounts to conceptually letting both the commonality and the collectivity disappear. They are
replaced by overlapping orders of boundaries and exclusions within and between
discursively constituted multiplicities of human beings. Instead of underlining
commonality with others, differences towards others are emphasized. The conclusion may be seen in abandoning the cultural form of reasoning about selfhood
and identity altogether.

However, abandoning could look easier than it is. Charles Taylor's inquiry into
The Sources of the Self starts out from the widely familiar argument that the
advent of modernity indicates that common frameworks for moral evaluation can
no longer be presumed to exist. The key contention in the remainder of the book
is then that the ability and inclination to question any existing such framework
does not lead into a sustainable position that would hold that no such frameworks
are needed at all, a view he calls the 'naturalist supposition' (Taylor, 1989: 30). If
such frameworks are what give human beings identity, allow them to orient
themselves in social and moral space, then they are not 'things we invent' and
may as well not invent. They need to be seen as 'answers to questions which
inescapably pre-exist for us', or, in other words, 'they are contestable answers to
inescapable questions' (Taylor, 1989: 38–40). Taylor develops here the contours
of a concept of inescapability as part of a moral-social philosophy of selfhood
under conditions of modernity.

Identity and Modernity

The discourse that connects selfhood to modernity mostly – at least in all its more
sophisticated forms – starts out from an assumption of constitutive sociality (or
culturality) of the human being as well. Such assumption, however, does here

not lead towards the investigation of collective identities in relation to forms of socialization. Instead the conditions and possibilities of the formation of a self, of personal identity is moved into the centre of interest. Formation of self-identity is here understood as the forming and determining of the durably significant orientations in one's own life. Therefore, this discourse, which often has its roots in (social) psychology, stands in a basic tension to the culturalist concept of identity as sketched above. Whereas commonalities between human beings are of major concern in the latter, the former moves the singular human being into the foreground. No necessary connection is presupposed between identity-formation and individuality; human beings may well form the same or highly similar identities in great numbers. But the identity of the singular human being is in the centre of attention in this discourse, not the group, culture or community.

In such a perspective, identity-formation is sometimes considered to be an anthropological constant of human existence. It is related to the formation of a consciousness of one's own existence and thus biographically to the period of adolescence. Crises of identity occur accordingly during growing up; more precisely one should speak of life crises during the formation of one's identity.[3] Self-identity once constituted is seen as basically stable further on. Since the very concept of identity is connected to continuity and coherence, stability is turned into a conceptual assumption.[4]

More specifically, however, the creation of such continuity and coherence can also be declared a particular problématique of selfhood under conditions of modernity. Only modern human beings, it is then held, know that form of self-consciousness that would allow one to speak of the formation of an identity as well as, by implication, of crises of identity. Such a view may result as a conceptual consequence from a specific understanding of modernity. If modernity is seen to be characterized by the denial of all certainties, by the prevailing of a principled scepticism and of doubt about one's knowledge of the world, then a requirement to question one's own location in the world and the stability of the I follows immediately – and thus also the problem of identity (see, for example, Giddens, 1991). The view that human beings have to construct their self-identities themselves can similarly be seen as characteristically modern (see Hollis, 1985). Modernity is then precisely defined as a situation in which such a view prevails – rather than considering identity-formation and crises of identity as a consequence of modernity.

This relation between modernity and identity, though, would also need to be conceptualized historically. The historical analysis has points of intersection with the theoretical one, but proceeds quite differently. I have referred to this double approach to modernity in the Introduction and have provided ample demonstration of the varieties of ways of dating modernity in the two preceding chapters. What is of interest in the current context, as set out above, is that a more specifically social-scientific perspective on the self emerges as late as the early twentieth century. This appears as a considerable 'delay', compared to virtually all periodizations of modernity – provided that we indeed want to assume a close connection between modernity and identity. This delay merits more attention from sociologists of knowledge and of the sciences than it has hitherto found. It suggests, namely, that the 'classical' sociologists at the turn of the twentieth (not to speak of their 'predecessors') implicitly pursued a quite élitist approach to society – even beyond those explicit élite theories of society developed by Gaetano Mosca, Vilfredo Pareto and Robert Michels. Up to the early twentieth century, sociologists regarded human beings as basically socially determined. Under that assumption, there always is a relation between the singular human being and the 'social structure' that is not (co-)created by the human being her- or himself. That is why the question of identity did not pose itself. But by implication one would also have to deny the attribute 'modern' to such a social configuration, or at least strongly qualify its reach.

Against this background, it is easier to understand the significance of George Herbert Mead's contribution to the sociology of selfhood and identity. Mead regards the constitution of self as a problématique that concerns all human beings and for which there may be a variety of processes which can be generally determined only in their forms but not in their results. As a consequence, it becomes much more difficult to conclude from identities on social structure and political order. This has often been seen as a 'weakness' of symbolic interactionism, which Mead is said to have inaugurated, as a social theory that allegedly cannot address issues of societal constitution. But by the same move Mead allows for and recognizes a plurality of selves that has returned to the centre of discussion today – after the renewal of a regressive synthesis of identity and society in Parsons (to which – as is often overlooked – Erikson contributed as well).

This sociological discussion about identity and modernity has points of reference that differ considerably from those of the philosophical and literary ones. The social upheaval during the second half of the nineteenth century with industrialization, urbanization and the phrasing of 'the social question' is often seen as a first 'modern' uprooting of identities, as a first massive process of 'disembedding' (Giddens, 1990). The development towards so-called mass societies during the first half of the twentieth century lets the question of the relation between individuation and growth of the self emerge. This is the first time that the sociological discourses about identity find themselves in synchrony with the societal developments they are about. In such a perspective, totalitarianism can be analysed in terms of an imbalance between imposed individuation and delayed self-formation, the result having been the tendency towards 'escape from freedom' and into stable collective identities (Arendt, 1958b; Fromm, 1941). Most recently, the indications of dissolution and dismantling of the rather comprehensive set of social institutions of the interventionist welfare state are one of the reasons to focus sociological debate again on questions of identity.

Some contributions to this recent discussion diagnose the emergence of forms of selfhood that cannot easily be subordinated to conventional concepts of identity. No longer continuity and coherence but transience, instability and inclination to change are said to be marks of the important life orientations of contemporary human beings. Some irritation is caused by the fact that such orientations are called 'identities' despite the counter-intuitive etymology of the term, which is counteracted by adding the adjective 'postmodern' (see Lash and Friedman, 1992). Douglas Kellner, for instance, diagnoses major differences between forms of selfhood that could be found during the 1960s and those of the 1990s. In the earlier period, 'a stable, substantial identity – albeit self-reflexive and freely chosen – was at least a normative goal for the modern self.' In the 1990s, identity 'becomes a freely chosen game, a theatrical presentation of the self, in which one is able to present oneself in a variety of roles, images, and activities, relatively unconcerned about shifts, transformations, and dramatic changes' (Kellner, 1992: 157–8; see also 1995: 233–47).

If such diagnoses of a historical transformation of identities were correct, they would entail a questioning of the entire modernist concept of identity. If there were a transition to a 'postmodern' condition, in which the prerequisites and/or the necessity for the constitution of stable personal identities in a 'modern' sense were no longer given, then one would have to speak more generally about historically varying conditions of self-formation. Within a plurality of forms of selfhood, the 'modern' and the 'postmodern' ones would constitute two of the possibilities. It is highly doubtful whether those diagnoses are correct, though. Despite a high degree of methodological sophistication in some of those works, it just is very problematic to assume – and difficult to investigate, in the next step – that forms of self-formation are specific to social configurations and homogeneous within them. Rather, it is much more likely that a diversity of forms of selfhood coexists in the contemporary social world without any single form being predominant. The conceptual contribution of recent research on selfhood thus should not be seen in the introduction of a new, 'postmodern' understanding of selfhood and identity, but rather in breaking open the strong conceptual link between identity and modernity that had been postulated by some earlier theorists.

Such an opening of the understanding of selfhood loosens the relation between identity and modernity so that this discourse – like the discourse that links identity to meaning – shows signs of tension. The range of questions needs to be widened. Instead of continuing to ask in a straightforward empirical way how personal and collective identities are constructed, the construction of identity within the discourses of the social sciences needs to be moved into focus. The concept identity then inevitably enters into the constitutive relation to its counter-concept, difference, a relation that was always already present in the philosophical discussion.

Identity and Difference

A concept of identity is – at least implicitly – of central importance for any philosophy that works with a strong ontology. The basic phenomena are not only existent beyond any doubt and can be defined; they are also stable over time and accordingly traceable through time. Their stable existence makes phenomena also distinguishable. To state the identity of a phenomenon means to note its difference towards other phenomena. After such a step is taken, relations – such as of causality, or of dependence – between the thus identified phenomena can be determined. Difference, however, is then always already pre-constituted. One pretends to name a state immediately and positively that is always only created by the act of setting one thing apart from another one with which it is not identical. It is only by thinking identity and difference as part of the same move that the problématique becomes visible which the term identity aims to address.

Such logic of identity, which philosophy and the sciences often employ, turns the stable existence of the observed phenomenon as the one that has been described into a presupposition of the philosophico-scientific operation. However, the status of a possible result of the investigation should be reserved for precisely this assertion of existence. There is a pragmatic justification for such a procedure in terms of the necessary bracketing of aspects that are not part of the specific investigation.[5] But neither is the absence of any reflexive deliberation about the status of concepts that are constitutive for theories – such as 'identity' – justifiable nor can the competence for such deliberation conveniently be restricted to philosophers of the sciences whose discussions will then have little impact on actual research practice.

Stanley Cavell's reflections provide an example for a thinking about selfhood that does not presuppose an idea of identity. Characteristically, it straddles philosophy and social science in what Cavell himself calls an attempt at retrieving Emersonian perfectionism and Wittgenstein's philosophy of culture (Cavell, 1989; 1990). Cautioning against 'any fixed, metaphysical interpretation of the idea of a self' and against the idea of 'a noumenal self as one's "true self"' and of this entity as having desires and requiring expression', he warns that such an idea would entail 'that the end of all attainable selves is the absence of self, of partiality. Emerson variously denies this possibility'. In contrast, Cavell suggests that the 'idea of the self must be such that it can contain, let us say, an intuition of partial compliance with its idea of itself, hence of distance from itself' or, in other words, he advocates the idea of 'the unattained but attainable self': 'One way or the other a side of the self is in negation' (Cavell, 1990: xxxi, xxxiv and 12).[6] Cavell, drawing on Emerson and indeed also on Wittgenstein and Heidegger, proposes here a relation of the unattained and the attainable as constitutive for the self, that is, he makes the question of attainability a central feature of a theory of selfhood.

For such an elaboration, precisely the concept of identity is crucial – in a twofold way. On the one hand, the concepts of personal and collective identity have become a central element of social theorizing and at the same time a prominent topic of empirical research in the social sciences in a way that, as has been shown, has created new tensions between theorizing and research. On the other hand and partly as a consequence of those tensions, the linguistic constitution of categories and modes of thinking in the social sciences becomes problematic itself, not least the postulate of identity.

The 'deconstruction' of the logic of identity, elaborated in part through observation of the 'discourse of the human sciences' (Derrida, 1978a), has nevertheless only experienced a very reluctant and selective reception in the social sciences yet. On the one hand, one may well assume that more attention is now devoted to ruptures and inconsistencies in personal 'identities' as well as to asymmetric relations between collective 'identities'. A shift in perception has occurred that becomes visible in the presentation of empirical research. On the other hand, the discourse on difference keeps presenting a problem for the philosophy of the social sciences, the full consequences of which have been but little recognized or accepted. Sometimes one even gets the impression that the significance is perceived but repressed and denied at the same time.[7] To take deconstruction seriously, in contrast, would require critical reflection on some basic presuppositions in the theory and methodology of the social sciences. The discussions about identity can serve as an example to demonstrate in which directions such questioning would have to go. A first step into this direction is an exploration of the antinomies that are generated by the discourses on identity but can finally not be handled by the established means of the social sciences.

Antinomies of Identity

Identity as Choice or as Destiny
The discussion about identity reproduces the sociological distinction between ascribed and acquired features of the human being and thus also the utterly problematic boundary between the traditional and the modern. Modern human beings allegedly choose actively their personal identities, whereas their traditional predecessors do not even know the problématique of identity-formation since they are socially determined. A similar distinction is coined in the discussion about collective identity. Social formations that are characterized by commonality of 'natural' markers of community, such as skin colour or sex, can be distinguished on a modernity scale from others that have been created and are constantly re-created by choice, such as the (political) nation as a daily plebiscite, as Ernest Renan said.

Such distinctions have disappeared neither from social-science discourse nor from political debate. And indeed they refer to an existing problématique. At the same time, however, they formulate this problématique in such a way that a conceptual dichotomy is constructed that cannot be dissolved again by empirical findings of whatever kind. This situation becomes visible as soon as one takes an interactionist position on the constitution of identity, which at first sight looks as a middle ground connecting the other two views, but which indeed opens up broader perspectives. From an interactionist perspective, the understanding of oneself – or of the group to which one feels one belongs – is created by turning those images back towards oneself that others, with whom one enters into interaction, have of oneself and communicate to oneself. Thus, the very question of the ascribed or acquired character of identity becomes mute. Identity cannot be formed without those images; thus it is always the result of social processes. At the same time, it does not emerge without relating to those images whose mere existence is without any significance.

Once formulated, this view seems almost banal. Taken seriously, however, it should allow one to cast some of the empirical questions as well as some political implications of the debate about identity in wider terms. As an immediate consequence, for instance, it would need to be considered as a priori entirely indeterminate whether 'natural' characteristics of a person become criteria for this person's identity, i.e. whether they will be seen as giving significant orientations to one's life. Similarly, there will be no general way to indicate criteria for the creation of collective identities. The native language or spatial proximity may become relevant for a sense of belonging. If this occurs, however, this will always be as a consequence of the experience of the views of others, never by either isolated choice or by predetermination. The mutual constitution of national identities between French and Germans, for instance, has recently been investigated through historical analyses of interactions and exchange, in particular during the eighteenth and nineteenth centuries (Espagne and Werner, 1988; on institutional co-constitution Zimmermann et al., 1999).

Such critical position towards any presupposition about fixed forms or contents of personal and collective identity, thus, does not rob itself of the possibility to study the formation of identities in historical and empirical terms. In contrast, it returns to visibility a question that had always been in the background of the discussion about identity the discourse-orienting character of which, however, had remained largely hidden. This is the question about the human capacity to act, about agentiality.

When identity is predominantly related to meaning, the concept always carries the function of guiding action and that, by implication, also means constraining action. Identity then signals the interiorization of norms or — less strictly — the appropriation of patterns of meaning as a necessary resource and condition for action. The modernist discourse about identity, in contrast, conceptualized the human being as autonomous towards others. Identity as the perception of the continuity and coherence of one's own person then becomes a precondition for the capacity to act.

Analogously, collectivities create their existence 'for themselves' through their identity and thus turn into collective subjects and actors. This latter variant of the modernist discourse was a key element of nineteenth- and early twentieth-century debates; it finds only little attention today, and thus the parallelism between the modernist constructions of personal identity, on the one hand, and collective identity, on the other, are easily overlooked. In some versions of the discourse on difference then precisely the illusionary character of this modernist view is emphasized. The elevation of the individual (or the collectivity) from its context is regarded as a discursive construction rather than a description of reality. The theorem of the de-centring of the subject leads then consequently to the loss of the capacity to act in these discourses.

Summarizing the three discourses on identity in such a way, the question – raised at the beginning but then postponed – of the identity of 'identity' re-emerges with greater urgency. Does 'identity' refer in these discourses to anything else than the human capacity to act? Or is the concept not rather a stand-in for the position on this point and changes meaning in relation to the discourse of which it is made a part? The conjecture that 'identity' serves as a sign for the question about the (individual or collective) capacity of human beings to act provides the first element in our attempt to position the concept of identity in the social sciences.

Identity as Autonomy or as Domination

This aspect is most strongly – and affirmatively – emphasized in the modernity-centred discourse about identity. If agentiality is understood in a strong sense as the capacity to give oneself one's own laws, then continuity and coherence, i.e. identity, of the person must be presupposed. The emphasis on this capacity – capacity to autonomy – is at the same time a basic ingredient of the discourse of modernity in philosophy and political theory. Socio-historical studies of modernity mostly do not step outside such foundations either. At best, they become investigations into the social conditions for identity-formation that focus on the diffusion of precisely the idea that laws of human life are not externally determined but given by the human beings themselves.[8]

To presuppose autonomy entails the additional assumption of the capacity of human beings, in principle, to separate from the context of socialization in which identity-formation occurs. Neither internal ('psychical') nor external ('socio-historical') conditions determine human action entirely (see Castoriadis, 1991: 143–6). A 'modern' understanding of identity, which is oriented towards agentiality, cannot assume any strong 'embeddedness' of individuals in psychical or social contexts. Action in the 'modern' sense would otherwise be unthinkable.

The modernity-centred discourse, however, cannot provide itself the means to safeguard its own validity. The occurrence of 'autonomy' cannot be empirically determined since it can never be excluded that the entirety of contextual factors – could they only be integrated into the analysis – would explain specific human 'actions'. The discourse remains inevitably exposed to the (different) criticisms that emerge from the meaning-centred and the difference-centred discourse. As a consequence, the contours of modern identity get blurred again; it fades into its 'context'.

Furthermore, the 'modern' approach to identity casts a peculiar light onto this 'context' in which the acting human being operates. In a sense, this 'context' is only created by the assumption that an actor, gaining his identity, separates from his environment and then in turn acts upon this environment. The other two discourses aim to counteract the modernity-centred one also in this regard. Theories of difference, in particular, underline the will to dominate and the exclusion of otherness from the realm of modernity effected through this operation. Over the past three decades, numerous analyses have gradually created an image of the process through which the identity of modernity was constructed by emphasizing differences. 'Modern man' aimed at distancing himself from a variety of forms of alterity – nature, wildness and tradition outside of his own social world, and the lower, dangerous classes, women and the mad inside of it.

In such critical perspective on the emergence of the concept of identity in modernity, relations of domination become visible. The proclaimed conquest of autonomy is then seen as possible only through the marking of (asymmetric) differences and thus through boundary-setting and the exclusion of the other. That is why post-colonialist, feminist and other discussions that emphasize relations of domination underline the creation of difference. Initially, the orientation was often towards the construction of counter-identities, but more recently the fundamental problématique of the inescapable connection between identity and difference has moved into the centre of concern. Identity-formation is inevitably creating difference. But without any conceptualization of self and other or self and context, the problématiques that are discussed in the modernity-centred discourse under terms such as 'action' and 'freedom' would not be thematizable at all.

Thus, the exploration of the relation of identity and difference under the aspect of autonomy and domination leads to a second element in our attempt at locating the concept of identity in the social sciences. 'Identity' here appears as a discursive sign for the possibility of distancing from a context and of the separation from the other.

Identity as Construction or as Reality

Both of the preceding aspects of the discussion about identity refer to a third one, namely to the question about the reality of identity. If identity is experienced as fate, then it is seen as part of an objective reality. If it is however chosen, then it is in the first instance one of several possibilities and as such not (yet) real. If the term identity is taken to express human autonomy, then it is real; if that discourse however is seen as itself constructed to allow for autonomy of the self and for domination over others, then identity is a project and not part of a given world.

At this point, it becomes evident that the social-scientific concept of identity needs to add something to a philosophical understanding of the term (at least outside of modal logic), if the concept is to be maintained at all. There is a close connection to a concept of identity as sameness only in one of the above formulae: If identity is fate, then a singular human being or a group are and will remain identical to themselves by virtue of social determinations. Such a narrow social determinism, however, is practically no longer upheld at all. All other conceptualizations contain the idea that identity needs to refer to the imagination of sameness of one 'thing' with another one, rather than sameness itself. The formation of identity has then always aspects of a project, guided by orientations, even by theories (Berzinsky, 1988). And the safeguarding of identity entails steady work at the maintenance of continuity and coherence or, in other words, at the interpretation of one's own life or of the one of the group as a continuous and coherent one. Each identity contains always at least an element of construction. The strong condition that Wittgenstein formulated for identity to exist can then be relaxed. At the same time, however, the openness and ambivalence that are thus admitted need to be fully accepted.

Such acceptance requires first of all the insight that the question whether a particular identity is imagined or real can never be fully answered empirically. In each individual life there is a minimum of continuity, most basically of bodily existence, and there are always discontinuities. To pose the question of identity means to consider whether particular changes can be seen within a framework of continuity or as a rupture. A conversion, for instance, may mean for somebody a conclusive reinterpretation of her or his own – and 'same' – religiosity and spirituality, but for somebody else it may mean a break with the entire preceding life and identity. Something analogous holds for collective identities. Any observation of 'objective' commonalities between people, were it then possible, would not permit any conclusions about those people's sense of belonging together.

These reflections bring the argument back to the discussion about the construction of certainty in the social sciences in the first chapter. It was then argued that there was an inclination in the social sciences to overemphasize both the existence and the coherence of social phenomena, since such was demanded by the requirements for epistemic certainty to be met. The concept 'identity' has a central role in such an endeavour (and its recent rise to prominence may reflect some awareness of the endeavour being at risk). 'Identity' may often serve less to characterize observable social phenomena, but rather towards providing an interpretation of those phenomena that privilege their persistence and durability over their transience and volatility. 'Identity' – and this is the third element in our effort at determining its location – is thus a sign for the stability of the world and indirectly also for the certainty and reliability of our knowledge about it.

Identity and Beyond

Tendencies Towards the Decomposition of the Concept

Reviewing the course of those identity-related discussions in the social sciences over time, a rather clear direction is visible for all three of its aspects. The debate has led from an emphasis on the pre-given, fate-like character of identity towards the possibility of choice; from placing the accent on the objective reality of identity to its constructed nature; and from underlining the acquisition of autonomy as a result of identity-formation to an emphasis on aspects of domination. In all cases, however, some contributions – like this one – conclude from the course of both the research and the theoretical debate on the need, not to move from the former positions to the latter ones, but to dissolve the antinomies. If the shifts in the discussions indeed, as I aimed to demonstrate, expose the concept of identity to a tension that it is unlikely to be able to sustain, does this require that one abandon the concept entirely?

It would not be fruitful to reject studies of identity in the social sciences merely by demonstrating that the explicated understanding of the phenomenon is ridden with contradictions. There is 'something' that is being investigated even if this phenomenon could not be called 'identity' in any philosophical sense nor even in the understanding of many common definitions in the social sciences. Many people have or develop during their socialization a sense for the continuity of their person and the connections across their life-story. And many people are able to say to which group or groups they see themselves belonging, what they have in common with other members of that group and what distinguishes them from other groups. 'Personal identity' and 'collective identity' do occur.

Furthermore, the existing studies do show – despite all objections one may have in conceptual and empirical detail – that that which is referred to as identity can be analysed by empirical sociological means. The findings lead neither to anthropological constants nor to any sharp dividing line between modernity and non-modernity, but to a variety of possible forms of 'identity'. Identities can be more stable or more changeable, perceived rather as given or rather as chosen, rather seen as rooted in a substantive self or rather oriented towards the realization of a yet unknown self. Possibly one may even arrive at some propositions about the importance of different socio-historical configurations for the emergence of specific orientations for people's lives.

But exactly because of this variety, such investigations in their sum also suggest that the concept of identity be cast in wider terms. It will not be sufficient to define the intellectual space of the social sciences, its 'sphere of cognition', such that approaches that tend to raise issues in the philosophy of the social sciences themselves fall outside that space. This move, which can be observed, would be equivalent to narrowing the problématique and at the same time to denying relevance to many of the more recent – both conceptual and empirical – findings. In contrast, the recent theoretical and empirical attention to identity demands the work at conceptualizations beyond a more narrowly conceived social science and social theory.

With regard to the empirical reach of the concept, the question about the significant orientations in the lives of human beings needs to be uncoupled from any presupposition, as presupposition, about continuity and coherence. The latter terms would otherwise have to be cast so enormously widely that they would be emptied of their contents (when, for example, a radical break with former orientations in life is nevertheless considered in terms of continuity, because it is the 'same' person who performs this rupture). Or, vice versa, the assumption about continuity and coherence would constrain interpretation – in the sense, namely, that significant orientations that do not conform to the idea could not be conceived as parts of identity-formation. If abandoning the connotation with continuity and coherence suggests that the term 'identity' appears inappropriate when analysing the emergence and change of important orientations in human lives, then this conclusion may well be drawn.

More important than a change in terminology, however, is the question why the analysis of individual and collective orientations in life and their social conditions has been given the label 'identity' in the first place. The concept is borrowed from philosophical debates, but at the same time its former meaning and reach were not maintained but – without explicit discussion – considerably altered. The enigma in the debate about identity lies less in recent research findings but rather in the adoption and current defence of the term. We need to ask about the persistence of the concept in the light of its revealed conceptual insufficiencies.

To pursue this question, it may need repetition that there is a requirement of both an empirical and a philosophical opening in the discussion about identity. Empirical postmodernism is accompanied by a critique of social ontology. The idea of the identity of things with themselves is of central importance in the latter respect. In modernist thought, it is this idea that makes both social science and society possible. Summarizing the three elements assembled over the preceding discussion, 'identity' in both the senses of selfhood and collective identity represents the capacity of human beings to act, their capacity for critique and the stability of the world. The continuity of selfhood that is implied in all three aspects allows the construction of the 'individual'. The third aspect in particular, but indirectly the former two as well, invites one to assume the possibility of similarly unequivocally constructing a collective entity 'society', the existence of which is required both for social theory and for moral and political philosophy (as discussed in the preceding two chapters).

The observation that this formula cannot persist in any unquestioned way does not entail any 'end of the subject' or the end of sociality or even the end of any intelligibility of the social world. Rather, a question as old as philosophy itself has been returned to the agenda and has been particularly directed to the social sciences, the question namely of a thorough-going de-ontologization and de-essentialization of the philosophy of the social sciences. This question can be approached further by looking at the relation between the concepts of the social sciences and the temporality of those social phenomena the concepts are meant to characterize (for the following see also Friese and Wagner, 1999b).

Identity and Temporality

If propositions about identity as sameness appear either nonsensical or empty of substance at first sight, they gain meaning once one turns from the question of *being* to the question of *becoming*. As I tried to show above, it is only an opening towards understanding identity at least partly as a project to be realized over time that can justify the usage of the term in the social sciences at all.

The fundamental problématique of identity, both as selfhood and as a collective identity, is revealed by considering its reference to time. A reminder of the basic definitions will suffice. The question about the continuity and coherence of a person refers to biography, to the life-course. The same question directed to a collectivity refers to the idea of a common history, a common experience. Identity is constitutively temporal. The implications of such an observation can be illustrated by discussing the example of collective identity.[9]

A conventional analysis of collective identity would demonstrate the existence of common orientations within a group of people in the present and would conclude from this observation on a long history of common experiences as a cause for present commonality. A historical analysis could confirm the latter, and the collectivity would have been successfully established – as a 'culture' or a 'society'. Such a reasoning, however, would necessarily presuppose a considerable degree of historical constancy and causality, or, in other words, it would repress temporality (see Friese, 1993 as well as 1991; Game, 1991: 21).

The recourse to common history must remain an insufficient explanation for the existence and solidity of collectively shared orders of belief already on grounds of the impossibility, strictly speaking, of any such 'common history'. Rather than any 'common history', there is always only a variety of experiences each one of which differs from any other. The conjuration of 'common history', as in theories of national identity, is an operation that is always performed in the respective present – as a specific representation of the past with a view to the creation of commonalities. Such an operation may well 'work' in the sense that an idea of proximity and belonging is created between people in the present. But it is not the past in the form of 'common history' that produces this effect, but the present interaction between those who propose to see the past as something shared and those who let themselves be convinced and accept such representation for their own orientation in the social world.[10]

One may want to object that such a reading ignores the importance of history for sociological analysis and plays into the hands of a presentist empiricism the proponents of which have always doubted the accessibility of the past. Is it not the case that one risks developing an ideology and apology of a present without historical depth and thus also without any understanding of historical possibilities for action and social change (Jameson, 1991)? The intention here, in contrast, is not to reject historicity but rather to come to a more appropriate understanding of temporality and historicity. Such an approach requires us to question the status of the present and to reflect about the modes of appropriating history. The social sciences have long only assigned a marginal significance to such reflections.

Still today most research in the social sciences falls into one of two categories, both of which are equally helpless in the face of this issue. Either 'timeless' snapshots are taken of the social world, or history is invoked to deterministically explain the present. In the former case, empirical evidence – such as answers to interviews – are analysed synchronically as present facts without considering their historical constructedness and possibly limited durability. This is true theoretical presentism, and it comes in characteristically modernist guise. In the latter case, in contrast, researchers appropriate the past selectively to explain the present. The identification of continuities between past and present is a methodological a priori in this procedure. Therefore, it becomes impossible to ascertain whether the coherence of the findings is a result of the selection or indeed the consequence of a causally effective connection between past and present actions (de Certeau, 1988; Friese, 1997).

It may appear that these reflections merely add more problems to social research and social theory and do not indicate any solutions. There is indeed no master approach to the epistemological implications of the temporality of the social world. What was argued in this chapter, however, is by far not the end of the debate. Starting out from identifying the assumption of the continuity of selfhood, both personal and collective, as crucial to current debates about identity, I have demonstrated some basic problems with that assumption and have tried to identify some reasons why it is nevertheless held. In the end, I hope to have established the inescapability of a consideration of temporality in social theory. The variety of ways in which temporality has indeed already been dealt with in debates around modernity, however, has not yet been fully explored. The following two chapters will try to do exactly this.

Notes

1 Wittgenstein himself later arrived at the view that, while there may be little more to say about the concept of identity, the problématiques that are circumscribed by this term lend themselves indeed to further discussion. The question about criteria of identity is central to the *Philosophical Investigations*. There, however, Wittgenstein no longer provides answers, rather he acknowledges a fundamental problem. The so-called analytical and continental traditions in philosophy share – despite all differences – the insight into the centrality of this problem. To bring some of those reflections back into the social sciences is one of the objectives of this chapter.

2 In the terms introduced in the preceding chapter, this significantly entails that priority is given to pre-political ties between human beings instead of the post-political forms of the social bond.

3 This would be the normal assumption. But major ruptures in later life can also be analysed under the aspect of the attempt of maintaining one's identity or as a crisis of identity in analogy to the equally crisis-prone first formation of identity during adolescence. Migration into a different cultural context or the growing consciousness of a minority position in one's own society, for instance, may fundamentally shatter existing orientations and lead to identity crises (see Chapters 4 and 5 as well as the interlude between them for an elaboration of the argument about migration).

4 See Cohen, 1994. Furthermore, the concept of personal identity can be connected to role and status; thus, a linkage to societal analysis would be created – such as in some anthropological theories and in Parsons-inspired sociology.

5 This is an observation Anthony Giddens quite rightly makes in the methodological conclusion of his *Constitution of Society* (1984). In his own later work, however, he seems to have reinterpreted such legitimate bracketing as a licence to avoid awkward conceptual and theoretical problems – with the result that the research programme that is entailed in *Constitution of Society* has thus far not been pursued further.

6 Cavell adds that there is a 'companion concept of society' which goes analogously with 'partial compliance with its principles of justice'. This remark could be used analogously for a discussion of collective identity in relation to moral and political philosophy.

7 It is not the ambition of this chapter or even of this book to continue the debate over deconstruction, which keeps being led with quite some fervour and more competence in philosophy. The significance of deconstruction can rather easily be demonstrated even in analytical language, see Wood 1990. My own references to deconstruction throughout this book are confined to two objectives: to widen the space of social theorizing and to underline the idea of a necessary reference of social theory to problems and situations.

8 This perspective also guided my own socio-historical investigation of modernity (Wagner, 1994a). A modernist standpoint however was not presupposed; rather, its occurrence was made part of the analysis.

9 An analogous discussion of temporality for the question of personal identity would have to consider in addition the status of the 'subject', a subject that in modernist perspective functions as the speaker for identity who guarantees sameness over time and becomes both subject and object of continuity and coherence.

10 Such critical reflection on the idea of 'common history' does not entail that its opposite, the idea that one can freely choose one's – individual or collective – history, is adopted (see Chapters 4 and 5).

4

The Accessibility of the Past

By identifying the dilemmas into which both an ahistorical empiricism and a history-laden cultural determinism run when analysing personal and collective identities, the preceding chapter has shown that 'some conception of the past is inescapable' in the social sciences (Abrams, 1972: 19). Both these methodologies try to answer this quest by suppressing temporality, however in two forms that are opposed to each other. Presentist empiricism neglects, or even rejects, the temporal character of the social world and confines its ambition to the only temporal state that is accessible – the present – turning an epistemological dilemma into a methodological virtue by means of self-restraint. Cultural determinism, in contrast, resorts to the past for explanation of the present, thus closing an explanatory lacuna by epistemological fiat. Whereas in the former case, that which is difficult to access – the past – is assumed not to matter for the present, in the latter case the problem of the accessibility of the past provides the scope for inferring its structuring impact on the present.

Presented here as an issue of the philosophy of the social sciences, the variety of ways of relating to the past can be translated into the debate about modernity. The occurrence of modernity assumes a rupture in time, the effect of which is to generate both modernity and its antecedent counterpart: tradition. The modernist discourse about modernity presupposes this break; in this sense, presentist empiricism can be regarded as one of the modernist methodologies in the social sciences. Since modernity however exists in and through its opposition to tradition, the question of the relation to tradition remains part of the discourse of modernity. The attempt to explain the present by recourse to tradition or, in stronger terms, to 'origins' emerges thus as a discourse about the past under conditions of modernity that insists on the rootedness of social life.

Unlike modernists tend to think, this latter discourse does not wither away with modernity taking its course. It is not a remnant, a residue that has persisted although it is doomed. (Such thinking itself shows a significant and largely untheorized temporal component.) On the one hand, a key characteristic of the discourse of modernity is indeed the decisive break with any concern about 'origins'. On the other hand, however, it appears that it is exactly this claim of modernity to have overcome the authentic rootedness of human existence that provokes resistance. Such resistance, in turn, re-emphasizes the need for origins and seeks to identify and specify them for the given situation. In both forms, modernity is defined through a reference to 'origins', be it as a denial or as an affirmation. In recent debates, this concern for origins and the attempts to overcome this concern have been associated with nostalgia as a philosophical condition.

Nostalgia as a Contemporary Theme

The intellectual situation of our contemporary time is marked by a double denial of the relevance of nostalgia. The modernist claim to have superseded any need for a reference to origins is countered and surpassed, for instance, by the claim of deconstruction to have detected a nostalgic longing in the modernism of the human sciences. Deconstruction then demands to overcome this longing. As Jacques Derrida (1978b: 27) writes, 'there will be no unique name, even if it were the name of Being. And we must think this without nostalgia, that is, outside of a myth of a purely maternal or paternal language, a lost native country of thought. On the contrary, we must affirm this.'

To a considerable extent, the issue at stake in what is loosely called postmodernism – and in particular in the works of those French authors that are grouped together under the label of post-structuralism – is exactly a radicalized critique of nostalgia.[1] The self-understanding of modernity is found wanting. The intellectual constructions that were erected to prove that modernity means a liberation from externally imposed constraints, from 'self-incurred serfdom' (Kant), are shown not to live up to their own exigencies. They are built on foundations that may conceal their reference to 'origins', but they nevertheless rely centrally on such rooting. What could arguably make these analyses 'postmodernist' (though most of these authors do not use this term themselves), is the call for a step beyond such modernism, a step defined as the effective break with nostalgia.

This step recurs in several otherwise quite different writings – and it can be detected despite differences in the precise terminology in which it is cast. The idea of the end of the grand narratives, put forward by Jean-François Lyotard in *The Postmodern Condition* (1984), defines modernity in a first step – I shall come to the second step later – as a social configuration dependent on a story that provides its self-understanding. More narrowly conceived than Cornelius Castoriadis's idea of the 'imaginary signification of society', Lyotard holds that such self-understandings are temporal accounts of the unfolding of a process of emancipation that have a beginning in time and foresee the possibility of accomplishing the project of emancipation in some future time. In a famous and much-debated passage, he argues that all available such narratives of emancipation have been invalidated by historical events over the past fifty years.

All that is real is rational, all that is rational is real. 'Auschwitz' refutes speculative doctrine. At least that crime, which was real, was not rational. All that is proletarian is communist, all that is communist is proletarian: 'Berlin 1953, Budapest 1956, Czechoslovakia 1968, Poland 1980' [...] refute the doctrine of historical materialism: the workers rise up against the Party. All that is democratic exists through and for the people, and vice versa: 'May 1968' refutes the doctrine of parliamentary liberalism. If left to themselves, the laws of supply and demand will result in universal prosperity, and vice versa: 'the crises of 1911 and 1929' refute the doctrine of economic liberalism. And the '1974–9 crisis' refutes the post-Keynesian adjustments that have been made to that doctrine.[2] (Lyotard, 1984: 318)

As a consequence, the contemporary situation is characterized by the end of any such common narrative and the resultant coexistence of mutually untranslatable languages, so that no reference to any beginning is any longer possible.

Jean Baudrillard, in apparent contrast, radicalizes the concept of modernity (rather than talking about postmodernity) when he – in ambivalent language – considers American modernity as the 'original version' precisely because it breaks with the claim for originality and authenticity:

> America is the original version of modernity. We are the dubbed or subtitled version. America ducks the question of origins; it cultivates no origin or mystical authenticity; it has no past and no founding truth. Having known no primitive accumulation of time, it lives in a perpetual present. [...] America was created in the hope of escaping from history, of building a utopia sheltered from history. (Baudrillard, 1988: 76 and 80)

Thus, he sees European – French – modernity as maintaining a connection to its origins. At the same time, he regards a break with origins – or maybe rather a denial – a present possibility, at least under certain conditions outside Europe.

Jean-Luc Nancy's discussion of 'community' argues that no story that posits the rupture of modernity from an earlier situation, its exit from another time, can be upheld. But he rephrases the question by focusing on those stories that posit an unbearable present and long for a harmonious past. Referring to political debates between the 1930s and the 1960s, he suggests that the critique of capitalism has often taken the form of a longing for 'community', for 'communism'. In his view, however, we have to recognize that

> community has not taken place, or rather, if it is indeed certain that humanity has known [...] social ties quite different from those familiar to us, community has never taken place along the lines of our projections of it according to these different social forms. [...] Community, far from being what society has crushed or lost, is what happens to us – question, waiting, event, imperative – in the wake of society. (Nancy, 1991: 11)

Thus, one may want to say, Nancy provides for a 'dislocation' of the search for community; from having been projected into the past, it is now being placed in the present.[3]

The issue has most comprehensively and also most strongly been put in Jacques Derrida's insistence on having to think philosophical problématiques without recourse to origins and to do this 'without nostalgia'. The passage quoted above – from a text introducing *différance*, the key idea of his early work – reads like an interdiction to have any recourse to nostalgia at all. Nostalgia stands here for the longing for foundations of thought. Since such foundations do not exist and since every postulation of any such foundations would limit the 'play' of thinking, the interdiction of nostalgia appears like the only interdiction deconstruction will emit and itself accept.

However, Derrida himself has considerably nuanced his position in other writings. In conclusion of his deconstruction of Lévi-Straussian structuralism, a theorizing in which he sees structure taking the place of the absent origin, he writes:

Turned towards the lost or impossible presence of the absent origin, [the ...] thematic of the broken immediacy is therefore the saddened, negative, nostalgic, guilty, Rousseauistic side of the thinking of play whose other side would be the Nietzschean affirmation, that is the joyous affirmation of the play of the world and of the innocence of becoming, the affirmation of a world of signs without fault, without truth, and without origin which is offered to an active interpretation. (Derrida, 1978a: 292)

This threefold distinction of philosophical positions – structuralism, i.e. in my terminology, modernism, and its two readings, Rousseauism and Nietzscheanism – basically mirrors the distinction of modes of discourse made here. Now followers and critics alike often take Derrida, and post-structuralism in general, to opt for Nietzschean affirmation, as the second response to modernism. This view, however, is not only not warranted by any overall assessment of Derrida's work, it is also directly contradicted by himself. 'For my part', he goes on, 'I do not believe [...] that today there is any question of choosing'. This statement quite unequivocally asserts that, in Derrida's view ('I [...] believe'), there is a justification for all those positions, and that there is a certain undecidability regarding the superiority of any of them over the others – at least under current circumstances ('today'), at the time of Derrida's writing (Derrida, 1978a: 293; see Friese and Wagner, 1999a). Or, in other words, there is not now any way of entirely doing 'without nostalgia'.

In a 1980 debate, Lyotard underlined Derrida's critique of modes of philosophy that retained nostalgia for origins. Derrida, however, responded by pointing out that Lyotard's own thinking was marked by an obsessive will to break with nostalgia. 'In the resolute break with nostalgia,' he said, 'there is a psychoanalytic-Hegelian logic, a rigid relation [...] there is perhaps more nostalgia in you than in me.' And he declared himself as not entirely sharing this obsession with the rupture: 'In regards to nostalgia, I said I wanted to break with it, but I guard [...] a nostalgia for nostalgia.' And in conclusion he observed that 'the relation to nostalgia is always badly regulated' and that 'to dismiss it purely and simply' would seem to be a case of a bad rule (Lyotard, 1989b: 387–9).

At a closer look this intuition is confirmed for the overall critique of modernity as pursued by so-called post-structuralism. In trying to explain the proposition of *The Postmodern Condition*, Lyotard (1984: 79) suggests a relation of postmodernity to modernity that is not one of straight posterity. 'The postmodern [...] is undoubtedly a part of the modern. [...] A work can become modern only if it is first postmodern. Postmodernism thus understood is not modernism at its end but in the nascent state, and this state is constant.' The relation is then the one of a liberating challenger to any kind of established rules and views. This is an acknowledging of both, the existence of hegemonic sets of rules with some claim for legitimacy, but no metaphysically groundable one, and the possibility and indeed need to uproot any such hegemony. We have here the idea of a sequence of modernities, each one of which, since metaphysically ungroundable, is exposed to a critique that appears 'postmodern' because it follows on this modernity, but which is exactly modern in its challenging of established rules. Any such critique thus has to adopt the mode of a 'rupture with nostalgia' (Derrida about Lyotard), but it does so only in the situation in which it formulates its quest. The denial of nostalgia is thus temporalized, and instead of the unequivocal adoption of one politico-philosophical position we arrive at an oscillation between questioning and affirmation.

This contemporary rejection of nostalgia, in the guise of so-called postmodernism and post-structuralism, rather than ending discussions about nostalgia, has revived them – and its protagonists are conscious of this revival. There is a hesitation on their part to enter into any strongly historicizing debates. Nevertheless it seems fairly obvious that their desire to identify nostalgic longings in socio-philosophical modernism, the validity of their claim notwithstanding, needs to be set into the socio-intellectual context of the 1960s and 1970s. During this period, such modernism and the social configuration of organized and technocratic modernity to which it belonged appeared to be unquestioned and beyond any possibility of critique. If one of the main thrusts of these contributions was to identify a concealed nostalgic longing in previously this modernism, then our next step will have to be an investigation into such modernist nostalgia – and that is, into the other and earlier thematization of nostalgia by way of denial.

Nostalgia as a Classical Issue of Modernity

The 'rupture with nostalgia', which Derrida, Lyotard and others demanded, needs to be related to the 'rupture with tradition' that is characteristic of the discourse of modernity. As discussed earlier, it is the defining feature of modernist discourse in social theory and philosophy that it aims to accomplish its objectives by positing a distancing from a context. This context is variably understood, in relation to the subject matter in question. What all these varieties of distancing have in common, however, is a temporal dimension. That from which modernity distances itself remains in the past; or, in slightly different terms, the state in which distance was lacking, is the state of the past. It is a well-known difficulty of both the history of philosophy and of historical sociology to locate the advent of modernity in historical time. All out of the variety of dates and periods that have been proposed, reaching from the end of the fifteenth century to the beginning of the twentieth century, have an identifiable, even if always contestable significance. However, the greater significance is in the quest itself, the attempt namely to trace the moment of distancing from a context in historical time. Hardly any contemporary discussion of modernity can do without it (see, for instance, Bauman, 1991: 3–4; Berman, 1982: 16–17; Giddens, 1990: 1; Habermas, 1985: Chapter 1, drawing on Koselleck, 1979; Toulmin, 1990: 5–6).

There is thus a common concern of identifying a rupture, a concern that is more important than the precise nature, not to speak of the overall consistency, of the breaking-away itself. Thinking about modernity is therefore always marked by a clear conceptual distinction between a before and an after. Without spreading the argument out too far, we may just briefly look at the form this distinction took in socio-historical debate, i.e. in the realm between philosophy of history and the sociology of entire social configurations.[4]

Socio-political thought has long distinguished major forms of societal configurations, has aimed at providing typologies of regimes. From the late eighteenth century onwards, however, this procedure gained distinct temporal connotations.

Adam Smith's analysis of commercial society unfolded against the backdrop of a feudal-agrarian society that was seen as preceding the commercial one.[5] A few decades later, in the works of Hegel and Comte, the full deployment of a philosophy of history can be found. An approach to history that sees the latter proceeding in stages should become common in the evolutionism of the later nineteenth century. It always worked with a major distinction between the present and the period that immediately preceded it. At the end of the nineteenth century, then, what is now known as classical sociology worked with a fundamental conceptual distinction between modern and traditional societies. This approach shaped its key concepts – such as mechanic and organic solidarity in Durkheim, and community and society in Tönnies – such that they reflected and expressed this dividing line.[6] The distinction was both formalized as well as translated into a global context of expected and desired 'development' in the modernization theories of the 1950s and 1960s.

I will not enter here into a discussion about the appropriateness of strong distinctions between societal configurations in terms of historiographical evidence. What is more important at this point is that the conceptualization of socio-historical time in term of dichotomies invited to take an evaluative stand that sets the present against the past. This is the major source for nostalgia as an attitude of social theory, and in particular the social theory of modernity.[7] As Rita Felski (1995: 38) put it, 'nostalgia emerges as a recurring and guiding theme in the self-constitution of the modern.'

To explore this attitude further, we need to distinguish possible ways of relating to the alleged rupture in history and to the socio-temporal dichotomy that it created. First, there is a current of sociology – indeed the disciplinary mainstream in one understanding of the field – that straightforwardly affirms the rupture and the thus established societal modernity. This is a line of thinking that runs from nineteenth-century evolutionism and Durkheim's early discipline-building writings to post-Second World War functionalism and modernization theory. The modern rupture is seen as a progress of reason in the earlier versions and as the evolutionary assertion of functional superiority in the later versions of this thinking. While new exigencies in the new situation are acknowledged, this is a sociology that largely denies nostalgia and claims to work without it.[8]

Second, there is a tradition of sociological thinking that acknowledges both the irreversibility and the desirability of the modern rupture but sees a need for, and also a principled possibility of, readjusting society towards a harmony that was thrown off-balance by the advent of modernity. In this tradition we find Hegel as well as Tönnies and among contemporary thinkers both Jürgen Habermas and Alain Touraine. We may draw a further distinction here between those who envisage truly new harmonies and those who rather aim at a balance between different exigencies that is rather negatively defined. The former, such as Hegel, envisage a fundamental reconciliation of different exigencies, whereas the best the latter hope for is the absence of pathologies (Habermas) and the control of dissociation (Touraine). The latter also conceptualize such balancing as possible in historical time and under a persistent modern condition. Others, most notably Marx, envisaged a further rupture that was required to achieve reconciliation, and it is arguable that such future rupture was conceived as happening in eschatological time.[9] In the former case, nostalgia is ('rationally') controlled, whereas in the latter it is transformed into utopian longings.

From a third position in sociology and social philosophy the onset and development of modernity is more or less strongly deplored. In a strong version, conservative social thought rejects modernity and holds it even to be reversible. Much more ambivalently, thinkers such as Max Weber, Theodor W. Adorno and currently Charles Taylor recognize an irreversibility of modernity that is founded not least on its attractions, on the achievement of individual freedom and instrumental rationality in particular. But they see dangers and existential threats arising from exactly the moral and political consequences of those achievements, once they are socially diffused or generalized. From this position, a non-conservative critique of modernity emerges that has strong tragic-nostalgic features.

Charles Taylor's observations on 'the malaise of modernity' provide a recent example for the way in which such an argument is elaborated in temporal terms and focused on losses as a consequence of the modern rupture. Taylor sees in the upholding of morality and community, in the relation to nature, and in the viability of a good polity the three crucial concerns of contemporary modernity. He describes these concerns in the following terms: 'Modern freedom was won by our *breaking loose* from *older* moral horizons. [...] Modern freedom came about through the discrediting of such orders [..., which] has been called the "disenchantment" of the world. With it, things *lost* some of their magic.' The awe of nature subsides '*once* society *no longer* has a sacred structure, *once* social arrangements are *no longer* grounded in the order of things or in the will of God [...], then 'the yardstick that *henceforth* applies is that of instrumental reason.' And finally, '*once* participation declines, *once* the lateral associations, that were its vehicles wither away', then loss of political freedom will occur. Taylor sums up the three malaises of modernity and the three fears that go with them as 'a *loss* of meaning, the *fading* of moral horizons [...,] the *eclipse* of ends, in face of rampant instrumental reason [..., and] a *loss* of freedom' (Taylor, 1991: 3–10; emphases added; see also Habermas, 1981: 447, on Weber).

Taylor's description is a most recent example of a kind of conceptualization that emerged – at the latest – at the turn to the nineteenth century and the first comprehensive articulation of which was probably Hegel's notion of the 'unhappy, inwardly disrupted consciousness' seeking 'its true return into itself, or its reconciliation with itself' (Hegel, 1977 [1807]: Chapter B IV). Using a formula proposed more than a century later, it can be characterized by the emphasis on the 'discontents' (*Unbehagen*) with modernity (Freud, 1985). It needs to be underlined that most of the thinkers in this perspective do not reject modernity, and be it only because of its inescapability. Rather, they place the accent in their analyses on features of social life that modernity has made unattainable. The construction then supposes that those features were attained or at least attainable in some past before the modern rupture, and that they cannot be forgotten. It is precisely this construction then that gives itself to an attitude of unsatisfied and unsatisfiable longing, to nostalgia.

Despite the marked differences between the three sociological perspectives on modernity, they all allow for such nostalgia or indeed even create the very possibility for (intellectual-theoretical) nostalgia to emerge. The modernist claim produces the dichotomy from which nostalgia for the past becomes a possible attitude once modernity appears to fall short of its promises. It is, however, only the third perspective that acknowledges the nostalgic possibility – and it does so not even by the use of this term, which – under the reign of the imaginary signification of modernity – smacks of 'backwardness'. The second one recognizes the possibility of nostalgia, but reasons it away by means of balancing or reconciliation, i.e. through intellectual constructions that cannot fully do away with the rift opened in the fundamentally dichotomical conceptualization. Proponents of the first perspective explicitly deny nostalgia any place, but this is because their construction locates 'tradition' and 'origins' entirely outside of modernity, since the rupture is basically accomplished. In this case, the rift is between their conceptualization and those of others, but such an almost explicit denial also gives nostalgia its place – outside of this theorization.

In our context, this commonality is more important than the differences between these positions. Overcoming, balancing and longing all not only use a dichotomy of modernity and tradition, but also create a determinate relation towards tradition from the viewpoint of (inescapable) modernity. The three positions together occupy the space between modernist social philosophy and the first response to it, with the balancing position deliberately applying a dualism using both modes. They share a conceptualization in which the modern is linked to the origins by an explicated understanding of the rupture; the relation to tradition is thought of as entirely intelligible.

The second response to modernist social theory challenges precisely this view. It focuses on the notions of time and history that enter into these conceptualizations and aims at questioning the import of the 'rupture' itself. Rather than using such a notion as an explanatory tool to conceptualize the difference between 'modernity' and 'tradition', it opens the space for a variety of ways to conceive of that relation.

Arguably, this mode of thinking was inaugurated with Friedrich Nietzsche's (1972 [1874]) 'untimely meditation' on the 'use and disadvantage of history for life'. In this text, Nietzsche discerned three major ways of constructing the relation between history and the present and tried to assess the respective impact on present life of each of these. Starting out from a critique of the historicism and evolutionism that was so dominant in nineteenth-century intellectual life, in particular in Germany, he is often read as favouring a less oppressive view of history. Rather than deriving present possibilities from the past, one should be encouraged to cast off the burden of history to liberate the forces of life in the present. Such reading situates the text quite appropriately in the problem-context Nietzsche was addressing in the 1870s. Re-reading it later, however, different and wider interpretative possibilities come to the fore. By distinguishing a multiplicity of ways of relating to the past, Nietzsche had opened up this relation to indeterminacy. Rather than only attacking one particular conceptualization of that relation, namely historical determinism, he had rejected any single and determinate relation between the past and the present. At the same time, he did not unequivocally favour the liberation from the past. He demanded an active, creative relation to the past – not a deliberate creation of one's own convenient past.

This step was recognized as well as considerably sharpened and accentuated between the two world wars by thinkers such as Martin Heidegger, Walter Benjamin and later Hannah Arendt.[10] In early writings, already during the First World War, both Heidegger and Benjamin radically questioned the accessibility of the past. Heidegger (1978 [1916]: 427) emphasized the 'qualitative otherness of past times', which entailed that the past was never available to the present as such, but only through a relation of present valuation.[11] Drawing on Heidegger, Benjamin developed then the ideas about the course of history that he should last express in the theses 'on the concept of history'. Already in 1916 he noted that 'the determining force of historical time cannot be fully grasped by, or wholly concentrated in, any empirical process. Rather, a process that is perfect in historical terms is quite indeterminate empirically' (Benjamin, 1996 [1916]: 55). In the essay on the work of art in the age of its technical reproducibility he spoke about 'the shattering of tradition' (1978 [1935]: 439). Reading Kafka and reflecting about the politico-philosophical choices during the inter-war period, Hannah Arendt later described the present as a 'gap between the past and the future'. The present is a moment of openness in which thinking and acting can intervene and liberate human beings from the thought of being caught between two adversaries, past and future, approaching from opposite sides and leaving no room (see Friese, 2001b).

If such a perspective is adopted, none of the three sociological approaches to modernity can be upheld. Modernity is no longer timeless and taken out of history, as the modernist view of the rupture implicitly suggests. But neither is it in any strong sense tied to the past via a dependence on tradition or on 'origins', as some of the critics of modernity hold. Nor can the two interpretations just be linked to each other and some need for balancing constructed. The 'opening of the time horizon', which Reinhart Koselleck (1979) described as the emergence of a distinction between the past and the future, does not clearly divide a past from a present and future, as the modernist view both in philosophy and in sociology often puts it. Rather, it opens the relations between them. The ambivalence and uncertainty about one's position in time can no longer be avoided or reasoned away.[12]

At the same time, these considerations allow us to further elucidate the relation of the post-structuralist critique of modernism that demands a 'rupture with nostalgia' to the modernism that proceeded on the assumption of a 'rupture with tradition'. As is well-known, post-structuralism in various ways draws on Nietzsche, Heidegger, Benjamin and to a lesser extent Arendt, those thinkers who rephrased the idea of historical time. In this light, it is now recognizable how 'postmodernism', as discussed above, becomes the radicalization of modernity. First, it demands to overcome the longing that was produced by the dichotomical foundation of modernist thought. Thus, it emphasizes – rather than denies – the modern claim of distancing and does not revert back into a relation with tradition. Second, however, unlike modernist theorizations of modernity this distancing is no longer seen as effectively taking social configurations out of time and historicity. It is in this sense that Jean-Luc Nancy, in the above quote, tried to transpose the question of 'community' into a present one, into one of present urgency, rather than either abandoning the question or searching for 'community' in a lost past.

Like all critique, however, post-structuralism remained marked by the object of its criticism – and this is at the core of the debate between Derrida and Lyotard quoted above. While developing the thought along the lines of one each of the two ruptures – rupture with tradition and rupture with nostalgia – both modernist social thought and deconstruction make generic claims about the 'origins' that are at stake – 'a purely maternal or paternal language' or 'a lost native country of thought', to quote Derrida again, or whatever else. Neither modernism nor the post-structuralism that provides the second response to modernism need or can specify the location of those origins, since their basic attitude is to deny the validity of the quest. Social thought that acknowledges nostalgia (even if under different terms), however, appears in different versions which distinguish themselves not least by the places where the origins are sought. Any closer investigation of nostalgia will have to take such varieties of longing into consideration. We shall then see that the contemporary liveliness of the double denial of nostalgia is on the one hand an indication for the inescapability of 'some conception of the past' (Abrams, 1972). On the other hand, it takes its particular form and urgency from the historical context in which it itself emerges.

Varieties of Longing

Nostalgia is about loss. Our more specific question will now have to be: what is it that is lost, why was it, or is it still, important to attain it, and why can it no longer be attained? The basic presupposition – and the commonality across strands of thinking – is that there is some original situation from which we are now separated and for which we long but which we can no longer reach. This always involves the idea of a break, a rupture that has occurred in the past, a current state of being in a situation of separation as a state of some sort of lack and, therefore, of suffering, and 'nostalgia' as the longing for the return to the earlier state. Without any ambition at systematicity, a variety of ways of identifying the longed-for past can be distinguished.

Most comprehensively, there is a religious-cosmological longing for an overall harmony of the world. The reference to the past is then – to use the themes of the first part of this book – to the time when knowledge was certain; the time when the polity was united; and the time when the self was an undamaged whole. In religious terms, this is also the time when God gave reassurance. The story of the Fall in all its varieties is the religious expression of nostalgia, and it is at the same time a mode of overcoming nostalgia by offering a return to the situation before the Fall through redemption. But the longing for a harmonious being-one-with-the-world does not have to carry any – explicit – religious connotations. In romanticism, it appears as a reaction against the attempt at distancing the thinking and willing subject from the world, which was characteristic of the Enlightenment. Eighteenth-century thinking about the sublime and the feeling of awe at the wonders of the world, while certainly being related both to religious conceptions and to classic Greek philosophy, gave a new expression to such oneness. The feeling associated with it was then also called enchantment, the counter-concept to which, 'disenchantment', was borrowed from classic German literature and turned into a key concept of a sociology of modernity by Max Weber a century later.

In the course of such reconsideration of both the oneness of being-in-the-world and the loss of it, the philosophical-religious topic was displaced. The experience of lack and loss was dissociated from its predominant, namely philosophical-religious, interpretation. This step subsequently allowed the experience to be re-entered into a variety of different interpretations. As we shall see, this variety included importantly an instrumental one, as one may want to call it, one that allows to 'treat' the experience, to come to terms with it.

Beginning in the seventeenth century, nostalgia entered into the medical vocabulary as the technical term for a disease that occurred during extended absence from one's home, often indeed during absences that were forced or only semi-voluntary, such as those of soldiers in the army. The debate intensified during the eighteenth century to reach its height in the first half of the nineteenth; it was also widely taken up in literary form. After that it subsided to finally disappear from medical discourse towards the end of the nineteenth century. Nostalgia, also known less technically as homesickness, *mal de pays* or *Heimweh*, was seen as causally related to the absence from home and turned out to be indeed largely curable by sending the soldiers back home (Chase and Shaw, 1989; Roth, 1992). It was not least in this connection, i.e. nostalgia as having a physical appearance and a remedial practice, that a discourse on loss emerged that is sufficiently different from the philosophical-religious discourse on the loss of being-one-with-the world to allow another access to the problématique. At the same time, this approach is sufficiently close to the former to recognize the issues dealt with as part of a similar problématique and indeed to allow for a reconnection of both discourses. A discussion of this relation can serve to further explore this problématique.

In the medical discourse, nostalgia is clearly a physical state and an experience of singular human beings. It is observable and it is, in principle, treatable once its source, the distance from home, has been recognized. By implication then, this discourse introduced a concept of 'home' and of 'at-home-ness' as counter-concepts to the disease and to the site of its occurrence. Apparently, nostalgia refers to a distance in space, a strangeness that results from being in an unfamiliar place. In the literature, one can indeed observe a shift over time from an early emphasis on the spatial aspect towards a later one on distance in time. However, that distinction was blurred from the beginning owing to the fact that nostalgia refers to the movements of a human being across time-space, namely over a part of his or her life-course. The experience of the other space, for which one longs, is always past, and the absent space of home is simultaneously the absent time of the past.

The scholarly medical literature of the nineteenth century tried to specify as precisely as possible what it was that was lacking and created the illness. Summarizing the debate, Roth (1992: 275) observes that it was 'family, native soil and earliest memories' that appeared as the basic objects of nostalgic affection, thereby creating indeed what for many people was a unitary time-space of childhood and growing up. Recent anthropological research similarly identifies the feeling of loss in a biographical perspective. The point of reference, to which orienting thinking in the present always returns, is the 'site of original remembrance' or 'the original space' (Friese, 1996: 60, 75).

For the feeling of lack and loss to emerge an event or process of separation from such original space is required. Logically, one may want to argue, no such feeling should emerge if and when people remain on their native soil and within the realm of their family. This is, however, the point where the discussion here relates in an equivocal way to the preceding one about selfhood (see Chapter 3). The modernist socio-psychological stream of the latter debate, as we have seen, relates identity-formation to socialization and expects a separate, stable identity, individually distinct from the identities of other family members, at a certain age. Such identity is the precondition for the formation of the modern, autonomous subject per se. Modern selfhood has essentially to do with separation. In the debate about nostalgia, in contrast, separation creates a divide in the human being and makes him or her long for something outside of his or her present state. The 'nostalgic' idea of one's own self is related to the wish that the separation had never happened or could be undone.

Despite some practical, medical successes in curing nostalgic patients by sending them home, however, as a matter of principle there is no return to the time-space of the 'before' after a separation. That to which one returns is always different from that from where one has gone. This is the guiding theme of Vladimir Jankélévitch's (1983) discussion of 'irreversibility and nostalgia'. Jankélévitch (1983: 8) underlines the constitutive nature of temporality for human life; time is not merely the way of being or the mode of existence of human beings; it is their being itself, their 'only substantiality'. Time, however, is not manipulable according to human will; its irreversibility leaves us radically powerless. Facing this situation, human beings have found two ways of compensating for their powerlessness – spatiality and intelligence. The former explains why the longing for a past time takes the form of the desire to return to a space where one once was. 'But the finite being is above all a mobile being, and its mobility is partly compensating for its finitude: the movement by which a finite human being displaces itself from place to place, the locomotion by which it puts itself from one site to another one compensate laboriously for the omnipresence of which it is deprived' (Jankélévitch, 1983: 17–18). And the latter helps to understand why, as discussed in the preceding chapters, conceptual work in philosophy and science operates through a repression of time. 'The fullest liberty of circulation is assured to us between places as well as between concepts' (Jankélévitch, 1983: 18). However, there is no overcoming the irreversibility of time. 'Irreversibility being our a priori powerlessness, we achieve over the invincible only imagined victories' (Jankélévitch, 1983: 70); the origins are always unattainable (see for a broader discussion Prete, 1992).

In a way, Sigmund Freud can be considered the writer who re-conceptualized the experience of irreversibility for a social philosophy of modernity, or, in other words, who turned the experience into a theorem on the human condition. The feeling of separation from 'family, native soil and earliest memories' (Roth) is then turned into the driving motive for the historical process of civilization as a means to overcome that feeling or at least to compensate for the loss. 'Writing was in its origin the voice of the absent person; and the dwelling-house was a substitute for the mother's womb, the first lodging, for which in all likelihood man still longs' (Freud, 1985 [1930]: 279). This step, however, displaces the experience. More unequivocally and more determinately than Jankélévitch, it turns the experience of lack into a drive and relates it to a projection, to an orientation towards the future in the present. Significantly, such a displacement of nostalgia can be found already throughout the nineteenth century.

In 1832, just after the 1830 revolution, Pierre-Urbain Briet noted that the homeland is not necessarily the place where one comes from, but could be the place where the lover is, the place where freedom is or, in conceptual terms, 'anywhere [where] he would find principles in accord with his own less vulgar prejudices, and the wherewithal to live as a man' (quoted after Roth, 1992: 275). Thus, we find here the idea of a longing, an apparent homesickness that is turned into something else. The connection to the actual origins can be cut, and the desire can be turned towards a future that is defined as attainable.

At about the same time, the medical debates started to indicate that nostalgia as a disease may be disappearing. 'Fortunately, nostalgia diminishes day by day [...]. Everything that touches civilization, in perfecting the human species, makes man understand his role as an individual, his part in the common work, and, in enlightening his spirit, submits the impulses of his heart to reason' (Morin, quoted after Roth, 1992: 278). Medical practitioners based this statement in the first place on the observation of a decreasing incidence of the illness. They did not refrain, however, from giving for this development an explanation, which was manifold but in all its parts focused on the advent of a higher civilization. Better education would allow people to overcome the rural attachment to the soil and to recognize the advantages of the modern times. New technologies in general would create a new human being, a self-reliant individual and conscious participant in the 'common work'. And at the same time, technologies of information and communication would allow those human beings to remain in touch with their native soil even while living a modern life elsewhere.

The mode of reasoning of one central stream of social theory should be easily recognizable in this medical discourse. The reference to the 'common work' in which the moral 'individual' engages, for instance, prefigures Durkheim's idea of the division of social labour creating organic solidarity. Overall, the nostalgic relation to the past is here displaced through an opposition of tradition and modernity, in which the reaching of 'modern' society – contractual and willed – relegates the experience of the past to the status of being superseded in all important respects and thus successfully overcome. The central tradition of social science constitutes itself thus as a modernist discourse with regard to temporality.

Already during the nineteenth century, however, critics pointed out that such overcoming was not to be had without important losses. While there were achievements of modernity, they could never fully compensate for the kinds of attachments one had before. And if it was one of the achievements of modernity to have let nostalgic longings disappear, then this disappearance itself was a loss that could not be compensated for. Nostalgia, with all its pain, had a density of feeling that no modern attachment could provide. Michael Roth (1992: 279) calls this attitude a 'nostalgia for nostalgia', referring by the second term literally to the disease. The nostalgia for nostalgia that we identified at the outset of this chapter in current post-structuralism, however, can be interpreted analogously. The deconstruction of modernist longings risks leaving us without any longings at all, and at that point nostalgia for nostalgia arises.

This parallel discourse about nostalgia as an experience and a disease, on the one hand, and about philosophical-theoretical nostalgia, on the other, leads to two conclusions. First, it confirms our identification of the space of modern reasoning with regard to the past. The reference to 'origins' of all kinds – language, the mother's body, childhood experiences, family, native soil – creates a discourse that is characterized by a substantive grounding. Our brief sketch, though, has also shown that this grounding can take a variety of different forms. The attempt then at overcoming such rootedness of human existence, which is seen as a constraint, aims at dissolving any substantive linkage to the past and thus produces a modernist discourse. Against and beyond such view, the insufficiencies of any modernist presentism can be pointed out. In sum, the double movement, while not exactly leading back to the beginning, demonstrates the inescapability of the issue, since the ways of overcoming it are deemed unsatisfactory, and the always open nature of the attainability of a solution, since no superior approach within this plurality can be identified.

Second, the parallelism between these two discourses returns us to the question of the relation between an historical-empirical and a philosophical approach to modernity, albeit in more radical form. An experiential-biographical concern for 'origins' exists next to a philosophical one, and though there are but few linkages of the discourses, they show a very similar structure. The socio-historical discourse, which is, so to say, situated in-between the other two, rarely reasons explicitly about origins, because it has developed a determinate relation to the past – even if in a variety of forms, as argued above. Returning indeterminacy to the socio-historical discourse demands, in a next step, to locate specific forms of nostalgia and of its counterpart, the identification of origins, in historical time, and to do so without either repressing the experiential aspect or denying the philosophical import.

Nostalgia in Historical Time

The immediately preceding discussion has identified the nineteenth century as a period when nostalgia moved into the centre of medical discussion, but also entered into a first form of a critique of modernity. At the beginning of this chapter, the early twentieth century, and then in particular the first and second post-war periods, were presented as a time when the argument that the relation to the past has to be conceptualized as radically indeterminate was put forward in philosophy, but also in literature and in social and political thought. I now want to come back to these two observations on discourses and relate them to some elements of a broad historical sociology. This will be an attempt to *argue* that there is *for us today* a particular meaning and significance of the reference to 'origins', one that emerges interpretatively, not deterministically, from the past. Several features of this attempt will need to be discussed before I enter into it.

First, I will 'argue' for such significance, but I will provide no full demonstration or give conclusive evidence. Any construction of a relation to the past occurs in the present and tries to understand the present, and so will this one. And in the light of what was said before, such construction can only be one out of a plurality of possible interpretations: Its power to convince can only be measured by the degree to which it appears plausible and is accepted. Second, although the 'for us' can also only be understood as the 'we' to which this argument is addressed, it is nevertheless problematic, in particular after Lyotard's (1989a) forceful questioning of any such 'we'. I will indeed propose that there is such a 'we', largely 'we Europeans', and I think that even Lyotard works with such a 'we'.[13] However, and here I follow and accept Lyotard's suggestion, this is mostly not a 'we' that 'can', but rather a 'we' that 'cannot' or 'can no longer'. It is a collectivity that is incapacitated by its past experiences and the interpretations it holds of them. And it is from this situation that the particular demands of our present emerge. Thus, thirdly, and this should by now almost be self-evident, the argument is made from a particular historical location and for a particular time – 'today'.

After these prefatory remarks, I feel enabled to suggest that our current ways of referring to origins are related to two major events in the European history of the past two centuries.[14] These are the concomitance of large-scale emigration from Europe and the emergence of nationalism during the nineteenth century, first, and the extended warfare – both military and civil – during the first half of the twentieth century, second. These events are rather familiar – which is not to say that they are known – to historians and to everybody else with some interest in the past. Why should they be singled out and seen as shaping our ways of relating to the past?

To anticipate the argument: each of these events radically altered the ways the past was seen, or even, could be seen, by those who lived through them or came after. Certainly, not all change went into the same direction and the new views of the past were not exclusively held. But a new discursive formation emerged, as a space of possible positions with a certain variety, but with a common frame that held it together. In each of these cases this change was brought about by a double move. On the one hand, there was the experience of actual displacement of such a large share of the European population that this experience could not but become a formative element of a new view of history and society. On the other hand, each of the events is also an event in intellectual history, through which the conceptual apparatus applied to the past and present social world was reshaped. The events mark a dislocation of thinking. And finally, and maybe most importantly, these two events stand in a relation of tension to each other. This relation is conditioned by its own temporality, the one event preceding the other in time. But it does not exhaust itself in the temporality. The first event is an experience of loss that is responded to by a conceptualization that aims at regaining. The second attempt marks the insight into the loss of the former conceptual possibility. That insight emerges through new experiences of loss, now accompanied by the conceptualization of loss itself. Or, in other words, what the first event proposes is withdrawn – Lyotard would say 'refuted' – by the second. But since the withdrawal remains *sans issue*, without a proposition of its own, the first proposal cannot be cancelled out. It stays with us, pointing to an inescapability, to the impossibility of its own negation.

The history of nineteenth-century Europe is not least a history of massive displacements of human beings. The movements from the countryside to cities and from rural-agrarian ways of life to urban-industrial ones have long been a key object and reference for economic and social history and for the sociology of industrial societies. Next to those movements and in their shadow, however, hundreds of thousands of Europeans went to North America, out of despair over their prospects in the Old World and/or in the hope of a more prosperous future in the new one. All of these migrants left the place of their original experiences, often forever, and knowing that it would be unlikely for them to return. Nostalgia in both of its forms, as a disease and as a critique of modernity, emerged in this context. And so did its proposed remedy.

The idea that people were tied to each other by the commonality of the original experiences at their places of birth, of natality, had been known long before the nineteenth century. It was after that massive experience of exodus, however, that it was rephrased and turned into the guiding orientation for social and political life – in the guise of nationalism. The conceptual innovation was twofold. First, the space of origin was extended beyond any possible experiential qualities, to the territory of the linguistically conceived nation-state. In as far as this rephrasing appeared convincing, it entailed that many of the migrants actually stayed 'home' despite enormous experiential changes.[15] And, second, this enlarged space of original 'experience' was designed to be the container of socio-economic and political life at the same time. The progressive view of history saw the institutionalization of modernity in the form of an industrial society with a division of labour that created organic solidarity and in the form of the nation-state with increasingly inclusive political rights. The displaced human beings would become members of this new order and thus autonomous but socialized individuals of a new kind.

This construction provided a double ground for nostalgia to wither away. There was no need to long for the past because, on the one hand, the present had superseded the past in all respects and, on the other, because the rewritten past remained present in the life of the nation as a home that had never been left. Nationalism was a response to the fear that modernity would leave people 'homeless'. It turned the argument around by offering a way of building 'homes' of a new kind under conditions of modernity (see Wagner, 1994a: Chapter 3). As much as indeed European modernity was organized with the help of such a conceptualization, during the twentieth century it became more and more obvious that, rather than providing a solution, the re-embedding through nationalism did nothing but displace the more fundamental problématique. The extended warfare during the first half of the twentieth century then demonstrated beyond doubt the absence of any solution.

As a war for which exalted nationalism was an important background condition, the First World War ended peculiarly in the reiteration of this nineteenth-century principle of national self-determination. With hindsight one recognizes, and not only because of Nazism and the project of the annihilation of the European Jewry, that this once embarked-on path of displacing nostalgia was thus continued, although with increasingly dim hopes. The nationalist wars in the Balkans write the most recent chapter of that story. With the First World War itself, however, the counter-story was inaugurated, the one about the shattering of all tradition.

Already as it was waging, the First World War meant to many observers the abandonment of any hope that 'modernity' was on an essentially peaceful and progressive path and, with this, it conveyed the undeniable insight that 'modernity' included the possibility of unprecedented horrors. The Russian Revolution marks a watershed between two eras. While on the one hand it was drawing on a dissident tradition of the nineteenth century, the Marxist reading of the workers' movement, on the other hand it inaugurated a regime that made the total dissolution of social ties and their planned reweaving its programme. The inter-war years – with hindsight nothing more than an extended cease-fire – witnessed then the increasing confrontation between nation-based and class-based proposals to organize a modernity that had proven more shaky and crisis-prone than its proponents had expected. Not much after the radical wing of nationalists in Germany had decided that struggle in its favour, the Nazi government reopened the war and led it recklessly against the populations of Europe including a major part of its own and the entire European Jewry. When this war was over at mid-century, Central Europe was emptied of any possibility to resort to tradition. The accumulated experiences of this whole period provide the historical background to the emergence of the philosophical debate about the shattering of tradition that was mentioned above. At the same time, such shattering of tradition found expression across a broad range of practices far beyond philosophical debate.

In art, literature and architecture, this expression is now commonly labelled modernism, although the strict association with the idea of shattered tradition is not always made. Rather, the prevailing understanding interprets modernism in terms of liberation from conventions. Seen as the movement from impressionism through expressionism and cubism towards abstraction, modernism in painting is then interpreted as the liberation from the need to represent a perceivable reality. Analogously, modernism in literature is related to the breaking up of the conventional narrative with an identifiable narrator, developing narrated selves, and an ordinary grammar and syntax. With varying degrees of radicality, all these conventions were broken in early twentieth-century literature. In architecture, finally, there has also been a break with representation, the representation of the status and power of the owners or inhabitants of a building namely through forms of decoration. Modernist architecture puts functionality over representation.

I do not want to challenge in any significant way the prevailing interpretation of those modernisms as liberations. This is what they certainly were and what their lasting contribution is. However, this view may underestimate the extent to which the originators of these movements saw themselves forced to go into this direction, because other ways were no longer available or acceptable. It may neglect their feeling something imposed on themselves because of a lack of alternatives, rather than choosing the path of liberation from the requirement to represent. Although there are important exceptions, it is noteworthy in this context that many of the protagonists of the various modernisms have been, in different ways, 'displaced persons', people who have emigrated from the places where they grew up or were forced into exile. The history of modernism in painting, as displayed in a canonized way in the New York Museum of Modern Art is a history of emigration and exile. In the great majority of cases, citizenship, country of birth and country of death, as indicated in the legend to the exhibited paintings, do not coincide.[16]

While the origins of all those modernisms lie – by and large – after the experiences of industrialization, urbanization and the First World War, but before those of totalitarianism, organized genocide and the Second World War, the latter experiences mark a further radicalization. In intellectual life, two reactions stand out as particularly significant. In political philosophy, the advent of totalitarianism was interpreted by some thinkers from the European continent, such as Isaiah Berlin, Karl Popper and Jacob Talmon, as demonstrating the inescapability of some form of liberalism as the founding philosophy of modern societies with a commitment to human rights and values (see also Chapter 2). The most famous statement in this respect is certainly Isaiah Berlin's somewhat tortuous plea for negative liberty to be given preference over positive liberty (Berlin, 1969). It is important to note that all of these thinkers, Berlin and Talmon in particular, had affinities to more substantively rich alternatives of political philosophy and that they did not abandon those alternatives lightly (see Horowitz, 1991). It also seems worthwhile to note that Berlin and Popper found in England their places of residence, thus rooting themselves anew in a philosophically analytical and politically liberal context. Historical experience had demonstrated, in their view, that all more substantive political philosophies, once they served as underpinning for political orders, were prone to produce catastrophic results, all worthy intentions of their intellectual originators notwithstanding. After a number of such experiences had been made, no further such experimentation seemed permissible.

In broader social philosophy, a related reasoning took more radical shape. It referred to the attempted annihilation of the European Jewry in particular, rather than to totalitarianism more generally. And from this specific event in human history it concluded on the loss of all language of representation. This is Adorno's intellectual trajectory from his remark on the impossibility of poetry after Auschwitz to the *Negative Dialectics* and similarly Lyotard's path from his early writing about Auschwitz to the idea of the historical refutation of all narratives of emancipation. Writers such as Paul Celan, Primo Levi and Sarah Kofman have struggled with the question of the possibility of language and representation after this experience for all of their lives, and the question, though it can be temporarily repressed, is bound to stay with us (Friese, 2000).

In the light of these observations in social and intellectual history, and beyond them, a step towards a reinterpretation of European societal developments during the second half of the twentieth century can be taken. The predominant view sees the social world gradually take its modern organized form during the second half of the nineteenth century up to the First World War in parallel processes of industrialization, urbanization, rationalization (through the modern sciences, but also though bureaucracy) and democratization. While some of these processes advance faster than others and in some societies more than in others, everything accelerates after the end of the Second World War, and by the 1960s socio-political modernity is in full place in Northwest Europe and North America. Although much historical research is devoted to it, the interim period between 1914 and 1945 remains precisely that, an interim, and does not gain any significance in a conceptual sense. Histories of social policy, for instance, regularly jump from 'the early welfare state' around the turn of the century to its 'full' development during the 1950s and 1960s. In the self-understanding of the social sciences, the 'classical' or 'neo-classical' period after 1890 finds its continuation in the 'modern' social sciences of the 1960s. Economic and social history detect the emergence of mass production and of the organized workers' movement in the second half of the nineteenth century and see an economic order erected on those twin foundations after the Second World War, organized corporate capitalism or 'Fordism'.

At most, the significance of events during the inter-war period is seen in the blocking of societal alternatives in the West, such as most importantly Soviet socialism and Nazism. Still today, intellectual and political activities during that period are interpreted mostly in terms of how they related to these grand alternatives. Violent and contested as the struggle about these and other alternatives was, however, once its victorious outcome was assured, Western modernity seemed to have re-embarked on its successful historical trajectory, if we are willing to believe the standard view. In contrast to this view, I propose to see this struggle itself and, to speak loosely, the damages it has inflicted as the major reason for the shaping of European societies after the Second World War. Thus, there was no continuation on a path of modernization, but conclusions drawn collectively, although in their specific results unintendedly, from a historical experience.

Such an alternative view entails to see a major societal transformation having occurred in European societies between 1913 and the 1950s (these are standard dates of reference in long statistical series in Europe). The former societies may have contained the germ of the latter, but they are in important respects different kinds of societal configuration. To give some illustration: social policies that cover residual risks in societies with strong ties of family support and a high degree of subsistence are quite different from a comprehensive welfare state in thoroughly commodified societies. The 'classical' social sciences conceived of the social bond and of the viability of social order quite differently from the 'modern' social sciences, and they used different means to provide evidence. An economy with pockets of mass production for basic investment and bulk goods is quite different from an economy that links mass consumption to mass production and can thus generalize the production model.[17] The International Style that dominated the architecture of the 1950s and 1960s and produced faceless cities is not merely a diffusion of *Neue Sachlichkeit*, but a style that is subject to quite different criteria.[18]

Obviously, any such assertion of a transformation of social life can rather easily be contested.[19] The case for continuities does not become invalid just because one emphasizes differences. And indeed I am far from denying the strength of continuities; I rather aim at underlining an overlooked feature of post-war European societies. Returning to the preceding discussion, this feature is a perceived loss of origins that has now moved far from the philosophical or religious-cosmological issue towards the possibility of making actual reference to a 'morality of custom' in everyday social life (see the – slightly misleading – discussion in Rose, 1993: 55–6). It is not that the avant garde modernism of the early century has trickled down to the masses by the 1960s as a 'sunk culture', as Daniel Bell (1976) has it. Rather, the break with all established ways of judging the good, the true and the beautiful was imposed twice – first by the political and military mass mobilizations of the early century and then by the destruction through totalitarianism, war and genocide. And this break was imposed in such a way that large segments of society could not escape the reach of that destruction. The massive material need for reconstruction after the war as well as the re-education programmes in the defeated societies and the silenced rift between resistance fighters and collaborators in the liberated societies assured the presence of that experience until far into the post-war period.[20] Without wanting to overemphasize the point, the preceding suggestions should suffice to give the notions of the shattering of tradition and of the loss of origins a socio-historical meaning – beyond and, so to say, in-between the biographical and the philosophical ones.

If the broad socio-historical argument set out here can be accepted, then important conceptual insights follow from it. First, while it is a characteristic of the thinking of modernity to create the possibility of nostalgia, as demonstrated above, modernity is not inherently nostalgic as such. Rather nostalgic longings exist in a variety of forms that need not co-exist or emerge at all. The distinction between biographical-experiential, socio-historical and philosophical forms of nostalgia, crude as it may be, opens up the path towards a more specific and differentiated investigation into modernity's (or capitalism's, for that matter) tendency towards the destruction of tradition and, as a consequence, the generation of nostalgic longings. By implication, even modernity 'without nostalgia', as called for by Derrida, is thus well conceivable in principle. Nostalgia is a possibility inherent in modernity, but nothing determined by the advent of modernity.

Once such considerations have led towards the path of a specific inquiry into our current condition, in contrast, it emerges that there is a current form of nostalgia that forms an integral part of the self-understanding of contemporary Europe and which one cannot easily do without. This nostalgia is related to particular historical events of recent European history. It is in principle possible to deny those events any overarching importance for our current situation; this is what the achievement of opening the relation to the past towards indeterminacy permits us. However, precisely any such attempt at denial or neglect by some is very likely to create as a reaction a call for endowing those historical events with central significance. This is what recent historians' disputes and revisionisms are about; and their emergence itself can be understood against the background of an optimistic theory of modernization that claimed to have settled the relation to the past once and for all, to have fixed its interpretation.

Even though there is a considerable leeway then in the significance given to the two events discussed, there can be much less doubt about the reflection upon them having added a new socio-historical meaning to the notions of tradition, loss and nostalgia. This meaning is now inevitably part of our repertoire of thinking about tradition and about loss.

It cannot be my ambition here to provide a full argument for taking the specificity of the two historical events into account when rethinking the concept of nostalgia under current conditions and when proposing a way of relating to the past today. The previous description may suffice to state the inescapability of creating a relation to this past. The argument is supported by the double evocation of the past in the contexts of continuous (and persistently violent) nationalism as a way of claiming origins, on the one hand, and of so-called globalization (both economic and cultural) as a way of allegedly clearing away the rubble of the past, on the other. At the same time, the twofold and contradiction-ridden nature of this evocation decreases the likelihood of attaining any single plausible and acceptable relation to the past. Or in other words, there is contingency that demands a contemporary specification.

Notes

1 Thus, Rita Felski (1995: 58) describes post-structuralists as tending 'to read any appeal to an originary unity as symptomatic of a reactionary metaphysics of presence.' This view, however, needs to be qualified, as will be argued below.

2 Lyotard, 1989a: 318. The way Lyotard sees (historical) events here as refuting theories (of history) would need further discussion – into which I will not now enter, however.

3 Andrew Benjamin (1997) analyses modernity on the basis of the idea of a 'founding dislocation', and Rémi Brague (1999) puts a similar insight to use for a philosophical history of Europe (see also below).

4 The sociological self-understanding is often founded on such distinction between philosophy of history and historical 'macro-sociology', without though entirely succeeding in overcoming the problématique. I shall address this question more fully in the next chapter.

5 And it is arguable whether his analysis was inspired by the contemporary difference between the early industry of the Scottish lowlands and the rural character of the highlands of his time; see Stafford, 1989. On temporal distancing, see Fabian 1983.

6 See Abrams, 1972. It is noteworthy that Georg Simmel reworked this distinction such that it explicitly operated in the present, in particular between the social worlds of women and those of men; see for a critical discussion Felski, 1995.

7 See Shaw and Chase, 1989, Mazlish, 1989, Tester, 1993; but also already Nisbet, 1959 and 1969, for related discussions of social theory. For social theorists who in their majority were Western throughout most of the history of social theory, this entailed a confrontation of the modern, Western present with an imagined Western past or with the present elsewhere, in non-Western, i.e. non-modern societies. The dichotomy, however, also works the other way round, such as in the case of political élites in the Ottoman Empire during the nineteenth century who found their image of the good life in the Western present and compared this with their own situation. Thanks are due to Ibrahim Kaya for discussions about this theme.

8 Although a deconstructive effort may show that nostalgia is merely better hidden in functionalism than it is in the structuralism of Lévi-Strauss. Nevertheless their lack of interest in this mode of thought points to weaknesses in Derrida's and Lyotard's conceptualization – for the former with regard to the absence of an explicit theory of modernity, for the latter with regard to the place of the scientific-technical language game in his theory of modernity.

9 The question whether 'modern' social theory and political philosophy operates with 'secularized' religious concepts has been a key theme in German history of ideas and

philosophy, see i.a. Löwith, 1949, Taubes, 1991, Blumenberg, 1985 and now Assmann, 2000. The question recurs in recent post-structuralist debates about religion, see Derrida and Vattimo, 1995.

10 Related ideas can be found in the works of William James and George Herbert Mead in the pragmatist tradition (as well as, in France, Henri Bergson). My neglect of these authors stems from a concentration on those works that had a direct impact on the recent resurgence of this aspect of temporality. Evidently, however, the question of the precise position of pragmatism in the map of modes of social theorizing I aim to provide thus arises. Broached only in the first chapter with regard to the epistemological problématique, I hope to deal more explicitly and comprehensively with this question in the future. Thanks are due to Hans Joas for a discussion of this issue.

11 Caygill (1994) offers a comparison of Heidegger and Benjamin in this respect, on which I draw here. See now also Friese 2001b.

12 This 'opening of the time horizon' has historically been located in the era of the Enlightenment and the late eighteenth-century revolutions. Conceptual historians have quite convincingly demonstrated an overall transformation in political language during this period. Modernity, however, seems to be limited to a particular form of political modernity in this view (see also Chapter 2). Rémi Brague (1998), in contrast, has argued that the very constitution of 'Europe' could be related to the displacement of the philosophical quest for origins into historical time. In both religious and politico-philosophical terms, the sources of Europe are outside of itself. European Christianity sees itself as 'secondary' to Judaism; and European politics and philosophy see themselves as 'secondary' to their Greek origins. This impossibility of identifying or providing any foundations inside oneself makes persistent quest and openness the specificity of Europe, since the eternal (philosophical-religious) and the transient (socio-historical) are thus related to each other. Despite many objections that could be raised against his argument in detail, Brague considerably widens the debate about the specificity of 'the West' and about the historical location of 'modernity'. His position, for instance, has the merit of historicizing Derrida's critique of philosophy and thus modifying the latter's scope. It also links up to other attempts at tracing modern specificities, such as Freud's interest in the emergence of 'spirituality and intellectuality' (Bernstein, 1998; Freud, 1967) and connects to recent attempts by Massimo Cacciari and Derrida at writing 'geo-philosophies' of Europe. I will return to the latter in Chapter 5 below.

13 Philosophers and social theorists in Europe – and the West in general – are still too little aware of the possibility and indeed likelihood that the historical moment is being defined quite differently from other points of view.

14 I deliberately use the term event in a rather broad sense, for every occurrence, or sets of occurrences, that is held together by some constitutive commonality, even if the occurrences themselves may stretch over considerable periods of time. The usual alternative term, process, suggests an understanding of historical time as flow that seems inadequate.

15 But this re-conceptualization also created a new divide between those who moved to the industrial areas of the 'same' country and those who went 'elsewhere', in particular to North America.

16 Ironically or tragically, the 'conservative' accusation that those painters were not proposing healthy and organic modes of representing the world has a true ring to it. What it fails to recognize, though, is that the world itself, to paradoxically say so, had disassociated itself from those conventional modes of representation.

17 The sections on work and labour in Hannah Arendt's *Human Condition* (1958) display a strong awareness of this transformation.

18 Friese and Wagner, 1993; thanks are also due to Daniel Monk for discussions about this topic.

19 It should also be noted that the background imagery to my description draws on some societies, for instance the German one, more than on others, for instance the English one – and these differences point precisely to different historical experiences and their

interpretation. A more elaborated comparative discussion of European societies would have to distinguish degrees of rupture and of continuity.

20 In *A Sociology of Modernity* (Wagner, 1994, Chapter 4) I have discussed the tendency of modernity towards self-cancellation as inherent in certain societal implications of the liberal notion of self-regulation; thus, the focus was on self-cancellation of liberal varieties of modernity. Continuing on that train of thought, one might say that the accumulated experiences of the first half of the twentieth century bear witness to a related tendency towards self-cancellation in organized modernity.

Interlude: Modernity and Exile

In the light of these reflections, the current requirement is to broaden the notion of nostalgia to live up to those two historical experiences. This is a double exigency: to take the experiences into account but also to assess the stakes in terms that go beyond each single one of them. Going beyond the experiences is inevitable for the very reason that the experiences are incongruent, that they are in an important sense even opposed to each other. The experience of nineteenth-century nationalism was an attempt to recreate a sense of origins in the face of the disembedding effects of early modernity and capitalism, whereas the experience of the twentieth century demonstrated the violent failure of the first and created a stronger sense of loss than ever before. If, currently, we live after those two moments then it is tempting to re-conceptualize the losses as the necessity of exile under modern conditions and nostalgia as something to be overcome.

Should the conclusion then be, as is certainly possible, that we theorize the nineteenth- and twentieth-century experiences as the generalization of emigration and exile and define our current situation in such a way? Generalized exile is then precisely *the condition of modernity after an extended experience with modernity*, and the call for a break with the modernist version of nostalgia, as described at the outset, can be sustained in such a light. Thus, the basis for an exploration of the contemporary human condition would be laid, an exploration the key to which is exile in its combined occurrence as an individual experience, as a phenomenon of socio-historical dimensions and as a condition of philosophical thinking.

To do this, one would need to disentangle the various aspects of the exilic experience and to relate them to both the double historical context and to a philosophic quest. In the first instance, then, there is the moment of leaving, or of being forced to go. In literature, not least, this experience has been a persistent theme in terms of an existential experience, a moment in which the view of the world undergoes a fundamental change because the safety of that which preceded one's own existence goes. There where one was born, where one was thrown into being, there the foundations have always already been in place and did neither require nor permit radical doubt and questioning. To lose this place, in particular if one was or felt expelled rather than going voluntarily, has often been described as the loss of a kind of ontological security, of the confidence of the availability of the world as it was.[1] In particular, the human condition threatened to be robbed of its existential temporality. Once the safety of that which is given was gone, that which was and that which can be could no longer be relied upon either.

Within philosophical discourse, exile can take a variety of connotations, but they all have in common the questioning of an – initially both implicit and prevailing – discourse of substantive rootedness. Exile tends to doubt the there-ness of the world; it introduces a split in consciousness. Among the more recent formulations of this issue, one finds the notion of the diremption of modernity (Rose, 1992) or of modernity as a dislocation (Benjamin, 1997). Along similar lines, disregarding important differences for the moment, Lev Shestov has understood the essence of life being about leaving home. Stanley Cavell has noted that 'the task of the human being, contrary to Heidegger's discovery of it, is not to learn how to dwell but to learn how to leave, to learn abandonment'. In what he termed the Rousseauistic side of interpretation, Derrida (1978a: 292) has read the act of interpretation as a stepping out of the text, 'as an exile'. Very comprehensively, Christian Miquel (1992, 1996; Dufresnois and Miquel, 1996) has recently written about exile as the human condition. Across all differences, these writings share the attempt, which is existentialist in a broad sense of the term, to relate an existential experience to a philosophical quest as the only means by which one can hope to grasp it.[2]

As recent writings, these views can be set against the two experiences discussed above. What is specific to the (predominantly nineteenth-century) context of emigration is that this decision then meant to leave the nation at the moment of actual nation-building. One left precisely at a point when nationalism aimed at offering a remedy against nostalgia in the form of a re-embedding. More than at other times, European emigration in the nineteenth century meant to go to live at a place that was not one's home. And what is specific about the (predominantly twentieth-century) experience of exile is that it meant to be expelled at a moment when the existential re-founding of the polity was claimed, a moment that turned out to become the moment that spelt the end of tradition as well. It is against this background that the many biographical experiences that added up to a socio-historical experience acquired a strong philosophical connotation, the connotation namely of questioning the viability of any discourse that insisted on the substantive rootedness of human existence.

In the second instance, such questioning then generates the search for new answers. After the questioning, the answers can no longer be the same as before. They have to be different answers, answers that oscillate between the possibility of liberation and the inevitability of negation. Having illustrated this ambivalence above when proposing elements of a reinterpretation of twentieth-century European history, I now want to briefly recast the argument in the terms developed up to this point.

The distancing from all that which appeared as given and natural can liberate the mind to think of the world in different terms. It is the common denominator of spatial utopias that they are constructed according to the will and intention of their authors, and the fact that those utopias are elsewhere permits such construction. No experience and no perception block the way to pure construction. Emigration and exile as forms of distancing therefore lend themselves towards a modernist discourse in social theory and political philosophy, which works precisely by avoiding or eliminating any contextual and particular information. In the history of philosophy, the predominant form are thought experiments, such as those employed by Descartes or more recently Rawls. However, we may assume that the actual experience of distancing enhances the readiness to engage in such a form of thinking.[3]

If the experience of distancing they have gone through is one rather formal feature of the new answers, one may inquire further whether one can also say something about their likely substance on that basis. Two possibilities emerge. First, the experience of going away is likely to change the character of the social bond to other people, at least on the level of the entire society or polity. Raymond Williams compared the experience of the exile with the one of the rebel: 'The exile is as absolute as the rebel in rejecting the way of life of his society, but instead of fighting it he goes away. [... Usually,] he will remain an exile, unable to go back to the society that he has rejected or that has rejected him, yet equally unable to form important relationships with the society to which he has gone.' Williams suggests that there is something unrecoverable, once one leaves one's place of origin. The social bond cannot be recreated in the same way in which it existed before; the same density of social relations and the density of meaning in the world around oneself can no longer be reached.

Sometimes emigration has even been related to a radical loss of the ability to give meaning. As a consequence, the possibility of involvement tends to wither away as well. The liberating effect that distancing may have turns into the inevitability of negation and, normatively speaking, into cynicism. The immigrants of all origins, having lost those origins, become 'the spent people, in whom the god impulse had collapsed, so they crossed to the great continent of the negation, where the human will declares itself "free," to pull down the soul of the world' (Lawrence, 1987: 77–8).

Such orientation is a possible, but not a necessary, consequence. There is at least one other systematic possibility, based less on the experience of leaving one's origins than on the experience of being somewhere else. For the émigrés, the lived experience of a social world that one has actively entered, rather than one that has been given, may arouse a feeling of disappointment, of falling short of expectations. For them, and even more so for the exiles, this feeling may be at the root of nostalgia and at the wish to return. Over such considerations, however, the impossibility of any return to origins may become evident, as Jankélévitch points out. At the same time, the feeling may transform itself into the perception of an experienced confrontation of incompatible worlds and, as or even more importantly, an experience of fragmentation, of collage, of 'social things' no longer fitting. In this sense, this experience may lead to the adoption of discourses that emphasize the impossibility of both distancing and re-embedding. What is underlined instead is the non-solid nature of the world, its varieties and possibilities and thus the relativity of any position in it.

One of Paul Claudel's protagonists in *Conversations dans le Loir-et-Cher* (1959: 148) speaks about America as 'something provisional and something ever to be started again. [...] It is peculiar though,' he adds, 'to see such a major part of humankind in this precarious state, alert and tense, in a state that belongs both to exile and to waiting.' While Claudel draws here on a notion of exile that relates to the historical experience of European migration towards America, his usage of it transcends the familiar connotations of origins that are lost and a destination that cannot turn into a new home. Exile, 'this precarious state', has become permanent and a feature of an entire civilization. We may well presume that the reference is here no longer exclusively to an actually existing 'America', but to a new situation in which 'a major part of humankind' finds itself in general. For European consciousness, the philosophical import of the American experience was something like a practical critique of ontology. And this seemed to imply a farewell to philosophy and history as they were known – an implication that was mostly seen as an unacceptable loss, though was sometimes also welcomed as a great relief. But the American experience can also be read differently, not as the end to all philosophy of the human condition, but as its truly 'modern' transformation. The existence of American modernity appeared to make the future transparent.

Notes

1 See for recent accounts Papastergiadis, 1993 (as I write Papastergiadis, 2000 arrives, which continues to explore the theme), Kristeva 1991; thanks are due to Yannis Stamos for important help with research on this topic as well as discussions about it.

2 As important as the current context is, such formulae should not lead into the temptation of thinking that the experience they refer to – of modernity, whatever the temporal connotation of the term may be – is a recent one. One of the classic and still most striking ways of putting that experience can be found in Shakespeare's *Tempest* – from which Marx may well have taken the idea that everything that is solid melts in the air.

3 There has been a long debate about the role of the intellectual and the possibility of critique in which the effect of distancing is discussed, reaching from Mannheim and Elias to Lyotard and Walzer. What for some observers is the condition of possibility of a critical standpoint turns for others into a remoteness from the problématiques of social life that leads directly into aridity. An analogous discussion can be led about the relation between academic practices – often seen as relieved of the need to act – and other social practices.

5

The Transparency of the Future

'Among the classical figures of sociology, Max Weber is the only one who broke with both the premises of the philosophy of history and the basic assumptions of evolutionism and who nonetheless wanted to conceive of the modernization of old-European society as the result of a universal-historical process of rationalization.' This is how Jürgen Habermas (1981: 207) opens the section on Max Weber in his *Theory of Communicative Action*. Later, he underlines that he sees it as one of Weber's achievements to have 'discharged the mortgages from philosophy of history and the nineteenth-century evolutionism encumbered by it' (Habermas, 1981: 209). And after having critically reconstructed the move from Enlightenment philosophy of history based on reason and progress to Weber's comparative-historical sociology, Habermas asserts that the question of the long-term development of societies, including the sense of their direction in history can be taken up again 'through the empirical sciences'. In his words, this is 'the question of how the emergence and development of modern societies can be conceived of as a process of rationalization' (Habermas, 1981: 223).

Habermas was aware of the fact that, at the time of his writing, numerous objections had already been launched against the very possibility of such a project, and he has certainly tried to take them into account. Since the writing of the *Theory of Communicative Action*, the situation has become even more complicated, and overall certainly not more favourable (as Habermas still thought, 1981: 223) to Habermas's ideas of the early 1980s. One strand of intellectual debate was ever more persuaded by the force of the objections. It included most prominently all that goes under the name of postmodernism, but also the majority of middle- or short-range social research and theorizing. My own discussion in the preceding chapters of this volume also reflects some scepticism, although the particular question of the direction of history has not yet been addressed.

At the same time, however, a strand of thinking (re-)emerged in which the assumption of an intelligible historical directionality was made without too much concern about its philosophical conditions of possibility. Rorty's (1989: 68; also 1998) attempt at narrating 'the rise of liberal institutions and customs' is a part of this strand as is Fukuyama's (1992) over-debated revival of the idea of an 'end of history'. Neo-modernization theories, which see globalization, individualization and reflexivity as the marks of a new era of modernity, provide the sociological underpinnings to such interpretations of history. Compared to Habermas's approach, with which they share the interest in evolutionary trends, those views are not only much more bluntly optimistic about societal developments, they also shift the focus from a comprehensive concept of 'societal rationalization' towards an emphasis on liberty and individualism. While my own observations force me to abstain from both the theoretical and the normative confidence these approaches display, I hope to have demonstrated throughout the earlier chapters, in particular the immediately preceding one, that the question of the direction of history cannot be entirely escaped from. But the means to address it have to be considerably recast.

This chapter will offer a modest proposal to start such reconsideration. It will proceed by focusing on a particular episode in, loosely understood, comparative-historical societal analysis. Following up directly on the period of prevailing evolutionism, which saw Europe itself as the forefront of history, European thought developed the shocking idea that there was a society that in many respects appeared superior to Europe and thus more advanced. This society was the USA, mostly briefly called 'America', and the period in which this discourse emerged was the early twentieth century.[1] In the light of this comparative observation, we can return to the hypothesis, as discussed in the preceding interlude, that a condition of extended modernity should be understood as the generalization of the experience of emigration and exile. Rather than seeing human beings as normally rooted in a socio-cultural context from which values and orientations can be drawn, the normal condition is then one of separation from any such context. In the view of many Europeans, this was precisely the condition that upheld in the US and that generated a new and different kind of society. This chapter will portray the development of European images of America as the future and will use such analysis to redescribe ways to reflect about the direction of history.

Images of America (1): Otherness or Origins

'It meant so many things, America. First of all, the inaccessible [...], a myth will not let itself be touched. [...] It was the future on its march, abundance, the infinity of the horizons, it was a crazy hullabaloo of legendary images' (de Beauvoir, 1963: 28). 'America' has occupied European consciousness since its discovery. Simone de Beauvoir like many others before and after her – emigrants, travellers, writers, philosophers – saw 'America' as a place that could not really be conceptually grasped, but that nevertheless – or maybe for that very reason – took hold of their thoughts and strivings.

During the past two centuries or more, and between the two World Wars in particular, American ways of living and of thinking have become the object of European reflections on modernity. The affirmation or rejection of modernity in Europe has been channelled through observations on America. And at the same time, the variety of European ways of looking at America also demonstrates the range of forms that are available to social theory for thinking the social world under conditions of modernity.

For Europeans, America was distinct from the moment it emerged. Unlike in the case of Asia and Africa, the so-called discoverers did not expect anything or anybody there where America happened to be found. The inhabitants of Asia and

Africa had 'always already' – so it seemed – been known about; they thus had 'always already' had their place in the history of humanity. The native Americans, in contrast, appeared as the radical Other, the possibility of which was not even contemplated (Pagden, 1993; Todorov, 1982). Or, as D.H. Lawrence (1962: 17) recast this theme much later, 'now we must learn to think in terms of difference and otherness. There is a stranger on the face of the earth, and there is no use our trying any further to gull ourselves that he is one of us, and just as we are. There is an unthinkable gulf between us and America [...]. The present reality is a reality of untranslatable otherness.'[2]

Henceforth, this image of fundamental alterity should never quite disappear. It was transformed, though, when European settlers had almost exterminated the natives and destroyed their societies.[3] From then on, there was an American society, which may still have been fundamentally different from the European ones, but it was at least one that could be spoken about. It may have continued to resist full intelligibility, but it no longer escaped European categories entirely.

The most consistent early attempt to make 'America' accessible to European consciousness was aimed at, though not really developed, by John Locke. He intimated that it was something like the state of nature that had prevailed in America, the state before human order had been founded by social contract: 'Thus, in the beginning, all the world was America', as he said in the *Second Treatise of Government*.[4]

This image appeared convincing for quite some time. Hegel saw American society as not yet having quite made its entry into world history; this was in 1822 – almost half a century after the American Declaration of Independence. His *Lectures on the Philosophy of History*, which subdivide the world into the 'Oriental', the 'Greek', the 'Roman' and the 'Germanic' parts, deal with the 'New World' only briefly in the context of a discussion of the nature of the state, and what he was most interested in were the geographical peculiarities of America. Since Hegel's main striving was to anchor the experience of the French Revolution again in a flow of history the sources of which were for him indubitably Greek and Christian (Hegel, 1996: 87), the radicality of what went on on the other side of the Atlantic escaped his mind.[5] Both Locke and Hegel regarded America as a somewhat belated beginning of society and history, the major use of which was to provide a comparative angle for reflections about the origins of social and political life.

This is the *first major image* of America in social philosophy. America shows the more advanced regions of the world a picture of their own past. As such it could be of interest, since it enabled the European mind to verify its ideas about the foundations of social life, and such grounding in origins was a necessary element of thinking order and history. The interest was also limited, though, since once this act of thinking the origins had been performed, there was little else to be gained from 'America'. This was a stage that had been left behind.

Images of America (2): Pure Modernity

For quite some time then, Europeans did not really see any reason why America's presence should provoke them to shift the centre of history. When gradually, however, the impact – social, political, economic, cultural – of America on Europe increased, the insight gained ground that what had occurred in America was not just a reminder of how things began, but something essentially new, a *different* beginning. A new image of America took shape in Europe in the course of the nineteenth century, an image the full contours of which became visible after the First World War – and in an important sense *because* of the First World War.

In European consciousness, the advent of the French Revolution eclipsed the attention bestowed upon the American one.[6] Unrecognized by most of its observers, however, the American Revolution had effected a rupture with political traditions that was in some respects much more pronounced than the one produced by its French successor. The French revolutionaries had shifted the site of sovereignty, the centre of politics, within a well-known social structure – away from the monarch, towards the people. This possibility was unavailable to the American revolutionaries; there was no American people, it had first to be created in and through the revolution itself. The Declaration of Independence was loaded with multiple significations. By the act of speaking, the speaking subject had to bring, first, *itself* into being, 'we the American people'. Second, it had to create the actual *thing it spoke about*, a particular polity then named the United States of America. And thirdly, it inaugurated the very *kind of order* of which this polity became the first lasting exemplar, the modern republic (see Arendt, 1965; Derrida, 1986 as well as Chapter 2).

As a consequence of this founding act, the American Revolution gave a new impetus to the radical hope for a reconciliation of social knowledge and political action, at the dusk of the Enlightenment. Up to then, so it seemed, the knowledge about human social life had been limited by the fact that all societies had histories that preceded their conscious existence. Human beings, however, can only fully comprehend what they themselves create. American society appeared as the first social order for which this precondition seemed to hold – and of which the leading members, at the same time, largely believed that it held.[7]

A beginning from nothingness and complete self-knowledge; these were the basic ingredients from which images of America could be produced. By the middle of the nineteenth century, the idea spread among European observers that such features indeed marked some basic differences between America and Europe. Such differences were increasingly observed and – by travellers – experienced, but they proved difficult to grasp and were also often only hesitantly acknowledged. In such a situation of uncertain understanding, many Europeans reasoned about American society in terms of what it lacked, compared with the Old World.

America lacked *history*, this was something on which many observers agreed. It was a country without tradition, 'where no medieval ruins bar the way, where history begins with the elements of modern bourgeois society', as Friedrich Engels pointed out in 1887.[8] Or it was even 'the specific country of ahistory', as Alfred Weber, Max Weber's brother, remarked in 1925, after the First World War, in stronger tones (Weber, 1925: 80). In his *Scenes from the Future*, again a few years later, the French writer Georges Duhamel (1930: 19) described American society as 'an aggregate of human elements, free of tradition, of monuments, of history, and with no other ties between them than those, horrible ones, which their work in common is providing them with'.

Individualism was often seen as the key social and political characteristic of America. Hegel already spoke of the atoms of *individuals* in this society in which the particular interest dominated over the general. And Alexis de Tocqueville (1966 [1843]) provided that magisterial portrait of American society in which the founding situation could not but lead to an order based on liberty and equality, with which, however, isolation and conformity should become inextricably intertwined. By 1936, as William Spoerri (1936: 7) then noted in a comprehensive review of European writings on America, the question of individual liberty had been identified as the one fundamental issue of American society, from which almost everything else could be derived.

These American individuals, with their 'cold serenity bordering on the uncanny', as the disappointed emigrant Nikolaus Lenau (1971: 215), returned to Europe, put it, were free of all the fetters that prevented Europeans from becoming the *absolute masters over themselves as well as over nature*. Technical progress in America began to impress and frighten Europeans at least from the early twentieth century onwards. The slaughter-houses in Chicago and the car factories in Detroit were favourite examples of that major vice of America that went under names such as mechanization, standardization, quantification and growth of scale *sans mesure* and at the expense of the loss of all moral dimension.

For Europeans, this apparently limitless breakthrough of instrumental rationality was more than a mere relative specificity, otherwise unimportant, of the young sub-continent; it was the reigning principle in America, and as such it created a divide between America and Europe. Duhamel (1930: 12) – like similarly many others – distinguished the moral civilization of Europe from America's mechanical one, which relied exclusively on what he called the inductive method. Later, in post-Second World War Germany, Ralf Dahrendorf (1963) should call America the country of 'applied Enlightenment', with a markedly more positive undertone than can be found in Duhamel.

The balance between affirmative and critical views of America is an interesting topic in its own right, but cannot be fully explored here. Suffice it to say that 'America' had a positive image in wide sections of the lower classes, often indeed considering emigration, but that a majority of the published assessments by academics and journalists were highly critical, with only some liberal-progressive writers showing interest in the comparatively more liberal and egalitarian American society.[9]

Outraged as many European observers were when they visited America, there should have been little at stake as long as a theory of two civilizations could be maintained; difference should have been acceptable as long as it was kept at a distance. The problems began when America's principles were seen to endanger the European spirit. And this was what Europeans came increasingly to fear. The existence and increasing power of the Big Other across the ocean was a drain on the European way of life, on its hopes and on its means to create its own future. This idea of an adverse impact of America on Europe can be interpreted in multiple ways; I will just offer two versions, a sociological and a philosophical one.

The sociological interpretation emphasizes the effect large-scale migration has on the societies that are left as well as on the societies that are moved towards. As to the former, the poet Ludwig Börne (1868: 108) was troubled by the question 'Who emigrates?' after the failure of the Revolution of 1830 in Germany, and he gave himself the distressing answer: 'The one who finds bondage most unbearable, who loves freedom most dearly and who is most able to fight for it. [...] Isn't it a lamentable foolishness that Germans search for America under great toil and danger beyond the sea instead of creating America in a much more comfortable and secure way at home?' One may have doubts about the assessment of the relative toil or comfort on the two sides of the ocean, but it seems safe to assert, even though necessarily counterfactually, that the loss of many of its most adventurous minds made a difference to Europe's more recent history.[10]

The related effect on the receiving society is precisely the creation of a society of exiles (beyond Williams, 1961; see also Kriegel, 1972: 93 and 95; Lawrence, 1964: 3). If, as I argued before, the social bond cannot be recreated in the same way in which it existed before its dissolution, America as a society of immigrants cannot but lack those elements of the social bond that prove to be unrecoverable. Sometimes an even stronger version of such an assertion can be found, trying also to specify that which is unrecoverable: having no roots, no history, no tradition of its own, America is incapable of any creation, and its very emergence in an extended process of migration is indicative of some degree of exhaustion of the creative power of humankind. Thus, in *The Plumed Serpent*, D.H. Lawrence (1987: 77–8) lets Kate Leslie wonder 'whether America really was the great death-continent, the great No! to the European and Asiatic and even African Yes!'

Here we move from the sociological to the philosophical interpretation. The 'crisis of the European sciences' was declared by Edmund Husserl in 1935, but it had already been felt several decades earlier. This crisis did not merely have its historical location in the course of the nineteenth century, which witnessed the rise of the specialized scientific disciplines and the withering away of any philosophy that could hold them together (see Chapter 1). It also had a geographical dimension which, among others (though not Husserl himself), Martin Heidegger pointed out in his *Introduction to Metaphysics*, also of 1935. 'From a metaphysical point of view,' he said, it is 'the same miserable frenzy of unfettered technology and the same bottomless organization of average man' that reign in both Russia and America. When 'time is nothing but speed, momentariness and simultaneity and when time as history has vanished from the *Dasein* (being-there) of the peoples', then 'spiritual decay' is far advanced, and 'perplexity and insecurity' gain ground in Europe.[11]

The perplexity of European philosophers was exacerbated by their perception that what they considered the deepest decline in the human condition was experienced by the Americans as something close to the arrival at the *telos*, the fulfilment of history. Without Nietzsche himself having given any such hint, some of his readers meant to recognize the Americans in the 'last men' of *Thus Spoke Zarathustra*: '"We have invented happiness" – say the last men and blink. They have left the places where living was hard: for one needs warmth. [...] Who still wants to rule? Who obey? Both are too much of a burden. No herdsman and one herd. Everyone wants the same thing; everyone is the same.' (Nietzsche, 1968: 'Vorrede', par. 5; see also Fraenkel, 1959: 23; Mathy, 1993: 214). And Alexandre Kojève went as far as turning Hegel upside down to see the end of history reached in mid twentieth-century America.[12]

Now, one may say that such assertions, whatever they may exactly mean, employ a mode of philosophy of history that contemporary sociology and philosophy have fortunately overcome. Even such a view would not relieve us of the burden of trying to understand such modes of thinking as a part of a comparative-historical sociology of Western societies. But these modes of thinking are of much more than historical interest; they provide, as I shall argue, keys to the range of our possibilities to understand Western societies. I shall have to come back later to more fully interpreting the socio-philosophical attitude behind this European thinking itself. First, the formal structure of this reasoning and of the view of America that it entails is to be considered.

All varieties notwithstanding, of which there were many, this European argument rested on two basic propositions. First, it posited some radical *alterity* of American civilization compared to the European one, or even to all Old-World ones. It is in this sense, as I mentioned at the outset, that the initial surprise in the face of the unknown should never again disappear. Second, the European view posited some principled *superiority* of the American civilization in a technical-economic as well as a socio-political sense, which went along, though, with the assumption of an American *inferiority* in a moral-philosophical sense. This is a quite complex argument, both in sociological and in philosophical terms, and it is far from self-evident how one could arrive at such a viewpoint.

If we draw together the elements of the characterizations of America that I offered up to this point, we can order and reassemble the basic ingredients. 'America' in this view is what we may call *presentist*, that is, without history and tradition. As Ferdinand Tönnies (1922: 356) wrote in 1922 about public opinion in America: 'Its knowledge of the old world, thus of the foundations of its own culture, is rather deficient; it thus lives much more in the present and in representations of the future which are exclusively determined by the present.' America is also *individualist*, that is, there are no ties between the human beings except for those that they themselves create. And it is *rationalist*, that is, it knows no norms and values except the increase of instrumental mastery, the striving to efficiently use whatever is at hand to reach one's purposes. Again Tönnies (1922: 357), here using Weber's concept of rationality, expresses succinctly his view on American public opinion as 'the essential expression of the spirit of a nation': it is '"rationalistic" [...] in the sense of a reason which prefers to be occupied with the means for external purposes'. Or, in D.H. Lawrence's (1962: 28) words, the American 'is free to be always deliberate, always calculated, rapid, swift, and single in practical execution as a machine.' And, finally, America is what we may call *immanentist*, that is, it rejects the notion of any common higher purpose, anything that transcends the individual lives and may give them orientation and direction.

Rather than an enumeration of distinct features, this is a cascade of characteristics where each single one refers to all the other ones. Individualism is directly related to the absence of history, which namely could have been a source of commonalities; and instrumental rationalism may be seen to follow from the absence of any common higher orientation. Trying to condense the imagery even further, we can say that the 'America' the Europeans perceived was the uncontaminated realization of the modernist principles of *autonomy* and *rationality*. America was *pure modernity*.

This is the *second image* of America. And at this point, it may need additional underlining that it is not the reality of American social life that I refer to, but images of it provided by Europeans, most of whom shared a relatively elevated social position and a certain degree of literacy. But such an account inevitably raises two related questions: what images did Americans themselves create of their own society, and how did the European images relate to American society and history? Not to evade these issues entirely, I shall just hint at the direction in which responses would possibly look.

There were some American self-images that largely corresponded to the European view, mostly without the normative connotations though. Louis Hartz's (1955) account of the American political tradition is one such example; Henry Miller's (1947) portrait of the 'air-conditioned nightmare' another one that indeed shared European evaluations – written, significantly, by somebody who had almost become an émigré. However, most American self-images complemented – at least – or contradicted European views. Americans may see themselves as having an historical mission, indeed based on the original covenant; as constantly building communities; and instead of adhering to instrumental and pragmatic world-views, they may see transcendentalism as one of their authentically own intellectual traditions.[13]

As regards the even more complex question of American history and society, many objections to the European point of view have been – and keep being – raised. It is indeed easily questioned. One may point to American religiosity, which lets the sociological theory of secularization rather appear as a case study of 'European exceptionalism'. Or one can emphasize the persistence of immigrant communities, which turn America into a community of communities, rather than a society of individualists (Walzer 1990). And the American obsession with history can only incompletely be explained by the alleged absence of history in their own country.[14]

'Americanization', the European Modern Tradition and the Transparency of the Future

The posited existence of such a pure modernity, cleaned of all contamination, demanded a more precise determination of the European condition, and this in particular if one objective was the identification of possibilities for resistance. The fiction of American modernity finds itself thus counterposed to a similarly fictitious portrait of European civilization.

In contrast to the icy freedom of the *homo americanus*, the Europeans – in their self-understanding – are connected to a history and to traditions; they are and feel a part of national memories. The European relies on the markers of a familiar environment, which provide security. Should they get lost, as they did for the America-traveller Bardamu in Louis-Ferdinand Céline's *Journey to the End of the Night* (1988: 169–214; see Mathy, 1993: 63), then loss of meaning, the feeling of a void will follow. Rather than liberating towards something, American freedom is a soul-fear, a flight from one's own self, one's real self, of which Europeans have both a notion and an experience, whereas Americans fear thinking and have replaced experience by innovation (Spoerri, 1936: 47).

In a similar counter-position, Adolf Halfeld (1927: 37; quoted after Schwan, 1986: 9) described an 'America of machine-men, which derives a normative order of offensive paltriness from the one basic principle of success and robs life of its eternal secrets'. He confronted this America with a 'European world of characters', where 'a spirit of community [...] is rooted in popular customs and makes the music speak, turns stones into meaningful images and life into a thousandfold allegory'.

Without a horizon that roots the individuals in time and brings them into touch with others, human beings cannot receive any great message and cannot recognize any great challenge that one has to accept. American life, however, lacks this horizon, argues Duhamel. It was no wonder, in his and many others' views, that the only philosophy that emerged from American soil was William James's and John Dewey's pragmatism, which precisely demonstrates such lack of any spirituality, reduces truth to utility and gives testimony to the aridity of the machine-age (Spoerri, 1936: 121; on the European reception of pragmatism see Joas, 1993: Part II).

There is a *third image* here, but this is not an image of America, it is a counter-image, developed by Europeans for their own social world, in the light of their perceptions of America. Where Americans emphasize presence, European life is rooted in history; Americans are individual atoms, Europeans are members of a community; Americans are driven by purposes, Europeans receive their orientations from values; Americans worship instrumental rationality, Europeans have a sense of spirit and spirituality.

It is significant that this particular European image of the world and its civilizations was created at that very moment when the unspoken certainties about the forms of its social and political life had been shaken, irrevocably shaken. This moment was, as argued earlier, the early twentieth century, the experience of the First World War and its aftermath. Not that European consciousness had not experienced major shocks before, such as the religious wars and the French Revolution. Now, however, internal eruptions in the context of rapid industrialization and urbanization coincided with the existence of an Other that did not appear to undergo a similarly deep-seated crisis. Furthermore, this other civilization seemed to show a superior form of social organization. The apparently explicit and explicable notions in the European discourse – of a common history that provides orientations, of a real self that one needs to search and realize, of the greater task that imposes itself – were all formulated in the face of the reality of an America where none of this appeared to apply.

This meant nothing less than that European thinking was trapped. The self-image of Europe had long been one of modernity – in philosophy, since Descartes; in politics, since the French Revolution; in the arts, since the success of the *salon des refusés*, or whatever significant dates one may want to mention (see, for example, Valéry, 1957). And now it had to adopt a discourse of tradition for its self-description. 'A traditional discourse about Europe' and at the same time a 'discourse on the modern tradition', as Jacques Derrida has called it, had emerged.[15]

This change had consequences for the whole intellectual edifice devoted to provide self-understanding by locating one's own position in the world. In earlier proposals, for instance, Europe had often been set off against the rest of the world, as that region of the spirit in which myth had been dethroned and where reflection reigned. Asia, in particular, often stood for the mythical as the pre-philosophical. This position was evidently no longer tenable (though obviously it had never really been). Asia, now standing together with Europe on this side of America, was accordingly re-evaluated. One of Paul Claudel's figures in *Conversations dans le Loir-et-Cher* (1959: 146–7) sees Asia 'in communication with the origin'; Asia forms 'the pole of gravity and plenitude, which strives to counterbalance the pole of movement and void that created itself over there in America.' In this imagery it seems as if Europe, rather than forming any front any longer, holds the balance between mythical Asia and modernist America. But this was a position that was much more difficult to describe than the earlier self-consciously proclaimed modernity of Europe.

This discourse on tradition, history, spirit, identity is not itself traditional. It is a thoroughly modern phenomenon, a response to the *social*, not merely *intellectual*, experience of a different variant of modernity, one that Europeans were unfamiliar with. One could say that it inaugurated the debate about varieties of modernity, or about multiple modernities, which is developing more fully now, at the turn of the twentieth century. And it seems as if a threat to the modern self-understanding was required to let such a debate emerge. This was a debate, furthermore, that did not develop its potential at all but remained caught in a simple opposition in which resistance against a particular variant of modernity, which was regarded as expanding, as colonizing Europe, expressed itself in the form of a resistance against modernity as such.

The problem for those Europeans was that there was not peaceful co-existence, but rather a 'clash of civilizations', as some political scientists would say today. And, worse, the outcome of this clash appeared to them to be decided in advance, at least under those twentieth-century political conditions that tended to work in favour of America. The American principles of individual autonomy and instrumental rationality would inevitably translate into techno-economic superiority. At least, they would do so wherever one had to accept a form of basically egalitarian mass society and individualist-liberal democracy, which namely would foster the lower desires for material objects and impede any collective attempt to apply moral brakes to such processes. This is how, in the European view, techno-economic and socio-political superiority of the American model translated into global moral-philosophical decline, that is, the undermining of ways of life grounded on morals and traditions. Europe was thus threatened by 'Americanization'. As Georges Duhamel (1930: 245–6) put it, 'there are on our continent [...] large regions that the spirit of old Europe has deserted. The American spirit colonizes little by little now this province, now this city, now this house, and now this soul.'

At the moment, namely, when the image of a pure-modernity-turned-reality as well as the counter-image of an Old-World-henceforth-lost had gained their full contours, this counter-position could not but turn problematic itself. Whatever 'America' exactly meant, it was always possible to show that it was not – geographically – where it was supposed to be. Neither were its alleged principles of individual autonomy and rational mastery completely alien to European soil, nor could American society itself be considered as uncontaminated by any cultural heritage. And with whatever original identity Europeans tried to endow themselves, each moderately plausible such account would have to contain elements of precisely that modernity that those besieged post First World War Europeans projected elsewhere. The idea of 'Americanization' was the way out of this theoretical impasse that many of those Europeans chose: there had been an intact Europe once, but American influence had destroyed its spiritual truths, they tried to say.

Thus, 'America' became an event in the history of social theory and social philosophy. The emergence of America stands, on the one hand, for the advent of modernity – in the sense, namely, that the diremption of modernity has become an inescapable condition. On the other hand, this diremption was turned into a dualism, and 'America' was made the location of the one side of this dualism. Having said that, the history of European social theory can be reread in terms of the relative presence of 'America' in European consciousness. At the time when Hegel and Marx wrote, 'America' was only distantly on the horizon. As a consequence, both had relatively few difficulties in emphasizing the possibility of reconciliation between contradictory tendencies in social life. At the end of the nineteenth century, 'America' had strongly entered into the European mind. Weber saw instrumental rationality on the rise and occasionally referred to this process as Americanization, a process that obviated any possibility for moral consensus in society.[16]

After the Second World War, along with a novel naturalness of 'America''s presence in Europe, explicitly dualistic social theorizing emerges, such as in the works of Jürgen Habermas and Alain Touraine. The misleading territorial metaphor has now disappeared, but the theoretical form that opposes instrumental rationality to sophisticated versions of authenticity and rootedness has been maintained. Both Habermas and Touraine conclude on a duality of social bonds in contemporary social life and see reconciliation in a single comprehensive form as neither possible nor desirable. Aiming to formulate the normative requirements for furthering the project of a viable modernity (or of societal rationalization, in Habermas's formula), they instead – in different ways – conceptualize the possibility to balance contradictory but simultaneous requirements. Ejecting 'America' and the residual philosophy of history that accompanied that term from their field, however, post-Second World War social theory also lost the historical perspective that had come with the idea of 'Americanization' and that allowed to at least ask about likely directions of history.

The idea that the future does not only lie ahead in time, where it is unknowable, but also elsewhere in space, where it can be glimpsed, is in many respects ill-conceived. If 'America', however, were just taken to refer to a way of speaking about the social bond, and 'Americanization' to the tendency of that form of social bond to spread, the discussion may have been interrupted prematurely. It is possibly in this sense that the inter-war authors tried to say that, wherever one is, there will now always be an 'America' somewhere else to which one will have to relate. After Duhamel (1930: 36) had angrily tried to explain to his American interlocutor that everything had been clearer and better before the war – he referred to the First World War – he let the latter answer: 'We are no longer "before the war", and you are not in Europe.'

Rationalist Individualism and the Direction of History

The formula that to be 'in Europe' may be similar to be 'before the war' suggests precisely the equivocal linkage between a spatial and temporal comparison that has been in the background of my discussion of images of America as a way to conceptualize the direction of history. Significantly, the formula not only suggests a connection between space and time, it also specifically entails that to be 'in Europe' means to be behind, that the future – whether it is desirable or not – is somewhere else.[17] Very plainly so, this spatio-temporal comparison is a rather helpless way of casting the issue – since that is what is at stake – of the consequences of modernity for the human condition. The previous analysis of the European images of America, however, allows us to identify specific claims, which can be exposed to scrutiny, about the nature of modernity and of the social bond and, subsequently, about the direction of history.

The idea of purity and purification provides the key to reading the European images of America as interpretations of modernity. The double imaginary signification of modernity as autonomy and mastery is clearly recognizable in those images, but both of these terms acquire a very specific – and much more narrow – meaning in the views of America. The former is exclusively interpreted as individual autonomy, and the latter as instrumental mastery, or instrumental, purposive rationality. Or, in other words, the hypothesis of 'Americanization' can be re-interpreted as the conjoining of the theses on 'individualization' and 'instrumental rationalization'. The question then is how this specific reading – which shall be called, for the sake of brevity, rationalist individualism – relates to the more general interpretation of this double signification.[18]

As a mode of social theorizing, rationalist individualism is – or, rather, relies on – a theory of modernity. It works with a postulate of autonomy; human beings have wills and are, in principle, able to act according to them. And on this basis, it takes the pursuit of their strivings with a view to accomplishing their objectives as expressions of rationality. In terms of Enlightenment philosophy, rationalist individualism takes a version of a combination of freedom and reason as its basis for social theory. It thus relates closely to a commitment to autonomy and mastery as the double imaginary signification of modernity.

Rather than merely situating itself within modernity, however, rationalist individualism provides a very particular interpretation of modernity. Both autonomy and mastery – freedom and reason – as meaning-providing terms are underspecified and ambivalent on their own and tension-ridden as a double concept. The social signification of modernity is widely open to interpretations. Autonomy, for instance, can be understood predominantly on individual terms, but it can also be read as collective self-determination. Rationality or mastery can be conceived in purposive, instrumental and then procedural terms, but it can also be related to substantive concerns. And these formulae for ambivalence – individual/collective, instrumental-procedural/substantive – by far do not yet capture the richness of possible interpretations – nor are they even necessarily the best way of framing the issue. Rationalist individualism, in contrast, proceeds from an unequivocal starting decision. Its social entities are individuals, and they behave instrumentally rational.[19]

If the imaginary signification of modernity as autonomy and mastery does not impose such a specific interpretation on inherent theoretical grounds, we may still ask whether there are *socio-historical* reasons to assume that this particular interpretation will tend to get adopted. If this question could be answered in the affirmative, its answer would at the same time provide an indication for the direction in the history of modernity and the future would become somewhat transparent.

In the history of social theory, basically two such reasons have been proposed, often in the form of alternative explanations. First, this interpretation will always tend to get adopted in the absence of forces that prevent people from doing so, because it is superior. This theorem brings us back to the Enlightenment combination of freedom and reason (discussed in Chapter 2), which gets translated into the combination of individualism and rationalism. The mode of explanation is ultimately functional, and as such it is sociologically tautological, since 'superiority' cannot be specified otherwise than through the observation of arrangements that indeed get adopted.[20] The second argument, in contrast, supposes that this particular individualist-rationalist interpretation of modernity will get adopted because established power-holders are capable of systematically imposing it on societies. These power-holders may be state élites who impose bureaucratic rationalization and an individualizing regime of 'governmentality' (Foucault) on their populations. Or they may be economic élites, the emerging bourgeoisie and capitalist class, who impose capitalist rationality and individualizing commodification on the workers. The richest of these theories have combined both explanatory modes. Thus, the imposition of a new arrangement by a dominant group has been possible because it also provided gains in overall rationality, i.e. some kind of experienced superiority. This is what Marx argued in terms of the increased productive power of capitalism, and Weber for the formal-legal basis of bureaucracy.

These two proposals inform the social theory of modernity until the present day, and they accordingly feature prominently in Habermas's account cited at the beginning of this chapter.[21] In two different ways, they indeed also provide a sense of the direction of history. The former and some versions of the latter work with a teleology of history, which is open to empirical-historical qualification only in terms of (temporary) impediments to the breakthrough of the superior arrangements.

They, thus, contain a stronger philosophy of history than most contemporary authors – including myself – would be willing to accept. The latter explanation can, however, also be historicized by arguing that the actual coming to power of those groups who enforce this particular interpretation of modernity was a contingent event (Mann, 1986 adopts such mode of reasoning). Even though these groups' grip on power may be quite forceful, history then would be open to future contingencies as well. Our reasoning, though, does not have to stop here. Within this latter frame of argument, an additional element for understanding how this particular, rationalist-individualist interpretation of modernity imposes itself can be introduced, one that relates socio-political history to intellectual history. This means taking the question seriously on which grounds a 'basic social theory' (de Tocqueville, 1966) is preferred to others at certain places and times.

To approach an answer to that question, a rapid survey of the history of rationalist individualism is needed. This thinking first emerged in theories of social contract, as unequivocally first spelt out in Hobbes's *Leviathan* and emphatically developed as a basic theoretical approach by thinkers such as Condorcet in the context of the French Revolution. In parallel to the latter, Smith's moral philosophy provided a space for rationalist individualism within the confines of the economy, an approach which also inspired Marx. Abolishing the elements of a separate moral-political philosophy, this thinking was radicalized during the marginalist revolution in economic thought, which led to what is now the dominant thinking in this field, namely neoclassical economics. During the inter-war years of the twentieth century, as seen above, European cultural critics identified a degraded version of rationalist individualism, in the form of a conjunction of atomism and conformism, as the prevailing attitude in mass society, in particular the North American one. Weber, though not a typical proponent of this thinking, laid many of its foundations. After the Second World War, rational choice theorizing gained the form in which we now know it and spread from economics to the other social sciences.[22]

With the help of these few historical reference-points, elements of a contextual understanding of the way in which the particular, rationalist-individualist interpretation of modernity imposed itself can be provided. I will anticipate the general argument and will then situate it in the various contexts. Rationalist individualism may emerge and find acceptance, or even impose itself, as a social theory by default. By default I refer to a move that is made in situations in which other interpretations of the modern condition, while they may be available in principle, cannot be reached. The default situation may arise as a consequence of the exigency of all other such interpretations to have recourse to stronger social presuppositions or, in other terms, to need more substantive social prerequisites than the individualist-rationalist one. To relate this idea to the signification of modernity: *not* to interpret autonomy as purely individual autonomy requires, if not a coherent and stable collectivity, then at least socially rich ways of relating to others, both singular others and networks of others. *Not* to interpret mastery or rationality in instrumental terms requires other substantive value orientations, which again need to be, if not shared with, then at least be communicable and agreeable to others (see Wagner, 1994a: 14, 31–3). If this observation can generally be accepted, the next task will be to identify the conditions under which such other interpretations become difficult or impossible so that the default situation arises.

Very abstractly speaking, such conditions prevail in times of destruction of a social configuration, in particular rapid and forceful ones, and in times of founding or re-founding of social configurations, in particular if this occurs under pressure or from a great diversity of sources. In such situations, human beings are seen to be left on their own, namely without substantive ties to others, and with 'reason' as the only resource they can reliably draw on, given that other resources presuppose that they are to some degree shared or recognized by others. Destruction may be caused by imposed social change, such as historically through the capitalist revolution and through the building of bureaucratic state apparatuses – here this reasoning meets Marx's and Weber's; but it needs now also to include totalitarianism.[23] But destruction of a social configuration also occurs through warfare and revolutions. Significantly, individualist-rationalist modes of theorizing made early breakthroughs in the context of the seventeenth-century religious wars and the eighteenth-century revolutions. In such situations, no other ways seemed available to think the return to peace and order.

The establishment of the European state system in the treaty of Westphalia and the creation of the French Republic in the course of the Revolution were obviously also moments of the founding or re-founding of social configuration. Nevertheless, in overall European consciousness these were events in which substantive resources to re-found social order were sufficiently – even if not abundantly – available. From the later European point of view, this was much less the case for the creation of the American republic, the master-case for the founding of a polity in the West. And this is the point where we can return to the significance of America for social theory.

Put crudely, the historical claim of the early twentieth-century European image of America held that an individualist-rationalist modernity had been established in America and that, owing to some of its features, it would expand from there to transform Europe in a similar way. Rather than referring to a territorially locatable society, 'America' stands here for a specific form of life. If we follow what I called the sociological argument, the emergence of this form of life can be traced back to the migratory experience. It is seen as related to the willingness to throw off the burden of history or equally to the impossibility to relate in the same strong way to a society into which one moves as to the society which was always already there. If it is the experience of migration and exile that sociologically accounts for the specificity of 'America', tendencies towards rationalization and individualization, in as far as they are observed elsewhere, can in general be connected to this particular condition.

Thus, the possibility emerges to develop an empirical-historical form of argument for some direction of history, i.e. an argument that no longer relies on a philosophy of history in the way in which such approaches have justifiably been denounced. The reasoning would have to have recourse to an existential-experiential theory of modernity, which works with notions of modernity as dislocation and modernity as exile. It would focus, on the one hand, on a decreasing historical depth of social life due to the constant recompositioning of societies that arises as a consequence of increased spatial mobility. On the other hand, it would emphasize the overburdening of the singular human beings with the task of recomposing not only their lives but also the guiding frameworks for the social world of which they become a part.

Social Theory and the Experience of Modernity

However, is this indeed the view that an existential-experiential approach to modernity would confirm? At a closer look, this perspective is based on an assumption about social bonds that reflects the simple dualism of socio-theoretical modernism and the first response to it, which was reproduced in European images of America. In this view, human beings may 'originally' – historically or biographically – be fully embedded in a social context that provides substantive roots for their self-identity and their motivations for action. Biographical as well as historical experience then tells that this rootedness will be shaken by events. Whenever that has happened, there is only one direction into which reorientations can go – towards individual autonomy and instrumental mastery, i.e. towards a rationalist-individualist outlook on the world as a consequence of the distancing from the context. It may be true that a full such reorientation only occurs subsequent to radical eruptions in life and history, so that all lesser events may leave space for some substantive ties. However, theoretically speaking, such lesser reorientations are only intermediate steps on the tatonnement towards rationalist individualism as a practical social philosophy.

As compelling as such reasoning may appear, it is theoretically flawed and, thus, misleading as a guide to both biographical and historical sociology. In the terms employed throughout this book, one could say that the problem with this reasoning stems from the flatness of the map of social theory that it employs. There are only two poles, and the movement from the one to the other is determined by some degree of theoretical as well as historical necessity. Thus, the consequence of a generalized condition of emigration and exile is that a common commitment of any collectivity of human beings, who aim to agree on an evaluation, becomes more difficult to attain. That such commitments could be attained historically at all can be analysed as the combined result of limited participation and the willingness to define long stretches of the past as common experience. Under conditions of a plural modernity, these features have become undesirable or unlikely or both. The temptation is thus considerable to search and adopt among the registers of evaluation those that are least equivocal in their application and most prone to be communicable across a range of different experiences. Although both criteria would require more detailed discussion, this argument is then taken to support the case for a combined individualism and rationalism.

A normative critique of such reasoning can be developed. Its general adoption would in the first instance entail an impoverishment of the range of possible modes of evaluation. Proposed as an exigency of a diverse world, it would tend to destroy diversity. Social theorizing that follows the line of argument in favour of rationalist individualism contributes to the realization of an individualist and rationalist social world by the effect of self-fulfilling prophecy. It would contribute to decrease further what I called historical depth by arguing for abandoning more substantively rich modes of evaluation. The idea of a direction of history towards individualism and rationalism, which repeats itself in a great variety of ways across the history of social theory, could well become a tragic possibility. The rapid succession of moments of destruction and re-founding of societal configurations is often enough seen to leave no other choice.

In addition to the normative rejection, however, there are also conceptual alternatives. Or more precisely, there is a conceptual error in the reasoning that can be detected and remedied, at least in principle. Some elements for a reconceptualization can indeed be detected in European observations on America. Umberto Eco (1986: 31 and 39), for instance, presented himself as initially shocked by what he regarded as simultaneously a denial and a playful fragmentation of history in American museums and historicizing entertainment worlds. Apparently using the familiar European imagery of America, he described them as nothing but 'the offspring of the unhappy awareness of a present without depth'. But in a second step he saw the need to 'in fairness employ[ing] this American reality as a critical reagent for an examination of conscience regarding European taste', the latter being marked by the habit of essentializing history. An understanding of the historicity of human social life should not remain caught in the opposition between American 'shrines of the Fake' and European 'sanctuaries of the Genuine', he argued. Thus, he rejects the theoretical dualism that enforces the move to one mode of thinking about social time – here: 'a present without depth', once the other one – essentializing history – has become impossible.

A similar operation can be performed with the opposition between the atomistic individual of America and the community-based human being of Europe. In his travel essays, Jean-Paul Sartre (1949: 130, see also 1968) tried to trace what one would nowadays call 'the American identity'. He starts out by borrowing de Tocqueville's observation of the simultaneity of individualism and conformism: 'There is anxiety in each American when he faces Americanism; there is an ambivalence in his anxiety, as though he was asking himself at the same time: "Am I sufficiently American?" and "How can I escape Americanism?"' But then Sartre takes a significant further step: 'A human being in America is a simultaneous answer to both of these questions; and each human being must find the answers alone.' To affirm the validity of both questions is to reject the alternative between an abstract concept of freedom, on the one hand, and a strong notion of social and cultural belonging, on the other. Or, as more recently Jean-Luc Nancy put it: freedom cannot be understood as 'simply a way of being "free" of causality or destiny, but [rather as] a way of being destined to deal with them.'[24] The questions about history, society and destiny do not disappear when human beings liberate themselves from their weight; but their substance changes. It is the inevitability of a critical reference both to origin and identity, on the one hand, and to the freedom of radical imagination and projection, on the other, that characterizes our contemporary condition.[25] Such formulations have the potential to open up the conceptual dualism that has reigned over the social theory of modernity in the wake of the American experience.

The idea of exile as constitutive for modernity should not be mistaken for just an empirical proposition about the ever more widespread diffusion of an exilic situation. Rather, it rephrases the modernist foundational notion of distancing from a context. It accepts the possibility of distancing, but the result of distancing is no longer taken to be a location on a higher plane, a plane of a categorially different order, as modernism presupposes. After distancing, one finds oneself somewhere else, in a different context, but in this same world. No principally superior insight is gained, but a different view, and an experience that adds to the previous experience. The experience and knowledge from a distance, therefore, does not necessarily form a unity. Exile does not necessarily turn human beings into individual atoms or make them incline towards adopting an instrumentally rational attitude to all their strivings. There is a plurality of distancing experiences. The enriching of human experiences that results from this possibility is one of the features modernity is rightly praised for. It is an essential component of the liberating promise of modernity.

Such liberation entails that the forms of human social life can be seen in terms of possibility rather than necessity. The range of available registers of political and moral evaluation increases.[26] At the same time, inevitably, the degree of unquestioned commitment to any specific register decreases. Modernity and the modern individual 'institute themselves by the experience of the dissolution of the ultimate markers of certainty; [...] their dissolution inaugurates an adventure – and it is constantly threatened by the resistance it provokes – in which the foundations of power, the foundations of right and the foundations of knowledge are all called into question' (Lefort, 1986b: 179). Lefort continued this characterization of modernity by adding that it is 'a truly historical adventure in the sense that it can never end, in that the boundaries of the possible and the thinkable constantly recede.' It is here that the task of a sociology of modernity lies. Since there are no modern institutions that, once consolidated, answer all questions once and for all, the historical struggles over the appropriate answers are likely to give rise to varieties of modernity, to variations in the location of those boundaries. We may possibly see the study of 'America' from a European perspective as the – rather implicit – beginning of such a comparative sociology of modernity, of a debate about – as it is now called – multiple versions of modernity.

Analysing those varieties of modernity, it is not at all certain that one will find a temporal movement from greater to smaller historical depth, collective commitment and substantive values. If we take the reconsideration of historical time proposed in these last two chapters seriously, then historical depth is never just there. To become actual, it needs to be drawn upon. Against the 'tendency' towards the loss of easily available common and substantive resources, human beings can always set their ability to creatively return such resources to availability and create them anew. Ultimately, there remains a gap between past and future.

Notes

1 Though some of the observations I will quote refer to all of America, the imagery I am centrally concerned with is the one of North America, and in particular the USA.

2 This historical discourse on otherness escapes most of the more recent post-colonialist discussions. Edward Said's *Orientalism* (1979), for instance, speaks rather indistinctly about European and American constructions of the Orient.

3 And one may ask, without though being ever able to find a conclusive answer, whether the genocide was not facilitated by the assumption of radical otherness.

4 Locke, 1966: par. 49. For an example of one of the relatively few detailed discussions of this aspect in Locke see Lebovics, 1986. In this tradition, see already Hobbes's remark: 'The savage people in many places of America [...] have no government at all' (Hobbes 1996 [1651]: Chapter 13, par. 11).

5 He was ready to consider, though, that America was a 'land of becoming, of the future, which does not *yet* concern *us*'. (p. 96, my emphasis). Richard Rorty's (1998: 20–2) creative reading of Hegel, aided by Walt Whitman, turns the position around. For Rorty/Whitman, Hegel tells a story about 'the growth of freedom' (p. 21) of which America is the end-point. The fact that Hegel declares himself unconcerned could by them be explained either through culturalism (Hegel, the European, is unconcerned, though 'we Americans' are) or through a very strong philosophy of history (Hegel, the man of the early nineteenth century, is unconcerned, but we, who are born later, are). Both explanations sit uneasily with Rorty's larger project of what he calls an edifying philosophy. Thanks are due to David Lambourn for directing my attention to this passage.

6 Henningsen 1974: 84. The 'special relationship' between the French and American intellectual worlds should not least be understood in the context of this historical parallel of revolutions with universalist claims that, though, were quite differently articulated.

7 Louis Hartz (1964) tried to compare the major European 'settler societies' – the USA, Canada, Latin America and Australia – with reference to the historical moment of their separation from Europe, that is, as a kind of socio-historical fragmentation of European consciousness in the process of colonization. The USA is then seen as a society frozen in the seventeenth and eighteenth century and, thus, characterized by Enlightenment optimism and Lockean individualism (Hartz, 1955). Alexis de Tocqueville (1966: 18) had already argued that the American colonizers 'in some way separated the principle of democracy from all those other principles against which they contended' in Europe.

8 Engels 1958: 354 (from the preface to the American edition of 1887). Karl Marx (1963: 9), too, saw America as a pure form; he characterized 'the free states of North America' as the country in which 'the state exists in its completely developed form', the country which has 'attained full political emancipation', falling short though of human emancipation.

9 See, for instance, Schwan, 1986; Trommler, 1986: 671. There are numerous accounts of European views of America, often focusing on specific countries, predominantly France and Germany, and periods, reaching from the early nineteenth century to the present. Among the most recent ones, with further references, see Mathy, 1993; Kuisel, 1993; Schmidt, 1997.

10 A century later, in 1938, Paul Valéry (1951: 85) offered a positive counterpart to this account. Should European civilization, with the advent of Nazism and the approach of another war, be inclined to destroy itself, remnants of it would be saved in America, which, after all, was an offspring of European civilization.

11 Heidegger, 1983: 40–1, 50. For Husserl and for Valéry, Europe was not a geopolitical, but a 'spiritual', for the latter even a 'functional' entity. Thus, they could include America, 'the English dominions' (Husserl), into Europe. See also Derrida, 1989: 120–4.

12 Kojève, 1969: 161. Rorty's (1998) view of America is a sophisticated and, some may want to say, postmodernist version of the Hegel/Kojève idea. It employs the metaphysical form of the argument that a post-metaphysical stage has been reached – as he says elsewhere (1989: 63): 'Western [sic] social and political thought may have had the last conceptual revolution it needs' – and locates this occurrence in space. Hegel himself had rather expected the desire for a kingdom to emerge when America would have approached the European condition. The idea of America approaching the European situation over time, 'Europeanizing' itself, is also used by Werner Sombart (1969) early in the twentieth century, but virtually disappears after the First World War.

13 One of the most interesting contemporary American philosophers, Stanley Cavell (see, for example, 1989), sees himself as part of an autochthonous intellectual tradition, of which Ralph Waldo Emerson is a key representative.

14 The further development of a cultural comparison that includes the 'practical' social ontologies and political philosophies, i.e. those that Americans and Europeans mobilize in their actions and disputes, cannot be pursued here. For an impressive example of such analysis see Lamont and Thévenot, 2000.

15 Derrida, 1991: 32. Paul Valéry's 'La crise de l'esprit' (1957) is a characteristic example of such an approach, probably more so than Derrida is willing to recognize. In this light, the current debates about modernity in non-European/non-American parts of the world, such as Japan and Korea or the Islamic countries, need to be compared with the European self-reflections between the two World Wars.

16 See, for instance, Weber, 1975: 7. Given that a key witness for 'the Protestantic ethic' is Benjamin Franklin, this major essay of Weber's could be read as a study in Americanization; see Henningsen (1974: 91–3), who also notes anticipations of the argument in Hegel.

17 In addition, though this feature is obviously owed to Duhamel's time of writing, the phrase suggests that it was the experience or the consequence of the First World War that altered the human condition.

18 To conceptualize a relation of specificity and generality opens the space for maintaining an idea of European modernity even in the face of the American 'pure' version. More broadly speaking, it introduces the possibility of varieties of modernity into comparative-historical sociology.

19 Furthermore, this particular – 'American' – interpretation of modernity, despite its claim to purity, is not self-sufficient. This is what critiques of neo-classical economics and of rational choice theorizing demonstrate, but it is not my intention to go into this issue here.

20 Two versions of such functionality co-existed in the history of social thought, one that focused on the functionality for individuals and one that focused on societies. Only the latter is usually given the label functionalism; and the critique of functionalism (for example, Giddens, 1977) has mostly focused on this version.

21 When Habermas reads the critiques of modernity as basically putting forward a one-dimensional rationalization thesis, he largely overlooks the theorem of individualization. This does not come entirely surprisingly, since this theorem used to be put forward only in the form of 'atomization' as a consequence of one-dimensional rationalization – with formulae such as 'decline of the individual' and 'cog in the machine'. More recent theories of modernity, in contrast, observe a resurgence of the individual in the broader understanding of a self-realizing subject (Bauman, Berman, Giddens, Toulmin, Touraine among others). Even if cast in a variety of different terms, such resurgence is also a key aspect of the sociology (in contrast to: philosophy) of postmodernity. Habermas was certainly writing before this wave, a fact that may explain why he failed to appreciate this basic tension at the very core of the imaginary signification of modernity. In any case, however, the institutional dualism of the *Theory of Communicative Action* avoids to problematize this core and tries to arrest the dynamics of modernity with the help of an overly strong substantive ontology – one that already now does not withstand the 'test of time'.

22 In the view of its own proponents, the real history of rational choice theory only starts in the middle of the twentieth century, but the insight into deeper roots or 'predecessors' can occasionally be found.

23 This is one of the main themes of the critical tradition from the eighteenth century onwards, in particular in the strand that runs from German idealism to the Frankfurt School. In those critical views, obviously, these tendencies are both diagnosed and denounced, and it is precisely the task of critical theory to identify the conditions under which they came about, or the forces that brought them about, with a view to challenging them. Rational choice theory basically provides for an inversion of that perspective. If it had an historical dimension (which it most often has not), it could broadly accept a Marxian-Weberian

narrative of individualization and rationalization, but rather than deploring the development, it would celebrate this course of human history as the progress of Reason.

24 Nancy (1990: 162–3) continues: 'This again means that history is the proper exposition of existence, which we are destined (this is "freedom") to think and/or manage as causality and/or chance, as process and/or happening, as necessity and/or liberty, as fugacity and/or eternity, as unity and/or multiplicity, etc.' See also Heller and Fehér's (1988: 14–43, esp. 41) observation on the 'modern' need to turn contingency into destiny.

25 Writing on Emerson, Cavell (1989: 10) noted: 'My judgment of the world expresses a search for a self, but not for a given state (call it perfection) of a given self (as it were, the one I represent).'

26 The significance of the works by Luc Boltanski and Laurent Thévenot on modes of justification can hardly be overestimated in this respect; see in particular Boltanski and Thévenot, 1991, Boltanski and Chiapello, 1999, Lamont and Thévenot, 2000.

Epilogue: Historicity, Plurality, Problématiques

Indeterminate Historicity

The reasoning in this book has adopted a double mode of argumentation. On the one hand, it has presented and discussed a set of issues in social theory. In this sense, it has proceeded along conceptual or philosophical lines. On the other hand, it has discussed each of these through the historically and contextually changing ways in which they have been set up. In this sense, it has proceeded along empirical and historical lines. The relation between these two lines of reasoning has necessarily been a central and explicit part of the discussion about the certainty of knowledge in the first chapter. Nevertheless, I have avoided committing myself to one of the two major standpoints in the debate about the relation between history and philosophy, or between empirical issues and transcendental issues. Throughout the subsequent chapters, I have tried to remain in this double mode, with shifting emphases depending on the specifics of the argument and its presentation.

Readers may nevertheless have got the impression that I lean towards a view that sees philosophical concepts as always historical, and this impression would not be entirely wrong. Throughout the book, I have aimed at indicating the – socio-historical and linguistic – contexts in which concepts emerged and which they tried to address. The insights that the work over the past few decades in 'conceptual history' or 'genealogy and archaeology' of discourses have provided are too strong a testimony to permit anybody to stay with a decontextualized pretence to universalism in philosophy and social theory. On the contrary, the move towards decontextualization (which I have called 'distancing') itself is a discursive device to re-interpret a given situation that is defined as problematic.

However, I hope it has also become clear that this move towards historicization is not meant to explain or even understand the discursive formations in philosophy and social theory by recourse to a socio-political history or a history of language use that is external to those discourses.[1] I do not see intellectual developments as somehow mirroring or shadowing a course of history. Neither does it seem appropriate to see human history running a 'course', nor do human attempts to interpret history relate to the latter in a merely derivative way. Rather, those attempts can be understood as problematizations, as the identification of problématiques. And problems do recur, so that an interpretation may quite commonly prove useful outside of the context in and for which it was elaborated. Thus, there is a relation of concepts to situations that is open and indeterminate, but nevertheless a relation of reference, be it of emergence in and for a situation or of application in a new situation.

Describable Plurality

This attempt at rethinking the contextual character of concepts, rather than forming itself the main objective, was a precondition for elaborating the central ideas of the book. Difficult as any brief summary is, I will try to sum up these ideas in two steps. First, this book is meant to have conveyed the idea that social theory and philosophy have to work with a plural discursive configuration, all elements of which are essential and none of which is fully substitutable by the others.

Now, the idea that there is a plurality of approaches, schools or paradigms in the social sciences is not at all new. It is rather a commonplace of reflection about the social sciences – deplored by those who aim and hope for the one true insight into the social world and praised by those who see in the open competition of ideas an important guarantor for the progress of knowledge. However, the plurality I wanted to have pointed out is very different from a weak, tolerant plurality of co-existence.[2] Rather, I refer to a plurality of commitment in the search for an adequate way of addressing key issues in the social world and at the same time a theory-laden plurality that acknowledges that single, superior answers to key issues are often not attainable. Rather than the correct 'approach' to a problem – resembling the path of an aeroplane approaching the runway for landing – there is a theoretical space in which multiple answers are situated.

Throughout this book, I have described this space as triangular. Before coming back to the features of the three outstanding positions in this space, it needs underlining that this space is not necessarily triangular, not for any meta-theoretical reasons. This is so because, on the one hand, there just may be other better descriptions of this space than the one I have been able to provide. I would merely like my description to be judged on the merits of what it makes visible. On the other hand, this current triangular constellation, if readers found my account somewhat persuasive, may just be the contours this space of theorizing has acquired at this point in time – or, crucially, at this point of reflecting the experience of modernity. This experience undergoes historical changes as does the thinking about the experience and, as a possible consequence, the contours of the space of theorizing.

I have chosen to portray modernism as the central position in this space, the one that orients and organizes the other ones. In terms of the spatial metaphor employed earlier, the other two modes of social and political thought have been presented as relating to modernism in critical terms from two different directions. But those modes do not merely flee from modernism in a critical reaction; they also turn in some respects towards each other – without, though, merging into each other or becoming reducible the one to the other.

The emphasis on difference in the discourse on selfhood that questions the unity of the self, for instance, resonates with the discourse on the 'same' topic that insists on the substantive rootedness of the self if multiplicity of meaning is allowed for, opening up the possibility of different registers for the understanding of one's own self. The two modes remain irreducible to each other, though, in the sense that the concept of difference cannot exhaust itself in the variety of socio-culturally available ways of making sense but points towards a more fundamental openness of what has been called identity. Analogously, the referral of knowledge claims to some pre-philosophical or pre-scientific rootedness of the human relation to the world may be seen to resonate with the deconstruction of 'scientific' concepts. At the same time, however, the former mode tends to affirm the search for origins in and of scientific knowledge, whereas the latter aims at laying open the problematic nature of this very search. Thirdly, the critiques of political representation in the call for 'rethinking the political' entertain important relations to the substantive attempts in the discourse that aims at enriching the thinness of liberal politics. But their ways of re-addressing fundamental issues, not least the historic separation of theological concerns from political ones and the expanded import of otherness for politics, go beyond any socio-historically identifiable substantive foundation of a political order.

Described in such systematic fashion, the irreducibility of each one of these modes to each other one becomes evident. Saying this, however, may in turn appear to give priority to the third position over the others, not least since it is with the latter's emergence that the triangle becomes visible in the first place. And, in the view of those who hold either of the other two positions, this stand may then lead into relativism, if not nihilism, with all the dangers that are often associated with these terms.

While, certainly, the acknowledgement of the irreducibility of any theoretical position to other co-existing ones must imply a certain relativism, or better: perspectivism, the apocalyptic reaction of modernists to those terms is unjustified. Such highly adversarial response takes perspectivism to assume that nothing can be said about the relation of the various theoretical positions to each other. Perspectivism takes an entirely different shape as soon as one is able to address the question of the point of view from which a perspective emerges; it turns into a pluralism of related and relateable perspectives. The three modes operate in a common space which, if it may not be well described and defined yet, it is at least describable and definable (see Ginzburg, 1998 for such an attempt). And if the answers the perspectives each provide are relative, they are relative, in the first place, to questions. An analysis of the questions, even if they are phrased differently in the various modes, then shows affinities between the modes of social theory discourses, even though, because of their irreconcilability, there often can be no full translation across the languages.

The attempt to talk about the problématiques of knowledge, polity, selfhood, past and future in such relational terms was meant to make commonalities between the questions visible. It is in the nature of such an attempt that one specific language has to be chosen to formulate it, and this language in turn may prove to be irreducible to one or more – possibly even all – of the interpretations it aims to relate to one another. Nevertheless it may succeed in demonstrating affinities between them.

If one wanted to, the analysis offered here could be read as a specific rendering of what Derrida (1978a: 293) sees as the task 'to conceive of the common ground, and the *différance* of this irreducible difference' between modes of interpretation in the field of the social sciences. The analysis suggested that approaches to this task will have to address two issues: first, what is it that we try to understand? This question points to the problématiques at issue. The expectation is that, even if the languages remain irreconcilable, there may be some proximity and affinity across such problématiques that may be inconceivable when merely looking at the divergence of the answers. And secondly, what is the situation in which we ask? This question points to the possibility of a commonality (or understandable difference) of discursive-intellectual moment – again, an aspect that may be inconceivable in a decontextualized analysis. The variation in the answers may be due to a variation in the assessment of urgency, and this variation itself may be analysable – instead of being considered a priori unbridgeable.

Persistent Problématiques

Social theorizing is essentially about key problématiques that human social life encounters. Those problématiques are actualized as problems that emerge in specific situations and to which solutions need to be found. The way human beings respond to problematic situations depends on the interpretation of the problem and the urgency with which it needs to be addressed. By implication, this means that the adequacy of any solution cannot be determined in any – however conceptualized – realm of theorizing alone, regardless of the situation, its interpretation and the assessment of urgency. Since there is – 'in the abstract', outside of time – no criterion for choosing from a plurality of answers, the attainability of answers must always remain a theoretically open issue.

Against the observation of such fundamental plurality, relating modes of theorizing to each other by recourse to commonalities of problématique presupposes what I called the inescapability of those problématiques. This is the second central idea of my reasoning I want to return to in these concluding remarks. The certainty of knowledge, the viability of the polity, the continuity of selfhood, the accessibility of the past, the transparency of the future have here been regarded as problématiques to which social thought will have to relate; they are questions that cannot be declined. Such assertion will not easily be accepted without further clarifications.

As usual, the issue of exhaustiveness will be raised; and I need to underline that no such claim is intended here. I hope to have demonstrated by the conjoint theoretical and historical presentation that there are good reasons to assume that these questions are inescapable, but I do not claim that there are no other ones, or even that those I selected are more central than other ones.

Then, one may ask whether the inescapability does not merely appear as a result of the form of presentation of the issues. More precisely, are not especially the first three questions posed in the way in which modernist theorizing would pose them as central questions – whereas the first response to modernism would assume that answers to those questions are always already given, and the second response would take the questions to be insignificant or overcome? It needs to be granted that each way of posing the issues entails some bias; there is no stepping out of the available space of social theorizing, only maybe some enlargement of it. The fact that the different ways of treating the questions co-exist with each other, however, demonstrates the persistence of the problématiques rather than their solution or insignificance.[3] My form of presenting the issues is likely to have many flaws. But before any bias there may be is taken to undermine the fundamental argument about inescapability, further evidence and reasoning would need to be provided against my claim.

Now, finally, I may have provided some such evidence and reasoning myself. Between the first three chapters and the final two, and without announcing so, I have introduced some change of register. Beyond the conjoint theoretical and historical presentation of the three modes of theorizing about a given problématique, as in the first three chapters, I have embarked on reflections about our current situation and the urgencies that may come with it. The historicization of approaches to the problématiques has then come close to saying that some modes of theorizing may get lost – in particular, the theorizing that insists on substantive rootedness – and that others may gain hegemony – in particular, the rationalist-individualist version of modernist theorizing. I have, however, guarded myself against formulating any such strong conclusion about total loss and final victory. Although the strength and persuasiveness of certain interpretations of situations over others is related to the socio-political and intellectual context, the fundamental plurality of ways of thinking about the social world does not therefore go away. To say otherwise is not a description of a situation, but an argument for some such change to happen.

What I have tried to do in those passages of the two chapters about time, is cautiously to move towards a socio-theoretical diagnosis of our own time – or rather, to explore some ways of enabling such a diagnosis to be made in the light of the considerations before. By warning of the impoverishment of registers of evaluation that would go with a discrediting of substantive, common answers, I wanted to indeed say that this is a current risk. But at the same time I excluded any determinism in that direction and pointed to the remedy. The central conclusion of my argument, if there is any, is that one needs to keep the full intellectual space occupied that is marked by the three modes of reasoning. This is the most adequate way both to think modernity and to preserve the full intellectual potential to deal with problematic situations of the present and the future. Guidance as to how to interpret specific such problematic situations, then, is nothing one should expect from theoretical fiat alone.

Notes

1 The inadequacy of such an attempt has recently at length been demonstrated in debates around the relation of deconstruction to historical analysis; see in particular Attridge et al., 1987; Derrida, 1990. Unfortunately, the significance of deconstruction for history and sociology has been much less debated, by either side.

2 Such tolerant co-existence is certainly also needed, but it far too often entails a practical relativism of indifference that always needs to be fought against, because it entails avoiding to ask crucial questions about the whole endeavour of social science.

3 Let me, as an illustration, briefly come back to an example I have quoted frequently, because of the clarity of the presentation. Richard Rorty's (1989) ambition may have been

to show the insignificance of certain questions, to call upon us to 'drop' them. But if all one would need to say about language, selfhood and community were that they are contingent, then there would be little to write about them philosophically. The fact that Rorty has written at length about these problématiques – and keeps doing so (about polity and knowledge: Rorty, 1998a and 1998b respectively) – gives testimony to their inescapability, even from what I take to be largely the position of a second response to modernism.

References

Abrams, Philip (1972) 'The sense of the past and the origins of sociology', *Past and Present*, 55, pp. 18–32.

Alexander, Jeffrey (1994) 'How "national" is social theory? A note on some worrying trends in the recent theorizing of Richard Munch', *Theory* (Newsletter of the ISA Research Committee on Social Theory), Autumn, pp. 2–8.

Apel, Karl-Otto (1991) 'Wittgenstein und Heidegger. Kritische Wiederholung und Ergänzung eines Vergleichs' in Brian McGuiness a.o., *Der Löwe spricht ... und wir können ihn nicht verstehen. Symposion an der Universität Frankfurt anläßlich des hundertsten Geburtstags von Ludwig Wittgenstein*. Frankfurt/M: Suhrkamp. pp. 27–68.

Arendt, Hannah (1958a) *The Human Condition*. Chicago: University of Chicago Press.

Arendt, Hannah (1958b) *The Origins of Totalitarianism*. Cleveland: World Publishing Company, 2nd edition.

Arendt, Hannah (1965) *On Revolution*. New York: Viking.

Arendt, Hannah (1978) *The Life of the Mind*, vol. 1: *Thinking*. New York: Harcourt, Brace, Jovanovich.

Arnason, Johann P. (1989) 'The imaginary constitution of modernity', in Giovanni Busino et al. (ed.), *Autonomie et autotransformation de la société. La philosophie militante de Cornelius Castoriadis*. Geneva: Droz. pp. 323–37.

Arnason, Johann P. (1998) 'Multiple modernities and civilizational contexts: Reflections on the Japanese experience', unpublished paper.

Assmann, Aleida and Friese, Heidrun (eds) (1998) *Identitäten*. Frankfurt/M: Suhrkamp.

Assmann, Jan (2000) *Herrschaft und Heil. Politische theologie in Altägypten, Israel und Europa*. Munich: Hanser.

Attridge, Derek, Bennington, Geoff and Young, Robert (eds) (1987) *Post-structuralism and the Question of History*. Cambridge: Cambridge University Press.

Baker, Keith Michael (1975) *Condorcet: From Natural Philosophy to Social Mathematics*. Chicago: University of Chicago Press.

Baker, Keith Michael (1990) 'Representation redefined', in *Inventing the French Revolution*. Cambridge: Cambridge University Press. pp. 224–51.

Balibar, Etienne and Wallerstein, Immanuel (1991) *Race, Nation, Class: Ambiguous Identities*. London: Verso.

Baudrillard, Jean (1988) *America*. London: Verso.

Bauman, Zygmunt (1987) *Legislators and Interpreters*. Cambridge: Polity.

Bauman, Zygmunt (1991) *Modernity and Ambivalence*. Cambridge: Polity.

Bauman, Zygmunt (1992) *Intimations of Postmodernity*. London: Routledge.

Bell, Daniel (1976) *The Cultural Contradictions of Capitalism*. London: Heinemann.

Benjamin, Andrew (1997) *Present Hope. Philosophy, Architecture, Judaism*. London: Routledge.

Benjamin, Walter (1978 [1935]) 'Das Kunstwerk im Zeitalter seiner technischen Reproduzierbarkeit' in Rolf Tiedemann and Hermann Schweppenhäuser (eds), *Gesammelte schriften*, vol. 1, 2. Frankfurt/M: Suhrkamp. pp. 431–69.

Benjamin, Walter (1996 [1916]) '*Trauerspiel* and tragedy', in Marcus Bullock and Michael W. Jennings (eds), *Selected writings*, vol. 1. Cambridge, Mass.: Belknap Press of Harvard University Press. pp. 55–8.

Berlin, Isaiah (1969) 'Two concepts of liberty', in *Four Essays on Liberty*. Oxford: Oxford University Press.

Berman, Marshall (1982) *All That is Solid Melts into Air. The Experience of Modernity.* New York: Simon and Schuster.

Bernstein, Richard J. (1998) *Freud and the Legacy of Moses.* Cambridge: Cambridge University Press.

Berzinsky, Michael D. (1988) 'Self-theorists, identity status, and social cognition', in Lapsley, Daniel K. and F. Clark Power (eds), *Self, Ego, and Identity. Integrative Approaches.* New York: Springer. pp. 243–62.

Bhaskar, Roy (1991) *Philosophy and the Idea of Freedom.* Oxford: Blackwell.

Blumenberg, Hans (1985) *The Legitimacy of the Modern Age.* Cambridge, Mass.: MIT Press.

Blumenberg, Hans (1997) 'Die welt hat keinen namen', *Ein mögliches Selbstverständnis.* Leipzig: Reclam. pp. 46–58.

Bolsinger, Eckard (1999) *State and civil war. A comparative analysis of the political thought of Carl Schmitt and Vladimir I. Lenin.* Ph.D. thesis at the European University Institute, Florence.

Boltanski, Luc (1990) *L'amour et la justice comme compétences. Trois essais de sociologie de l'action.* Paris: Métailié.

Boltanski, Luc and Chiapello, Eve (1999) *Le nouvel esprit du capitalisme.* Paris: Gallimard.

Boltanski, Luc and Thévenot, Laurent (1991) *De la justification. Les économies de la grandeur.* Paris: Gallimard.

Börne, Ludwig (1868) '114th letter from Paris, 15 March 1833', *Gesammelte Schriften,* vol. 12. Vienna: Tendler & Comp. p. 108.

Brague, Rémi (1999 [1992]) *Europe, la Voie Romaine.* Paris: Gallimard.

Brian, Eric (1994) *La mesure de l'etat. Administrateurs et géomètres au XVIIIe siècle.* Paris: Michel.

Bryant, Christopher G.A. (1990) 'Tales of innocence and experience: Developments in sociological theory since the 1950s', in Christopher G.A. Bryant and Henk A. Becker (eds), *What Has Sociology Achieved?* Basingstoke: Macmillan. pp. 69–93.

Burke, Edmund (1993 [1790]) *Reflections on the Revolution in France.* Oxford: Oxford University Press (ed. L.G. Mitchell).

Cacciari, Massimo (1994) *Geo-filosofia dell'Europa.* Milan: Adelphi.

Cacciari, Massimo (1997) *Arcipelago.* Milan: Adelphi.

Castoriadis, Cornelius (1990) *Le monde morcelé. Les carrefours du labyrinthe III.* Paris: Seuil.

Castoriadis, Cornelius (1991) 'Power, politics, autonomy', in *Philosophy, Politics, Autonomy: Essays in Political Philosophy*, Oxford: Oxford University Press. pp. 143–74.

Cavell, Stanley (1989) *The New Yet Unapproachable America. Lectures after Emerson after Wittgenstein.* Albuquerque: Living Batch Press.

Cavell, Stanley (1990) *Conditions Handsome and Unhandsome.* Chicago: University of Chicago Press.

Cavell, Stanley (1995) *Philosophical Passages.* Oxford: Blackwell.

Caygill, Howard (1994) 'Benjamin, Heidegger and the destruction of tradition', in Andrew Benjamin and Peter Osborne (eds), *Walter Benjamin's Philosophy. Destruction and Experience.* London: Routledge. pp. 1–31.

Cedroni, Lorella (1999) *Il problema della rappresentanza politica nel dibattito rivoluzionario inglese, francese e americano: Burke, Sieyès e Madison a confronto.* Ph.D. thesis at the European University Institute, Florence.

Céline, Louis-Ferdinand (1988 [1933]) *Journey to the End of the Night.* London: Calder.

Chase, Malcolm and Shaw, Christopher (1989) 'The dimensions of nostalgia', in Christopher Shaw and Malcolm Chase (eds), *The imagined Past. History and Nostalgia.* Manchester: Manchester University Press. pp. 1–17.

Claudel, Paul (1959) *Conversations dans le Loir-et-Cher.* Paris: Gallimard.

Cohen, Anthony P. (1994) *Self-consciousness: An Alternative Anthropology of Identity.* London: Routledge.

Critchley, Simon (1998) 'The other's decision in me', *European Journal of Social Theory* 1 (2): 259–79.

Dahrendorf, Ralf (1963) *Die angewandte aufklärung. Gesellschaft und demokratie in Amerika*. Munich.

d'Arcy, François and Guy, Saez (1985) 'De la représentation', in François d'Arcy (ed.), *La représentation*. Paris: Economica.

de Beauvoir, Simone (1963) *La Force des choses*. Paris: Gallimard.

de Certeau, Michel (1988) *The Writing of History*. New York: Columbia University Press.

de Tocqueville, Alexis (1966) *Democracy in America*. New York: Harper and Row.

Derrida, Jacques (1978a) 'Structure, sign and play in the discourse of the human sciences', in *Writing and Difference*. London: Routledge. pp. 280–93.

Derrida, Jacques (1978b) 'Différance', in *Margins of Philosophy*. London: Rouledge. pp. 1–27.

Derrida, Jacques (1986) 'Declarations of independence', *New Political Science*, 15: pp. 7–13.

Derrida, Jacques (1989) *Of Spirit. Heidegger and the Question*. Chicago: University of Chicago Press.

Derrida, Jacques (1990) 'Some statements and truisms about neologisms, newisms, postisms, parasitisms, and other small seisms', in David Carroll (ed.), *The States of "Theory". History, Art, and Critical Discourse*. New York: Columbia University Press. pp. 63–94.

Derrida, Jacques (1991) *L'autre Cap*. Paris: Minuit.

Derrida, Jacques (1994) *Specters of Marx*. New York: Routledge.

Derrida, Jacques and Vattimo, Gianni (eds) (1995) *La religione*. Bari: Laterza.

Desrosières, Alain (1991a) 'The part in relation to the whole? How to generalise. A pre-history of representative sampling', in Martin Bulmer, Kevin Bales, and Kathryn Kish Sklar (eds), *The Social Survey in Historical Perspective 1880–1940*. Cambridge: Cambridge University Press. pp. 217–44.

Desrosières, Alain (1991b) 'How to make things which hold together: social science, statistics, and the state', in Peter Wagner, Björn Wittrock, and Richard Whitley (eds), *Discourses on Society. The Shaping of the Social Science Disciplines*. Dordrecht: Kluwer. pp. 195–218.

Desrosières, Alain (1993) *La politique des grands nombres. Histoire de la raison statistique*. Paris: La découverte.

Dewey, John (1984 [1929]) *The Quest for Certainty*, in *The Later Works 1925–1953*, vol. 4. Carbondale, Ill.: Southern Illinois University Press.

Donzelot, Jacques (1984) *L'invention du social. Essai sur le déclin des passions politiques*. Paris: Fayard.

Donzelot, Jacques (1991) 'The mobilization of society', in Graham Burchell, Colin Gordon and Peter Miller (eds), *The Foucault Effect. Studies in Governmentality*. Chicago: University of Chicago Press. pp. 169–79.

Dufresnois, Huguette and Miquel, Christian (1996) *La philosophie de l'exil*. Paris: Harmattan.

Duhamel, Georges (1930) *Scènes de la vie future*. Paris: Mercure de France.

Durkheim, Emile (1976) *The Elementary Forms of Religious Life*. London: Allen & Unwin.

Dutschke, Rudi (1974) *Versuch, Lenin auf die Füße zu stellen*. Berlin: Wagenbach.

Eco, Umberto (1986) 'Travels in Hyperreality', in *Travels in Hyperreality*. San Diego: Harcourt Brace Jovanovich.

Eisenstadt, Shmuel N. (1998) *Antinomien der moderne*. Frankfurt/M: Suhrkamp.

Engels, Friedrich (1958) *The Condition of the Working Class in England in 1844*. Oxford: Blackwell.

Erikson, Erik H. (1968) 'Identity, psychosocial', *International Encyclopedia of the Social Sciences*, vol. 7. London and New York: Macmillan and Free Press.

Espagne, Michel and Werner, Michael (1988) *Transferts: les relations interculturelles dans l'espace franco-allemand, XVIIIe et XIXe siècle*. Paris: Editions Recherche sur les Civilisations.

Fabian, Johannes (1983) *Time and the Other*. New York: Columbia University Press.

Felski, Rita (1995) *The Gender of Modernity*. Cambridge, Mass.: Harvard University Press.

Foucault, Michel (1966) *Les mots et les choses*. Paris: Gallimard.

Foucault, Michel (1984) 'What is Enlightenment?' in Paul Rabinow (ed.), *The Foucault Reader*. London: Penguin. pp. 32–50.

Fourastié, Jean (1979) *Les trentes glorieuses ou la révolution invisible de 1946 à 1975*. Paris: Fayard.

Fraenkel, Ernst (1959) *Amerika im spiegel des Deutschen politischen denkens*. Cologne.

Fraisse, Robert (1981) 'Les sciences sociales et l'Etat', in *Esprit* (50), February, pp. 21–7.

Freud, Sigmund (1967) *Moses and Monotheism*. New York: Random House.

Freud, Sigmund (1985) 'Civilization and its discontents', in *Civilization, Society and Religion* (vol. 12 of the Penguin Freud Library). London: Penguin. pp. 251–340.

Friese, Heidrun (1991) *Ordnungen der Zeit. Zur sozialen Konstitution von Temporalstrukturen in einem sizilianischen Ort*. Ph.D. thesis, University of Amsterdam.

Friese, Heidrun (1993) 'Die Konstruktion von zeit: zum prekären verhältnis von akademischer "theorie" und lokaler praxis', *Zeitschrift für Soziologie*, 22 (5): 323–37.

Friese, Heidrun (1995) 'Zitationen der geschichte – zur (re)konstruktion von vergangenheit in einem sizilianischen ort', *Historische Anthropologie*, 2 (1): 39–62.

Friese, Heidrun (1996) *Lampedusa. Historische anthropologie einer insel*. Frankfurt/Main: Campus.

Friese, Heidrun (1997) 'Geschichte im Alltag', in Jörn Rüsen and K. Müller (eds), *Historische Sinnbildung*, vol. 1. *Sinnprobleme und Zeitstrukturen*. Reinbek: Rowohlt.

Friese, Heidrun (1998) 'Literal letters. On the materiality of words', *Paragraph*, 21 (2): pp. 169–99.

Friese, Heidrun (2000) 'Silence – voice – representation', in Robert Fine and Charles Turner (eds), *Social Theory after the Holocaust*. Liverpool: Liverpool University Press (Studies in Social and Political Thought).

Friese, Heidrun (ed.) (2001a) *Identities*. Providence: Berghahn.

Friese, Heidrun (ed.) (2001b) *The Moment*. Liverpool: Liverpool University Press (Studies in Social and Political Thought).

Friese, Heidrun and Wagner, Peter (1993) *Der raum des gelehrten*. Berlin: sigma.

Friese, Heidrun and Wagner, Peter (1997) 'Bild und wissen. Reflexionen zu erkenntnis und darstellung in den sozialwissenschaften', in Ute Hoffmann, Bernward Joerges and Ingrid Severin (eds), *LogIcons. Bilder zwischen theorie und anschauung*. Berlin: sigma. pp. 207–22.

Friese, Heidrun and Wagner, Peter (1999a) 'Inescapability and attainability in the sociology of modernity', *European Journal of Social Theory*, 2 (1): pp. 27–44.

Friese, Heidrun and Wagner, Peter (1999b). 'Not all that is solid melts into air. Modernity and contingency', in Mike Featherstone and Scott Lash (eds), *Spaces of Identity. City – Nation – World*, London: Sage, pp. 101–15.

Friese, Heidrun and Wagner, Peter (2000) 'When "the light of the great cultural problems moves on". On the possibility of a cultural theory of modernity', *Thesis Eleven* no. 61: pp. 25–40.

Fromm, Erich (1941) *Escape from Freedom*. New York: Holt, Rinehart, and Winston.

Fukuyama, Francis (1992) *The End of History and the Last Man*. New York: Free Press.

Fuller, Steve (1998) 'Divining the future of social theory. From theology to rhetoric via social epistemology', *European Journal of Social Theory*, 1 (1): 107–26.

Fyfe, Gordon and Law, John (1988) 'Introduction: on the invisibility of the visual', in Gordon Fyfe and John Law (eds), *Picturing Power. Visual Depiction and Social Relations*. London: Routledge. pp. 1–14.

Gallie, W.B. (1955–6) 'Essentially contested concepts', *Proceedings of the Aristotelian Society*, vol. 56: 167–98.

Game, Ann (1991) *Undoing the Social. Towards a Deconstructive Sociology*. Milton Keynes: Open University Press.

Giddens, Anthony (1977) 'Functionalism: après la lutte', *Studies in Social and Political Theory*. London: Hutchinson.

Giddens, Anthony (1984) *The Constitution of Society*. Cambridge: Polity.

Giddens, Anthony (1990) *The Consequences of Modernity*. Cambridge: Polity.

Giddens, Anthony (1991) *Modernity and Self-identity*. Cambridge: Polity.

Ginzburg, Carlo (1998) 'Distanza e prospettiva. Due metafore', in *Occhiacci di legno. Nove riflessioni sulla distanza*. Milan: Feltrinelli. pp. 171–93.

Griswold, Wendy (1994) *Cultures and Societies in a Changing World*. Thousand Oaks: Pine Forge.

Gunnell, John G. (1991) 'In search of the state: Political science as an emerging discipline in the US', in Peter Wagner, Björn Wittrock, and Richard Whitley (eds), *Discourses on Society. The Shaping of the Social Science Disciplines*. Dordrecht: Kluwer. pp. 123–61.

Habermas, Jürgen (1981) *Theorie des kommunikativen handelns*. Frankfurt/M: Suhrkamp.

Habermas, Jürgen (1985) *Der philosophische diskurs der moderne*. Frankfurt/M: Suhrkamp.

Halfeld, Adolf (1927) *Amerika und der Amerikanismus. Kritische betrachtungen eines Deutschen und Europäers*. Jena: Diederichs.

Hannerz, Ulf (1992) *Cultural Complexity*. New York: Columbia University Press.

Hartz, Louis (1964) *The Founding of New Societies. Studies in the History of the United States*. New York: Harcourt, Brace and World.

Hartz, Louis (1955) *The Liberal Tradition in America*. New York: Harcourt, Brace and World.

Hegel, Georg Wilhelm Friedrich (1977 [1807]) *Phenomenology of Spirit*. Oxford: Oxford University Press.

Hegel, Georg Wilhelm Friedrich (1996) *Vorlesungen zur geschichte der philosophie*. Hamburg: Meiner.

Heidegger, Martin (1978 [1916]) 'Der zeitbegriff in der geschichtswissenschft', in *Frühe schriften*. Frankfurt/M: Klostermann. pp. 413–33.

Heidegger, Martin (1983a [1933]) *Die selbstbehauptung der Deutschen universität*. Frankfurt/M: Klostermann.

Heidegger, Martin (1983b) *Einführung in die metaphysik*. Frankfurt/M: Klostermann.

Heilbron, Johan, Magnusson, Lars and Wittrock, Björn (eds) (1998) *The Rise of the Social Sciences and the Formation of Modernity*. Dordrecht: Kluwer.

Heller, Agnes and Fehér, Ferenc (1988) 'On being satisfied in a dissatisfied society I and II', in *The Modern Political Condition*. Cambridge: Polity. pp. 14–43.

Henningsen, Manfred (1974) *Der fall Amerika. Zur sozial- und bewußtseinsgeschichte einer verdrängung*. Munich: List.

Hobbes, Thomas (1996 [1651]) *Leviathan*. Oxford: Oxford University Press.

Hollander, Paul (1992) *Anti-Americanism. Critiques at Home and Abroad 1965–1990*. New York: Oxford University Press.

Hollis, Martin (1985) 'Of masks and men', in Michael Carrithers, Steven Collins und Steven Lukes (eds), *The Category of the Person: Anthropology, Philosophy, History*. Cambridge: Cambridge University Press.

Honig, Bonnie (1991) 'Declarations of independence: Arendt and Derrida on the problem of founding a republic', *American Political Science Review*, 85 (1): pp. 97–113.

Honneth, Axel (1995) *The Struggle for Recognition*. Cambridge: Polity.

Hont, Istvan (1987) 'The language of sociability and commerce: Samuel Pufendorf and the foundation of the "four-stages theory"', in Anthony Pagden (ed.), *The Languages of Political Theory in early Modern Europe*. Cambridge: Cambridge University Press. pp. 253–76.

Horkheimer, Max (1931) 'Die gegenwärtige Lage der Sozialphilosophie und die Aufgaben eines Instituts für Sozialforschung', in *Frankfurter universitätsreden*, vol. XXXVII. Frankfurt/M: Englert und Schlosser.

Horowitz, Irving Louis (1991) 'On Jacob L. Talmon', *Partisan Review*, no. 58, 101–6.

Husserl, Edmund (1970 [1935]) *The Crisis of European Sciences and Transcendental Phenomenology*. Evanston: Northwestern University Press.

Jameson, Fredric (1991) *Postmodernism, or The Cultural Logic of Late Capitalism.* Durham, N.C.: Duke University Press.

Jankélévitch, Vladimir (1983) *L'irréversible et la nostalgie.* Paris: Flammarion.

Joas, Hans (1993) *Pragmatism and Social Theory.* Chicago: University of Chicago Press.

Joas, Hans (1996) *The Creativity of Action.* Cambridge: Polity.

Joas, Hans (1998) 'The autonomy of the self. The Meadian heritage and its postmodern challenge', *European Journal of Social Theory*, 1 (1): 7–18.

Kant, Immanuel (1993 [1781]) *Critique of Pure Reason.* London: Dent.

Kellner, Douglas (1992) 'Popular culture and the construction of postmodern identities', in Scott Lash and Jonathan Friedman (eds), *Modernity and Identity.* Oxford: Blackwell.

Kellner, Douglas (1995) *Media Culture, Cultural Studies, Identity and Politics between the Modern and the Postmodern.* London: Routledge.

Kelly, George Armstrong (1992) *The Humane Comedy. Constant, Tocqueville and French Liberalism.* Cambridge: Cambridge University Press.

Kojève, Alexandre (1969) *Introduction to the Reading of Hegel.* New York: Basic Books.

Koselleck, Reinhart (1979) *Vergangene zukunft. Zur semantik geschichtlicher zeiten.* Frankfurt/M: Suhrkamp.

Kraynak, Robert P. (1990) *History and Modernity in the Thought of Thomas Hobbes.* Ithaca: Cornell University Press.

Kriegel, Annie (1972) 'Consistent misapprehension: European views of America and their logic', *Daedalus*, no. 101, fall.

Kristeva, Julia (1991) *Strangers to Ourselves.* New York: Columbia.

Kuisel, Richard F. (1993) *Seducing the French. The Dilemma of Americanization.* Berkeley: University of California Press.

Lamberti, Jean-Claude (1983) *Tocqueville et les deux démocraties.* Paris, Presses Universitaires Françaises.

Lamont, Michèle and Thévenot, Laurent (eds) (2000) *Rethinking Comparative Cultural Sociology. Polities and Repertoires of Evaluation in France and the United States.* New York: Cambridge University Press.

Lamont, Michèle (1992) *Money, Morals and Manners. The Culture of the French and American Upper-middle Class.* Chicago: University of Chicago Press.

Lapsley, Daniel K. and Power, F. Clark (eds) (1988) *Self, Ego, and Identity. Integrative Approaches.* New York: Springer.

Lash, Scott and Friedman, Jonathan (eds) (1992) *Modernity and Identity.* Oxford: Blackwell.

Lash, Scott (1994) 'Expert systems or situated interpretation? Culture and institutions in disorganized capitalism', in Ulrich Beck, Anthony Giddens and Scott Lash (eds), *Reflexive Modernization.* Cambridge: Polity.

Latour, Bruno (1993) *We Have Never Been Modern.* Hemel Hempstead: Harvester Wheatsheaf.

Lawrence, D.H. (1962) 'The spirit of place', in Armin Arnold (ed.), *The Symbolic Meaning. The Uncollected Versions of Studies in Classic American Literature.* Fontwell: Centaur Press.

Lawrence, D.H. (1964) *Studies in Classic American Literature.* London: Heinemann.

Lawrence, D.H. (1987) *The Plumed Serpent (Quetzalcoatl).* Cambridge: Cambridge University Press.

Lebovics, Herman (1986) 'The uses of America in Locke's Second Treatise of Government', *Journal of the History of Ideas*, vol. 47, pp. 567–81.

Lefort, Claude (1972) *Le travail de l'oeuvre machiavel.* Paris: Gallimard.

Lefort, Claude (1986a) 'La question de la démocratie', *Essais sur le politique. XIXᵉ–XXᵉ siècles.* Paris: Seuil. pp. 17–30.

Lefort, Claude (1986b) 'Réversibilité: Liberté politique et liberté de l'individu', *Essais sur le politique. XIXᵉ–XXᵉ siècles.* Paris: Seuil. pp. 197–216.

Lefort, Claude (1986c) 'Permanence du théologico-politique?', *Essais sur le politique. XIXᵉ–XXᵉ siècles.* Paris: Seuil. pp. 251–300.

Lefort, Claude (1991) 'Introduction' to Gordon S. Wood, in *La création de la république américaine 1776–1787*. Paris: Belin.

Lenau, Nikolaus (1971) *Sämtliche werke und briefe*, vol. II. Frankfurt/M: Insel.

Locke, John (1966) *The Second Treatise of Government*. Oxford: Blackwell

Löwith, Karl (1949) *Meaning in History*. Chicago: University of Chicago Press.

Lyotard, Jean-François (1984 [1979]) *The Postmodern Condition*. Manchester: Manchester University Press.

Lyotard, Jean-François (1989a) 'Universal history and cultural differences', in Andrew Benjamin (ed.), *The Lyotard Reader*. Oxford: Blackwell. pp. 314–24.

Lyotard, Jean-François (1989b) in 'Discussions, or phrasing "after Auschwitz"', in Andrew Benjamin (ed.), *The Lyotard Reader*. Oxford: Blackwell. pp. 360–92.

Maier, Charles S. (1970) 'Between taylorism and technocracy', *Journal of Contemporary History*, 5: pp. 27–61.

Maier, Hans (1980) *Die ältere deutsche Staats – und verwaltungslehre*. Munich: Beck.

Mann, Micheal (1986) *The Sources of Social Power*. Cambridge: Cambridge University Press.

Manent, Pierre (1994) *La cité de l'homme*. Paris: Fayard.

Marx, Karl (1963) 'On the Jewish Question' in Tom B. Bottomore (ed.), *Early Writings*. New York: McGraw-Hill.

Mason, Peter (1990) *Deconstructing America. Representations of the Other*. London: Routledge.

Mathy, Jean-Philippe (1993) *Extrême-Occident. French Intellectuals and America*. Chicago: University of Chicago Press.

Mazlish, Bruce (1989) *A New Science. The Breakdown of Connections and the Birth of Sociology*. New York: Oxford University Press.

Miller, Henry (1947) *The Air-conditioned Nightmare*. London: Secker & Warburg.

Miquel, Christian (1992) *Critique de la modernité. L'exil et le social*. Paris: Harmattan.

Miquel, Christian (1996) *La quête l'exil (Pratique de l'exil)*. Paris: Harmattan.

Morley, David and Robbins, Kevin (1995) *Spaces of Identity. Global Media, Electronic Landscapes and Cultural Boundaries*. London: Routledge.

Mouffe, Chantal (1991) 'Pluralism and modern democracy. Around Carl Schmitt', in *The Return of the Political*. London: Verso. pp. 117–34.

Mouffe, Chantal (ed.) (1999) *The Challenge of Carl Schmitt*. London: Verso.

Münch, Richard (1991) 'American and European social theory: cultural identities and social forms of theory production', *Sociological Perspectives*, 34: pp. 313–35.

Münch, Richard (1993) 'The contribution of German social theory to European sociology', in Birgitta Nedelmann and Piotr Sztompka (eds), *Sociology in Europe*. Berlin: de Gruyter. pp. 45–66.

Münch, Richard (1995) 'Geopolitics in guise of universalist rhetoric. A response to Jeffrey C. Alexander', *Theory* (Newsletter of the ISA Research Committee on Social Theory), Spring, pp. 2–10.

Münkler, Herfried (1998) 'Zwang und freiheit in der politik der moderne' (unpublished paper).

Murphy, Tim (1997) *The Oldest Social Science? Configurations of Law and Modernity*. Oxford: Clarendon Press.

Nagel, Ernest (1961) *The Structure of Science. Problems in the Logic of Scientific Explanation*. New York: Harcourt, Brace, and World.

Nancy, Jean-Luc (1990) 'Finite history', in David Carroll (ed.), *The States of 'Theory'. History, Art and Critical Discourse*. Stanford: Stanford University Press. pp. 149–72.

Nancy, Jean-Luc (1991) *The Inoperative Community*. Minneapolis: University of Minnesota Press.

Nietzsche, Friedrich (1968) *Also sprach Zarathustra*. Berlin: de Gruyter.

Nietzsche, Friedrich (1972) 'Unzeitgemässe betrachtungen. Erstes Stück: Vom nutzen und nachteil der historie für das leben', in Giorgio Colli and Mazzino Montinari (eds), *Werke. Kritische gesamtausgabe*. Berlin: de Gruyter. pp. 239–330.

Nisbet, Robert A. (1959) *The Sociological Tradition*. London: Heinemann.
Nisbet, Robert A. (1969) *Social Change and History. Aspects of the Western Theory of Development*. New York: Oxford University Press.
Österberg, Dag (1988) *Meta-sociology. An Inquiry into the Origins and Validity of Social Thought*. Oslo: Norwegian University Press.
Outhwaite, William (1999) 'The myth of modernist method', *European Journal of Social Theory*, 2 (1): 5–25.
Pagden, Anthony (ed.) (1987a) *The Languages of Political Theory in Early Modern Europe*. Cambridge: Cambridge University Press.
Pagden, Anthony (1987b) 'Introduction', in Anthony Pagden (ed.), *The Languages of Political Theory in Early Modern Europe*. Cambridge: Cambridge University Press. pp. 1–17.
Pagden, Anthony (1993) *European Encounters with the New World*. New Haven: Yale University Press.
Paine, Thomas (1993 [1791–2]) *The Rights of Man*. London: Dent.
Papastergiadis, Nikos (1993) *Modernity as Exile. The Stranger in John Berger's Writing*. Manchester: Manchester University Press.
Papastergiadis, Nikos (2000) *The Turbulence of Migration*. Cambridge: Polity Press.
Pettit, Philip (1997) *Republicanism. A Theory of Freedom and Government*. Oxford: Clarendon.
Pocock, John Greville Agard (1976) *The Machiavellian Moment. Florentine Political Thought and the Atlantic Republican Tradition*. Princeton: Princeton University Press.
Pollak, Michael (1979) 'Paul F. Lazarsfeld – fondateur d'une multinationale scientifique', *Actes de la recherche en sciences sociales*, 25: pp. 45–59.
Prete, Antonio (1992) *Nostalgia. Storia di un Sentimento*. Milan: Cortina.
Procacci, Giovanna (1993) *Gouverner la misère*. Paris: Seuil.
Rawls, John (1971) *A Theory of Justice*. Cambridge, Mass.: Belknap of Harvard University Press.
Rorty, Richard (1980) *Philosophy and the Mirror of Nature*. Princeton: Princeton University Press.
Rorty, Richard (1989) *Contingency, Irony, Solidarity*. Cambridge: Cambridge University Press.
Rorty, Richard (1998a) *Achieving our Country. Leftist Thought in Twentieth-century America*. Cambridge, Mass.: Harvard University Press.
Rorty, Richard (1998b) *Truth and Progress. Philosophical Papers*, vol. 3. Cambridge: Cambridge University Press.
Rose, Gillian (1992) *The Broken Middle. Out of Our Ancient Society*. Oxford: Blackwell.
Rose, Gillian (1993) *Judaism and Modernity*. Oxford: Blackwell.
Rosenblum, Nancy L. (1987) *Another Liberalism. Romanticism and the Reconstruction of Liberal Thought*. Cambridge, Mass.: Harvard University Press.
Roth, Michael S. (1992) 'The time of nostalgia. Medicine, history and normality in 19th-century France', *Time & Society*, 1 (2): 271–86.
Sahlins, Marshall (2000) '"Sentimental pessimism" and ethnographic experience, or, Why culture is not a disappearing "object"', in Lorraine Daston (ed.), *Biographies of Scientific Objects*. Chicago: University of Chicago Press. pp. 158–202.
Said, Edward (1979) *Orientalism*. New York: Vintage.
Sartre, Jean-Paul (1949) 'Présentation', in *Situations III*. Paris: Gallimard.
Sartre, Jean-Paul (1968) 'Individualism and conformism in the United States', in *Literary and Philosophical Essays*. London: Hutchinson. pp. 97–106.
Schmidt, Alexander (1997) *Reisen in die moderne. Der Amerika-diskurs des Deutschen bürgertums vor dem Ersten Weltkrieg im europäischen vergleich*. Berlin: Akademie Verlag.
Schmitt, Carl (1996) *The Leviathan in the State Theory of Thomas Hobbes – Meaning and Failure of a Political Symbol*. Westport: Greenwood.

Schnapper, Dominique (1998) *La Relation à l'autre. Au coeur de la pensée sociologique.* Paris: Gallimard.

Schwan, Gesine (1986) 'Das Deutsche Amerikabild seit der Weimarer Republik', *Aus Politik und zeitgeschichte*, 26: pp. 3–15.

Seidman, Steven (1983) *Liberalism and the Origins of European Social Theory.* Oxford: Blackwell.

Sellin, Volker (1978) 'Politik', in Otto Brunner, Werner Conze and Reinhart Koselleck (eds), *Geshichichtliche Grundbegriffe.* Stuttgart: Klett-Cotta, vol. 4, pp. 789–874.

Sewell, William H. Jr (1986) 'Artisans, factory workers and the formation of the French working class, 1789–1848', in Ira Katznelson and Aristide R. Zolberg (eds), *Working-Class Formation: Nineteenth-Century Patterns in Europe and the United States.* Princeton: Princeton University Press. pp. 45–70.

Shapin, Steven and Schaffer, Simon (1985) *Leviathan and the Air Pump.* Princeton: Princeton University Press.

Shklar, Judith N. (1987) 'Alexander Hamilton and the Language of Political Science', in Anthony Pagden (ed.), *The Languages of Political Theory in Early Modern Europe.* Cambridge: Cambridge University Press. pp. 339–55.

Shklar, Judith N. (1991) 'Redeeming American Political Theory', in *American Political Science Review*, 85 (1): 3–15.

Skinner, Quentin (1997) *Liberty Before Liberalism.* Cambridge: Cambridge University Press.

Skirbekk, Gunnar (1993) *Rationality and Modernity. Essays in Philosophical Pragmatics.* Oslo: Skandinavian University Press.

Slygoski, B.R. and Ginsburg, G.P. (1989) 'Ego identity and explanatory speech', in John Shotter and Kenneth J. Gergen (eds), *Texts of Identity.* London: Sage. pp. 36–39.

Smelser, Neil (1997) *Problematics of Sociology.* Berkeley: University of California Press.

Smith, Stephen B. (1989) *Hegel's Critique of Liberalism.* Chicago: University of Chicago Press.

Sombart, Werner (1969) *Warum gibt es in den vereinigten staaten keinen sozialismus.* Darmstadt: Wissenschaftliche Buchgesellschaft.

Spoerri, William T. (1936) *The Old World and the New. A Synopsis of Current European Views on American Civilisation.* Zurich: Niehans.

Stafford, William (1989) '"This once happy country": nostalgia for pre-modern society', in Christopher Shaw and Malcolm Chase (eds), *The Imagined Past. History and Nostalgia.* Manchester: Manchester University Press. pp. 33–45.

Stengers, Isabelle (1993) *L'invention des sciences modernes.* Paris: La découverte.

Sternberger, Dolf (1971) 'A controversy of the late-eighteenth century concerning representation', *Social Research*, vol. 38.

Straub, Jürgen (1998) 'Personale und kollektive identität. Zur analyse eines theoretischen begriffs', in Aleida Assmann and Heidrun Friese (eds), *Identitäten.* Frankfurt/M: Suhrkamp. pp. 73–104.

Taubes, Jacob (1991) *Abendländische eschatologie.* Munich: Matthes & Seitz.

Taylor, Charles (1989) *Sources of the Self.* Cambridge, Mass.: Harvard University Press.

Taylor, Charles (1991) *The Malaise of Modernity.* Concord, Ont.: Anansi.

Taylor, Charles (1995a) 'Overcoming epistemology', in *Philosophical Arguments.* Cambridge, Mass.: Harvard University Press. pp. 1–19.

Taylor, Charles (1995b) 'The importance of Herder', in *Philosophical Arguments.* Cambridge, Mass.: Harvard University Press. pp. 79–99.

Taylor, Charles (1995c) 'Heidegger, language, and ecology', in *Philosophical Arguments.* Cambridge, Mass.: Harvard University Press. pp. 100–126.

Tester, Keith (1993) *The Life and Times of Post-Modernity.* London: Routledge.

Therborn, Göran (1976) *Science, Class and Society. On the Formation of Sociology and Historical Materialism.* London: New Left Books.

Thévenot, Laurent (1985) 'Les investissements de forme', in Laurent Thévenot (ed.), *Conventions économiques, cahiers du centre d'Études de l'Emploi*. Paris: PUF, pp. 21–71 (an English version was published as: 'Rules and implements: investment in forms', in *Social Science Information*, 23 (1) 1984: pp. 1–45).

Thévenot, Laurent (1990) 'L'action qui convient', in Paul Pharo, Patrick Ladrière and Louis Quéré (eds), *Les Formes de l'Action*. Paris: Editions de l'EHESS. pp. 39–69 (*Raisons pratiques*, no. 1).

Thévenot, Laurent (1993) 'Agir avec d'autres. Conventions et objets dans l'action coordonnée', in Paul Ladrière, Patrick Pharo and Louis Quéré (eds), *La théorie de l'action. Le sujet pratique en débat*. Paris: CNRS Editions. pp. 275–289.

Todorov, Tzvetan (1982) *La Conquete de l'Amérique: la question de l'autre*. Paris: Seuil.

Tönnies, Ferdinand (1922) *Kritik der öffentlichen meinung*. Berlin: Springer.

Toulmin, Stephen (1990) *Cosmopolis. The Hidden Agenda of Modernity*. Chicago: University of Chicago Press.

Toulmin, Stephen (1984) 'Introduction' to John Dewey, *The Quest for Certainty*, in *The Later Works 1925–1953*, vol. 4, Carbondale, Ill.: Southern Illinois University Press.

Trommler, Frank (1986) 'Aufstieg und fall des Amerikanismus in Deutschland', in Frank Trommler (ed.), *Amerika und die Deutschen*. Opladen: Westdeutscher Verlag.

Valéry, Paul (1951) 'America as a projection of the European mind', in *Reflections on the World Today*. London: Thames and Hudson.

Valéry, Paul (1957) 'La crise de l'esprit', in *Oeuvres*. Paris: Gallimard. pp. 988–1014.

Vatter, Miguel (2000) *Between Form and Event. Machiavelli's Theory of Political Freedom*. Dordrecht: Kluwer.

Wagner, Peter (1990) *Sozialwissenschaften und Staat. Frankreich, Italien, Deutschland, 1870–1980*. Frankfurt/M: Campus.

Wagner, Peter (1992) 'Liberty and discipline. Making sense of postmodernity, or, once again, toward a sociohistorical understanding of modernity', *Theory and Society*, 21 (4): 467–492.

Wagner, Peter (1994a) *A Sociology of Modernity. Liberty and Discipline*. London: Routledge.

Wagner, Peter (1994b) 'Dispute, uncertainty and institution in recent French debates', *The Journal of Political Philosophy*, 2 (3): 270–289.

Wagner, Peter (1995) 'Sociology and contingency. Historicizing epistemology', *Social Science Information/Information sur les sciences sociales*, 34 (2): 179–204.

Wagner, Peter (1996) 'Crises of modernity. Political sociology in historical contexts', in Stephen P. Turner (ed.), *Social Theory and Sociology*. Oxford: Blackwell. pp. 97–115.

Wagner, Peter (1998a) 'Certainty and order, liberty and contingency; the birth of social science as empirical political philosophy', in Johan Heilbron, Lars Magnusson and Björn Wittrock (eds), *The Rise of the Social Sciences and the Formation of Modernity*. Dordrecht: Kluwer. pp. 241–63.

Wagner, Peter (1998b) 'Fest-stellungen. Beobachtungen zur sozialwissenschaftlichen diskussion über Identität', in Aleida Assmann and Heidrun Friese (eds), *Identitäten*. Frankfurt/M: Suhrkamp. pp. 44–72.

Wagner, Peter (1998c) 'Politik und moderne', in *Die grünen und die moderne*. Netzwerk Mecklenburg-Vorpommern der der Heinrich Böll-Stiftung (ed.). Rostock: Netzwerk Mecklenburg-Vorpommern (n.d.). pp. 35–68.

Wagner, Peter (1999a) 'The resistance that modernity constantly provokes. Europe, America and social theory', in *Thesis Eleven* (58): 39–63.

Wagner, Peter (1999b) '"Adjusting social relations". Social science and social planning during the twentieth century', in Theodore Porter and Dorothy Ross (eds), *The Cambridge History of Science*, vol. 7: *Modern Social and Behavioral Sciences*. Cambridge: Cambridge University Press.

Wagner, Peter (1999c) 'Das Politische denken. Claude Leforts Herausforderung an unser Politikverständnis' (publication in preparation).

Wagner, Peter (2000) '"An entirely new object of consciousness, of volition, of thought". The coming into being and (almost) passing away of "society" as an object of sociology',

144   Theorizing Modernity

in Lorraine Daston (ed.), *Biographies of Scientific Objects*. Chicago: University of Chicago Press, pp. 132–157.

Wagner, Peter (2001) *Not All That is Solid Melts into Air. A History and Theory of the Social Sciences*. London: Sage.

Walzer, Michael (1990) 'What does it mean to be an "American"?' *Social Research*, 57 (3): 591–614.

Weber, Alfred (1925) *Die Krise des modernen staatsgedankens in Europa*. Stuttgart and Berlin: DVA.

Weber, Max (1975) *Wissenschaft als beruf*. Berlin: Duncker & Humblot. (Engl. tr.: 'Science as a vocation', in H.H. Gerth and C. Wright Mills (eds), *From Max Weber. Essays in Sociology*. London: Routledge and Kegan Paul.)

Weir, Allison (1996) *Sacrificial Logics. Feminist Theory and the Critique of Identity*. New York: Routledge.

Williams, Raymond (1961) *The Long Revolution*. Harmondsworth: Penguin.

Wittgenstein, Ludwig (1969) *On Certainty* (ed. by G.E.M. Anscombe and G.H. von Wright). Oxford: Blackwell.

Wittgenstein, Ludwig (1984a) *Tractatus logicus-philosophicus*. Werkausgabe, vol. 1. Frankfurt/Main: Suhrkamp.

Wittgenstein, Ludwig (1984b) 'Philosophische untersuchungen', in *Tractatus logicus-philosophicus*. Werkausgabe, vol. 1. Frankfurt/Main: Suhrkamp.

Wittrock, Björn and Wagner, Peter (1992) 'Policy Constitution Through Discourse: Discourse Transformation and the Modern State in Central Europe', in Douglas Ashford (ed.), *History and Context in Comparative Public Policy*. Pittsburgh: University of Pittsburgh Press. pp. 227–246.

Wittrock, Björn and Wagner, Peter (1996) 'Social Science and the Building of the Early Welfare State', in Dietrich Rueschemeyer and Theda Skocpol (eds), *Social Knowledge and the Origins of Social Policies*. Princeton and New York: Princeton University Press and Russell Sage Foundation. pp. 90–113.

Wokler, Robert (1987) 'Saint-Simon and the passage from political to social science', in Anthony Pagden (ed.), *The Languages of Political Theory in Early Modern Europe*. Cambridge: Cambridge University Press.

Wood, David (1990) *Philosophy at the Limit*. London: Unwin & Hyman.

Wood, Gordon S. (1998 [1969]) *The Creation of the American Republic 1776–1787*. Durham: University of North Carolina Press.

Wuthnow, Robert (1989) *Communities of Discourse. Ideology and Social Structure in the Reformation, the Enlightenment, and European Socialism*. Cambridge, Mass.: Harvard University Press.

Yack, Bernard (1997) *The Fetishism of Modernities*. Notre Dame: University of Notre Dame Press.

Zimmermann, Bénédicte, Didry, Claude and Wagner, Peter (eds) (1999) *Le Travail et la nation. Histoire croisée de la France et de l'Allemagne*. Paris: Editions de la Maison des Sciences de l'Homme.

Index